EVERYDAY SCHOLARSHIP WINNER

EVERYDAY SCHOLARSHIP WINNER

A Proven Process Any Student
Can Use to Win Money for College

Jeremy Kaszycki

FOUR STONE PUBLISHING
an imprint of Kaszycki Consulting LLC

FOUR STONE

Four Stone Publishing is an independent imprint of Kaszycki Consulting LLC
Rockford, Illinois

1st edition, July 2026

For additional services, please visit everydayscholarshipwinner.com.

ISBN 979-8-9963766-0-5 (paperback)
ISBN 979-8-9963766-1-2 (hardcover)
ISBN 979-8-9963766-2-9 (ebook)
Library of Congress Control Number: 2026914368

PUBLISHER'S CATALOGING-IN-PUBLICATION
(PROVIDED BY CASSIDY CATALOGUING SERVICES, INC.)
Names: Kaszycki, Jeremy, author.
Title: Everyday scholarship winner : a proven process any student can use to win money for college / Jeremy Kaszycki.
Description: 1st edition. | Rockford, Illinois : Four Stone Publishing, an imprint of Kaszycki Consulting LLC, [2026]
Identifiers: LCCN: 2026914368 | ISBN: 9798996376605 (paperback) | 9798996376612 (hardcover) | 9798996376629 (ebook)
Subjects: LCSH: Scholarships--United States. | Student aid--United States. | Student loans--United States. | College costs--United States. | LCGFT: Self-help publications. | BISAC: EDUCATION / Counseling / Academic Development. | STUDY AIDS / College Guides. | BUSINESS & ECONOMICS / Personal Finance / General.
Classification: LCC: LB2338 .K37 2026 | DDC: 378.340973--dc23

Manufactured in the United States of America for U.S. orders, and internationally for global fulfillment.

To my mom and dad.

Thank you for making me all that I am.

I strive to bring to others what you have brought to me my entire life.

CONTENTS

Introduction

PROCESS OVERVIEW

1

Before the Process

WHY I WROTE THIS BOOK

One person can change the world. In fact, every individual leaves an imprint on it, but the significance of that imprint depends on the choices made during their lifetime. One of the earliest and most influential of those choices is whether to attend college. Although there are arguments on many sides of the topic of college, it remains a system that accomplishes meaningful growth in individuals—young or old. At its core, a college education was created to give people the opportunity to broaden their knowledge and understanding of the world—through a single discipline or many—and to use that knowledge to contribute to society, push human boundaries, transform the unimaginable into reality, and ultimately change the world. The same mindset exists in those who choose to attend college or university today. Their goal is to use the knowledge, skills, and experience gained through higher education to create change in the world, on any scale, in a way that aligns with their personal vision.

My name is Jeremy Kaszycki, and I am an alumnus of Bradley University, Class of 2017. I graduated Cum Laude with a degree in Manufacturing Engineering. Although I am greatly enjoying my current career in the manufacturing industry and using that skillset to drive positive change in society, I knew I wanted to formally write about something I found great success in during college that, if shared, would drive lasting impact in a different way. The success I am talking about is finding financial assistance in a world where it seems as if paying for the cost of college is the equivalent of climbing Mt. Everest and carrying massive amounts of student debt feels like carrying the weight of the world on your shoulders. Sharing my techniques, tricks, processes, strategies, and tips on how I was able to fund 57.5% of my college at no cost to me through scholarships and grants is one way I can make my own impact on the world. The goal of this book is to equip you with the knowledge of a proven approach to winning financial assistance for a college education to lessen the burden of the immense cost it takes to attend a college or university. I want to share what worked for me to help others see how easy it is, capitalize on their opportunities they may not know they have, and help make their dreams a reality.

The reason why I am so confident in this information is because of how much success I saw in my process of winning scholarships considering the type of person I am. I am very skeptical of the "Too Good to Be True" pitches that everyone hears every now and then, so I don't even bother giving them the benefit of the doubt. Too often, they are unrealistic results that people try to blow up out of context. What I am going to share in this book are **realistic results** that I **earned** through sheer willpower, work, and consistency. Those traits exist in *everyone*. I'm not the smartest person in the world, I am not the most talented, I was never considered in the top percentages of anything, and yet what I accomplished put me in a position of success that those at the "top of their class" wouldn't normally achieve. *The point I am trying to make is that the information I am going to share is what I did step-by-step on my way to winning as many scholarships and grants as I did.* I figured this out through trial and error. I am writing this with the hope that you will mimic a lot of what I am detailing in this book, use what I have learned, emulate what brought me success, and apply it to your situation. Everything in life happens for a reason, and I believe partly why I was blessed with the amount of financial assistance I received was so that I can share it to better the situation of whomever reads this information. I am a simple person. How I was able to do what I did regarding scholarships and grants is **simple**. That is why I am extremely excited to be able to finally share my experience and information in a proper way so that others can use it to their advantage. I guarantee you will find results by applying my process for finding scholarships and am confident that after consuming this information, you will see the task of paying off college tuition in a whole different light. Without further ado, let's begin.

MY COLLEGE BACKSTORY

Since the majority of people who will most likely read this book are high school students preparing to go to college or current college students, I will go into a bit of my backstory on the beginning of my college process so you can get a feel for my mindset as I approached this new chapter of my life. I am going to assume that for those of you who are planning to attend college (or maybe are in their first or second year already) and do not have a clear idea of what to major in, have a career in, or ultimately achieve at the end of your college tenure, you are not alone. That was also where my head was at going into college. The only reasons why I knew college was in my future plans were because my parents saved a little bit of funding for me in a college savings account (more on that later) and my older brother and sister, whom I was following in the footsteps of, both went to college. Therefore, I naturally gravitated toward planning to attend college, which I ended up doing.

Although they were not highlights of my life, I enjoyed high school for what it was. As I stated before, I was never really a standout in anything, but I was involved in extracurriculars throughout my four years which I will get into specifics on later. I was an average student. At the end of my freshman year, I had around a 2.8 Grade Point Average (GPA). I realized this was moderately bad, so I kicked myself into gear and really tried to put in effort into my high school classes. I ended up taking a good amount of honors classes and only one Advanced Placement (AP) class, AP Biology, which I ended up getting a two on the AP exam, ultimately not receiving any college credit. It did not bother me though. I took AP Biology to challenge myself, and because my older brother and sister, who also attended the same high school a few years earlier, took a majority of AP classes. I also took AP Biology because I was wondering if I would enjoy a biology-related field of study in college. At the end of the class, it still was not clear to me if I whole-heartedly wanted to study a particular field of science related to biology. This ended up not being the case as I ended up studying engineering. At the time, I should have taken my indifference as a signal that this was not the right path for me. I enjoyed animals and nature in general, but not how in-depth biology dives into the study of life. Now that I am growing older, *I realize that if things don't make you happy or there is something you don't particularly enjoy, it is best not to invest time in an idea that will not bring you fulfillment or one which you do not love in some way.* It's not because I wasn't good at it that I didn't enjoy it. Rather, it never interested me to the degree that a potential lifelong career should. Anyone can get good at things with enough time and practice, but it is up to that person to decide if they want to do that, and for what reason. When I was in high school, I did not know this fact. In a way though, life plays out how it is meant to. In this case, my ignorance in not recognizing my lack of enjoyment for the subject of biology played a part in leading me to eventually picking engineering. At the end of the day, these types of situations call for open-mindedness, curiosity, and an eagerness to explore the unknown and unfamiliar, because approaching situations in life such as this will help you get to the answers to your questions.

At the end of my senior year of high school, I finished with a non-weighted GPA (excluding any boost for honors and AP courses) of 3.334 and a weighted GPA (including any boost for honors and AP courses) of 3.609. I had already started my college search and knew I wanted to go somewhere relatively close by my hometown of Rockford, IL. I will mention here though, after looking back on the opportunity of going to college and not realizing at the time that I had the chance to pick where I lived for the next four years, I would have very strongly considered studying in places such as California or Florida since I absolutely love beaches and warm weather. That was not my thought process at that time though. Instead, I was thinking that it would be slightly cheaper if I attended an in-state school and it would be a good idea to be located a few hours from my hometown of Rockford, IL in case anything went awry during school.

I applied to several different schools including Bradley University, Butler University, Drake University, Illinois State University, University of Illinois, Marquette University, and Saint Xavier University. Despite my GPA being eligible, my American College Test (ACT) score was really the only thing that held me back from being accepted into a higher tier of universities. I scored a 23 my first try on the ACT and improved to 24 on the second. One bright spot I had was I received a 10 out of 12 on the optional essay writing section, which was a very competitive score but that did not play a major factor in college acceptance. Although, this was a nice prelude considering what would later happen with all the success I had with scholarship essays!

I visited most of the schools I had mentioned previously for on-campus tours, but a lot of their campus layouts reminded me of three or four big high schools mashed together. Also, it rained on most of those visits. When I got to Bradley University, I can honestly say I was impressed. The campus itself was big enough to my liking as I did not want a small campus community. I wanted the feel of a big school, and Bradley at the time had around 6,000 undergraduate students which was decently mid-sized. A lot of the buildings were newer, showcasing a more modern flare which really livened the place up and gave me the perception that the university is growing and constantly evolving rather than staying rooting in the past. On top of that, the majority of buildings were made of beautiful large white stone, a timeless look that you would not get tired of looking at. I fell in love with their athletic center immediately. The Markin Family Student Recreation Center was newly built and featured a vast and diverse option of athletic areas that students can utilize, but what struck me was the three shiny wooden full college-length basketball courts all in a row with advanced rims and backboards to go along with a fourth indoor mix-use basketball and soccer court. I fell in love with playing street basketball in high school so seeing this was a welcome site. On top of that, Bradley does not have a football team, but they do have a Division I basketball team. The absence of football in your prototypical college setting did not bother me whatsoever as the only sport I cared about was basketball, so it was a perfect fit! To go along with the jovial and truly enthusiastic student guide I had on the day of my tour, Bradley was the one campus that it did not rain on my visit! Lastly,

Bradley was located in Peoria, IL, which is two and a half hours away from my hometown—far enough away that I could have a sense of independence yet close enough to where I can still be close to home. Peoria is quite a large city with a big downtown area hosting a variety of older style skyscrapers that tower along the Illinois River. While picking my college choice, I wanted to have a big-city vibe since I lived close to Chicago. Peoria was big enough that I was content with it. My visit to Bradley was the best one I attended. I could see myself as a student there, so I chose to attend Bradley University in the fall of 2013.

I want to quickly touch on why I did not consider community college. Despite there being a great community college very close to where I lived in Rockford, I knew I did not want to attend community college for two years because I wanted to receive the full college experience of four years at a college or university. That is just how I pictured college to be in my mind. Looking back, this was not the wisest financial decision for me as I could have saved thousands of dollars by going this route, but I would not change my decision because this path has brought me to where I am today and I am happy about it. As you continue reading, please do not disregard the numerous benefits of going to a community college. It is up to you to weigh out all the options and choose what is best for you. Everyone is different.

I did not only pick Bradley for its aesthetic appeal, but also for the courses they offered. Ironically enough, with all the major choices Bradley had to offer, I entered as an undecided major. As described earlier, I really did not have a good idea of what I wanted to do in college. My first semester I enrolled in mostly general education classes along with an additional academic exploration class that was meant to touch on a wide scope of majors throughout the semester so I can get a good feel for what each field is about and eventually decide on one to move forward with. Honestly speaking, I was still flirting with the idea of majoring in some biology-related field, partly due to my brother going along that same route and he was a person I looked up to. That is when I questioned what I *actually* enjoyed doing, for example, as a kid, and at other points in my life. Some of the fondest memories of my childhood were playing with Legos, Bionicle, K'Nex, and other block-type toys. I enjoyed building all sorts of structures with these toys and I would really focus on the details of every elaborate building project I undertook. I even recall building a miniature pulley-powered conveyor that I jerry-rigged with string as the conveyor belt with the K'Nex blocks. Using this as a basis, I centered on Undecided Engineering. *This is the biggest tip I can point out here. If you are in the same situation as I was and struggling to find your "calling," so to speak, I'd recommend doing some internal questioning.* What do you find fascinating? What do you catch yourself doing hours of? What is something you lose your sense of time in? What is something you cannot get enough of? What did you genuinely enjoy doing as a child? What are some top qualities you have? Focus on asking questions and highlighting the positive traits you have. A lot of times we tend to focus on the things we are missing instead of highlighting and rejoicing on the key traits and characteristics we as individuals are uniquely blessed with. You may find the answers you are looking for by doing some internal questioning as I did. For me, it turned out for the best.

Going into college, I originally did not consider engineering because I thought it was too "mainstream," meaning I thought all guys do engineering. I could not have been more wrong. What changed my mind was, first of all, answering my internal questions, but secondly seeing the vast range of fields and opportunities that engineering can open for someone. It is an extremely boundless major. With my academic exploration class now focused on Undecided Engineering, I toured all Bradley's engineering-related majors such as Civil, Electrical, Chemical, Mechanical, Manufacturing, Industrial, Biomedical, and Computer Engineering, just to name a few. Don't get me wrong, my first glance of engineering had me worried. It is a tough subject. Touring the different types of engineering curriculum Bradley offered started making me question engineering. It wasn't until I toured the Industrial & Manufacturing Engineering and Technology (IMET) department that I found the right fit. What intrigued me instantly were the different types of machines in the laboratory of the department building. They had injection molding machines, mills, lathes, 3D printers, 3D scanners, and a plethora of other machinery that I would eventually come to know. They even had custom made an aluminum silver bullet keychain with my name engraved on it as a gift. I still have it on my car keys to this day. The tour of this department had piqued my interest, and at the end of the tour I started discussing my situation with the department's dean, who later invited me out to a lunch at his favorite restaurant for a further discussion on a major in either Manufacturing or Industrial Engineering. At lunch, I could see his passion and enthusiasm for his field of manufacturing, and he described to me the opportunities manufacturing has, not only within the walls of Bradley, but throughout the entire world. I concluded that I would study Manufacturing Engineering for several reasons. Firstly, virtually everything in the world is mass produced through manufacturing so this major offered job stability. Secondly, the subject matter interested me since I was fascinated with the types of machines there were and the things that they had capability of making. This aligned with my upbringing as a child while playing with Legos and things of that nature. On top of that, the compensation for an engineering degree is very generous. Lastly, I felt I would be able to endure the academic strain of this type of engineering. In my eyes, I saw Manufacturing and Industrial Engineering a little easier to handle than, for example, Chemical or Mechanical Engineering. With those factors in mind, I made the decision to major in Manufacturing Engineering with a concentration in Lean Manufacturing toward the end of my first semester freshman year. Lean manufacturing is a specialization within manufacturing that focuses on eliminating waste and reducing variation within manufacturing systems. I saw this as a key to how I would add value to a company to ultimately land myself a job out of school. Overall, I am happy about the direction I have chosen for myself. It has propelled me forward into the life that I lead today and I would not change one part of the journey of how I got here.

I wanted to share how I centered around my college major of choice before going into scholarships because I think it is important to be in school for the right reasons. A lot of you who are reading this are either at a crossroads of what you should study in college or university, or you have been in this position before. For those still struggling to decide, I hope my story helps you find the answers you need to discover what fits you best. Don't get discouraged. Everything happens for a reason. Try new things and explore not only inside yourself about what makes you happy or what you find enjoyable, but also outside to discover what is around you because you may not know what you will find. Become comfortable with the uncomfortable, because through discomfort comes growth to launch you forward to more challenging and uncomfortable situations in which the bounties and rewards waiting on the other side are unimaginable.

2

Cost & Financial Assistance Breakdown

COST

Now that I have painted the picture on the events leading up to and during my college experience along with some difficult decisions I had to make, I will now share about the difficult decisions surrounding my financial experiences while I attended college and how I was able to cope with the massive debt I was about to undertake.

The following is my overall cost breakdown for attending Bradley University starting in 2013. To note, the only number here that I generalized is books because I did not have a solid paper trail on how much it exactly cost me for each year in books. Therefore, I assumed that I paid an average of $300 per year on books. A lot of them were used and I sold back most of mine hence why the number is on the lower side.

Freshman Year Cost (2013-2014):	
Fall Semester 2013 Tuition	$19,407
Spring Semester 2014 Tuition	$19,407
Books	$300
Total:	**$39,114**

Sophomore Year Cost (2014-2015):	
Fall Semester 2014 Tuition	$20,612
Spring Semester 2015 Tuition	$20,732
Books	$300
Total:	**$41,644**

To note thus far, my freshman and sophomore year tuition included room and board and a meal plan. My junior and senior year tuition does not reflect this since I lived in an apartment with friends and cooked most of my own meals although I did buy a small off-campus meal plan. I have included the rent, which was $390 per month for ten months, and this off-campus meal plan as separate line items but they are still related to the overall cost of attendance. Also, I underwent a sixteen-day study abroad to London my senior year which amounted to an additional cost.

Junior Year Cost (2015-2016):	
Fall Semester 2015 Tuition	$16,340
Spring Semester 2016 Tuition	$16,340
Rent	$3,900
Off-Campus Meal Plan	$890
Books	$300
Total:	**$37,770**

Senior Year Cost (2016-2017):	
Fall Semester 2016 Tuition	$16,610
Spring Semester 2017 Tuition	$16,560
Rent	$3,900
Off-Campus Meal Plan	$890
Study Abroad	$3,900
Books	$300
Total:	**$42,160**

Summing up these numbers, the overall cost of my college education was **$160,688.**

FINANCIAL ASSISTANCE

Now that I have summarized the overall cost of college attendance, I will now summarize a breakdown of overall financial assistance while in college. Please note, my parents had a college savings account saved for me in the amount of $20,000 that I applied all to my freshman year. Despite this not being earned, I am still factoring it in as part of financial assistance. Also to note, these summary financial assistance numbers include all student loans, grants, internal scholarships, external scholarships, and all other forms of financial assistance that were applied to the overall cost. This is a high-level summary before breaking down into specifics.

High School Senior Year Financial Assistance (2012-2013):	
External Scholarships Awarded	$500
Total:	**$500**

Freshman Year Financial Assistance (2013-2014):	
Federal Student Loans	$5,500
Bradley Grant (University Scholarship)	$6,000
Bradley Grant (Normal)	$8,000
Parent's College Savings Account	$20,000
Total:	**$39,500**

Sophomore Year Financial Assistance (2014-2015):	
Federal Student Loans	$6,500
Private Student Loans	$16,000
Bradley Grant (University Scholarship)	$6,000
Bradley Grant (Need-Based)	$2,000

Bradley Grant (Special Enhancement)	$6,000
Internal Scholarships Awarded	$1,500
External Scholarships Awarded	$2,000
Total:	**$40,000**

Junior Year Financial Assistance (2015-2016):	
Federal Student Loans	$7,500
Private Student Loans	$7,000
Bradley Grant (University Scholarship)	$6,000
Bradley Grant (Need-Based)	$2,160
Bradley Grant (Special Enhancement)	$6,000
Internal Scholarships Awarded	$3,600
External Scholarships Awarded	$14,500
Total:	**$46,760**

Senior Year Financial Assistance (2016-2017):	
Federal Student Loans	$7,500
Private Student Loans	$12,760
Bradley Grant (University Scholarship)	$6,000
Bradley Grant (Normal)	$500
Bradley Grant (Need-Based)	$6,062
Bradley Grant (Special Enhancement)	$6,000
External Scholarships Awarded	$9,500
Total:	**$48,322**

Summing up these numbers, the overall financial assistance of my college education was **$175,082.**

Taking the overall cost of college at $160,688 and subtracting the overall financial assistance of college at $175,082, this gives a net negative value of **-$14,394.**

After paying the cost of college with my financial assistance, I came out with a surplus of $14,394. This extra $14,394 means I took out more student loans than I should have. I want to stress that this was not an extra check that was waiting for me at the end of graduation. Rather, whenever my financial aid exceeded the tuition cost for that year, I would be refunded that surplus amount. I will get into this more later, but junior year for example I had to take out a set amount of student loans at the beginning of each semester to make sure I was covered for the year. I did not know how much in scholarships I would win throughout the course of the year. As the year progressed and I started to accumulate scholarship winnings despite me already paying for the respective semester, Bradley's financial aid office would accept the scholarship check and then write me a refund check in the amount of my scholarship (the surplus amount) and direct deposit it into my bank account.

Also, there are other costs that you must plan for if you want to use student loans to cover them. For example, I bought a used 2006 Kia Spectra EX for $4,900 because I needed a car for my junior and senior years. I paid for part of the car with my summer internship earnings and covered the rest with student loans. Gas, repairs, and other living expenses were also supplemented with loans whenever my income didn't stretch far enough. Another example is I had to take out a loan for my study abroad trip to London my senior year. The total cost was $3,900 for a sixteen-day January Interim class; however, I took out a little more than that in the loan because I knew I needed extra money to facilitate my travel activities while on the trip. Not to encourage you to abuse this tactic because they are loans and you will need to pay them back, but I am just emphasizing to be smart and plan ahead to cover any future college-related costs as needed. Instances such as these explain as to why I ended up with a positive amount of $14,394 left over in financial assistance versus the cost to attend college.

FINANCIAL ASSISTANCE CATEGORIES

From my financial assistance total of $175,082, I can break this into separate categories to better understand what makes up this total. Below includes the total of each category and its impact over the four years of college. These categories are an introduction and will all be explained in greater depth as we go further in this book. How they are ordered will also dictate the structure of how I explain each of these categories.

Parent's College Savings Account:	$20,000
I know everyone's situation is different and may not have a savings account going into paying for college. I wanted to include this category for accuracy's sake so that you may understand the full picture of my college financial journey.	
Federal Student Loans:	**$27,000**
These student loans came from the FAFSA process through the government. Based on how an individual qualifies, you can only take out a limited amount of loans each year through FAFSA.	
Private Student Loans:	**$35,760**
I went through Discover for any additional student loans I needed for college attendance.	
Bradley Grant (University Scholarship):	**$24,000**
This was a standard award that Bradley University gives to all their incoming students. The amount you receive is based on your application, but mostly on high school GPA and ACT or Scholastic Aptitude Test (SAT) scores. In my case, based on my credentials, I was awarded a standard $6,000 per year.	

Bradley Grant (Normal):	$8,500
I labeled this type of grant as "normal" because how my university was structured was as they looked at each student's financial situation, that student was awarded certain amounts based on if they had further assistance or not. Therefore, anyone can receive this, and this was just the "normal" process for them.	
Bradley Grant (Need-Based):	**$10,222**
Although this is very similar to how the Bradley Grant (Normal) is calculated and applied to students based off need, the only difference with this is that this particular category is funded through resources outside the university such as private donors.	
Bradley Grant (Special Enhancement):	**$18,000**
This is the most important grant considering how I was awarded it. The main difference between this and the previous three categories of grants is that this grant category I was able to create, push for, and eventually get awarded all through my perseverance, intuition, and control. Without a specific action I took, I would have never had this applied to my financial assistance package. I am excited to share this strategy later on.	
External Scholarships Awarded:	**$26,500**
This funding came from outside organizations and donors who had set up scholarship programs for students. With the sheer number of scholarships that I applied for, I was able to create an easy-to-follow process that gives structure to any student seeking extra means of paying for college. This was my college lifesaver.	
Internal Scholarships Awarded:	**$5,100**
This is the same concept as the External Scholarships Awarded category, only that the organizations and donors came from within Bradley University. I still had to take initiative to apply for and win these scholarships.	

To conclude, I was awarded **$92,322** in total grants and scholarships, took out $62,760 in student loans, and was blessed to receive $20,000 from my family in order to make up my $175,082 financial assistance package. I cannot imagine life had that total number been all student loans. Unfortunately for some, that is a reality. The mission of this book is to help prevent that from occurring and to give a pathway for those who are wanting to attend or are already attending college to show them that there are endless opportunities to pay off the cost of college. The problem is these opportunities go unnoticed. I am happy I get to shed a light on what I found worked for me and provide a guide so that others may mimic my tips and strategies to achieve the same results in their lives.

PROCESS ON WINNING SCHOLARSHIPS

Now that I have shared a bit of my college journey and have shown how I managed to pay for school, I would like to introduce the process that I took in order to achieve the success I had in acquiring financial assistance.

Step 1: Know Your "Why"
Knowing why you're doing anything in life gives meaning to whatever it is that you are doing. By truly understanding why it is you want to achieve financial success in college, you give yourself the highest chance of actually following through on achieving the financial goals you define. In Step 1, I explain how you can find your "why" and the importance and effect that it brings.

↓

Step 2: Improve Yourself

It is great that you are reading this book and are really excited about embarking on a journey that will save you thousands of dollars in the future, but why should organizations pick you to give their scholarships to? Why do you deserve scholarships or grants more than another perfectly qualified and deserving applicant? In Step 2, I answer those questions and show you how you can improve yourself in order to better your chances at submitting a winning scholarship application.

↓

Step 3: Find Scholarships

In Step 3, I explain how to find the most applicable and highest quantity of scholarships you can apply for.

↓

Step 4: Apply

This step is the most crucial as it explains how to successfully fill out a scholarship application and helps you build your case for why you are the best candidate to win the scholarship you are applying for. There is so much in this section to cover: forms, essays, letters of recommendation, thank you letters, and more. In Step 4, I walk you through the steps to take and the mindset to adopt that will position you to win thousands of dollars in scholarships.

↓

Step 5: Repeat

Step 5 is the shortest step I will elaborate on but arguably the longest as you repeat Steps 2 through 4 until you achieve your goals or you graduate.

Out of all the financial assistance categories listed, this process is tailored for winning scholarships and helped me win **$31,600** in external and internal scholarships. Before I fully elaborate on each process step, I will explain exactly how every other form of financial assistance was granted in the order of the categories listed above. It's important to understand how you can influence financial assistance categories beyond scholarships, because these other areas can also play a major role in reducing your college costs, as they did for me. In order to fully take advantage of these other financial assistance categories, one must first understand Step 1 to truly grasp the magnitude each category has to your college financial assistance success.

Step 1

KNOW YOUR "WHY"

3

Executing Step 1

Growing up, children often use the word "why" as a way to explore and make sense of the world around them. Their use of the never-ending question of "why" uncovers answers to a world that is, at first, foreign to them, using those answers to shape their environment and continue to venture forward toward new horizons. As an adult, that same never-ending question, instead of helping us uncover the surface of our reality, guides us into a deeper realm of reflection. Constantly asking "why" can uncover a better understanding of one's internal self by answering questions that bring forth passion, vision, purpose, and mission in life. By discovering these ideas, it gives meaning to a person's life, and that meaning then drives that person to exhibit relentless commitment, motivation, and pursuit toward the actions that will eventually allow them to achieve what they want to gain out of life.

The above paragraph emphasizes the importance of knowing the reason you are pursuing whatever it is that you are pursuing in life. Giving a reason helps you to stay on course until you accomplish something because you want the fruit those actions will produce. In this case, the same idea applies for scholarships. Some may think that scholarships are a small aspect of college and therefore do not take them too seriously. They may start applying for some scholarships or start researching where to find them only to end up quitting, not following through, or not applying altogether. This shows they did not have a deeper meaning associated with "why" they want to win scholarships in the first place. *Energy flows where intention goes.* To them, scholarships held less value which led to weak actions that failed to generate scholarship winnings.

If you are reading this and you are in college or high school, most likely your purpose at this stage of your life is to be the best student you can be. To do that, you have to balance a multitude of responsibilities that come with being a student, so adding an emphasis on scholarships on top of how much you already have going on can feel a little overwhelming. College brings plenty of positives, but the part no one likes to talk about is the cost of tuition. Obviously, some students are granted full-ride scholarships that allow them to attend school for little to no cost. I cannot speak to those scenarios because I was never fortunate enough to be one of those people. I am talking about the average, everyday student that has to pay thousands of dollars in tuition every year, typically for four years. The only way most of these students manage to pay for the up-front cost of tuition is by taking out hundreds of thousands of dollars in student loans to attend over-priced universities. After completing their education, they are left to start off their careers in an immense financial debt hole that will take years to pay off, amplified by the interest that is accumulated during the payback period. This situation forces a lot of students to get a slower start in life after college and can often lead into worse scenarios if not properly managed.

Knowing the potential pitfalls that follow as a result of carrying massive amounts of debt at an early age from the cost of attending a university is what motivated me to begin a journey that ended up saving me thousands of dollars and years of time. Although I am a first-generation college student, I was not the first one in my family to attend. I have an older brother and sister that both attended Loyola University in Chicago, IL. Having siblings go through college first gave me an idea of what to expect from the college experience—especially the debt involved. When I was on the verge of starting my freshman year, my sister was concluding her undergraduate studies, while my brother had already been a few years into his post-college life. I saw first-hand how their student debt slowed down the trajectory of their starts in life, and here I was about to sign my name on the dotted line for the same fate. That is, unless I did something about it. Couple this with the fact that I came from a middle-class family with very minimal saved in a dedicated college fund to me. I knew that I would have to pay for college by myself because my parents did not have the funds to send me to school. *The combination of these factors answered "why" I needed to do whatever it took to win as many scholarships as I could to hopefully pay off as much tuition off as possible.* In essence, I learned from my brother and sister's mistakes in not prioritizing the importance of finding scholarships.

At the time of writing this portion of the book, I am officially student-loan free and yet both of my siblings still have thousands of dollars yet to pay back. Don't get me wrong, I had debt after college, but it was manageable. With the help of scholarships as well as responsible financial management, I paid off my student debt balance of $62,760 in less than three years after graduating. The power of knowing why I wanted to commit to going the extra mile to solidify whatever funding was available to me at the time caused me to be in the debt-free situation I am in today. It helped me through the journey and stay on course because during the difficult times, such as times when I did not win certain scholarships that I applied for, I was able to not get discouraged and instead keep consistently applying. This also directly correlated with how I was able to achieve my purpose of being the best student I could be. You can look at that from multiple angles: socially, spiritually, emotionally, physically, and the list goes on. All cases are valid and one should strive to achieve milestones in all those aspects of life; however, a lot of students overlook the importance of bringing out the best of yourself *financially* during this time. Don't get me wrong, students can do this by, for example, getting an on-campus job (which I did also), and that is great, but is that your best? What you need to realize is that scholarships are free checks in your pocket. Organizations want to give away free money to students. Not to take advantage of this fact is borderline irresponsible! Students during the time they are in school underestimate and do not realize the financial opportunity they have at their fingertips simply by being classified as such—a student. Some know but are too ignorant and lazy to act on it, and some simply have no idea! Whatever the case may be, I am here to shed light on the opportunity at hand in order to help you achieve your purpose as a student and eventually help tip the next financial domino in your life a little faster than if you did not find what I will share with you in this book. Use this to fuel your "why."

Out of all the financial assistance categories listed earlier, external and internal scholarships are the most important. Knowing your "why" is crucial if you want to maximize this category because it will allow you to be consistent in your effort throughout your scholarship journey. The right "why" will also make you conscious of all the potential that exists in the other financial assistance categories. Knowing Step 1 now, and before getting into the scholarship aspect of the book, let's take a look at how my "why" helped me take action to maximize all of the other financial assistance categories as much as I could so you can do the same.

4

Maximizing Financial Assistance Categories

PARENT'S COLLEGE SAVING'S ACCOUNT: $20,000

Not much to say here as I had no influence over this category of my college financial assistance journey. Again, I wanted to include it to give the full picture of how I went about paying off my college. This savings account was started for me by my parents when I was born. I came from a middle-class family. My parents saved whatever they could throughout the years and let the savings account grow as much as possible. They did what they could in order to give me the best opportunity for success at life. I am beyond blessed to be able to have had, not only this luxury of a college savings account, but also the luxury of being able to pursue higher education. *The lesson here is to be grateful for what you are given, and not to get distracted or bent-out-of-shape with what you do not have.* Sure, there are some kids that have their college paid for either with full-ride scholarships, their parents work at the university they attend, their family is simply able to pay for the tuition in-full, and the list goes on. I cannot control any of those things. What I can control is what has been given to me so that I can make the most with the cards I was dealt because, at the end of the day, only you are able to change your situation. In life, there are no handouts. Life is hard. You must embrace life for what it is because that is where the most growth happens—when you are challenged. Become comfortable with the uncomfortable. You cannot escape any uncomfortable feeling in life since we are surrounded by them. *You must recognize that through every period of discomfort and challenge, you are growing stronger and learning important lessons.* In my case, I was challenged with paying off my college. I knew that if I did not act, things were just going to stay the same and not get better. With hard work, I was able to change my situation. Simply put, hard work works. If things are not going well in your life, what are you doing to change your environment? The key word in that question is "doing." Doing means taking action. That is why I am beyond excited for those reading this book. It shows the first signs that you really want to make a change for the better in your life, and you are seeking the resources to help you do it. With this type of mindset, it doesn't matter if you started with $20,000 or $20 in a college savings account. No matter where you start, the point is **you can do it**. You can create change in your life for the better with effort and action.

One more thing I would like to mention in this category is that if you did receive a sum of money from your parents, other family member, or whomever, that went toward any type of education regardless of the amount, I recommend to go back to them once you graduate and ask if you need to pay them back if they did not explicitly tell you it was a gift. It is only right to do. It doesn't have to be immediately after. Do it on your own time. All I am saying is it would be a kind gesture and speak well of your character as a person if you were to ask whether or not you need to pay back what they gave you. In my case, it was about three years after I graduated and had my life somewhat under control at the time when I asked my father whether he wanted the $20,000 back. He said I did not have to pay him and that it was his responsibility as a parent to provide whatever he thought was necessary for me to have a better life. I thanked him and gave him a hug. It was a very quick two-minute conversation, but I could tell my father really appreciated the fact that I reached out in that way. He did not expect it. In my eyes though, I thought it was only right—because if there is anyone I would rather be paying back, it's my family and not some random bank.

FEDERAL STUDENT LOANS: $27,000

I don't like talking about student loans since this is the exact thing everyone wants to avoid while going to school. Of course, going into any kind of debt feels counterintuitive, and financial experts like Dave Ramsey—whose work I highly recommend—argue that you can pay for college in cash and avoid student loans altogether. However, many people face fixed timelines and, despite not having the funds readily available, choose to take out loans rather than delay their education. Now, I am not saying that Dave is wrong, I am only saying that people make their own choices in life. I am writing this book to share the steps I took, from beginning to end, on how I dealt with paying off my college. My audience, as they read the book, are welcome to emulate anything and everything that I did. If they do or do not want to take out loans, that is completely fine. I am merely explaining what I did and part of what I did was take out federal student loans.

As I started to slowly prepare for college, one step I took was apply for FAFSA. For those of you who do not know, FAFSA stands for Free Application for Federal Student Aid (FAFSA). To be completely honest, I did not fully understand the process behind FAFSA at the time. I only knew that my older brother and sister applied for it when they were entering school, so I figured it was something you're supposed to do when entering college. FAFSA, it turns out, is not that complicated. Based on an application that you fill out, the United States government loans you a certain fixed amount of money to pay for your schooling. You cannot take out an unlimited amount. The one nice thing about federal loans is that the total amount you borrow is divided into two types of loans: subsidized and unsubsidized. Despite both having interest rates tied to them, the interest amount on a subsidized loan does not start accruing until after you graduate! With unsubsidized loans, interest begins accruing immediately and keeps building until the loan is fully repaid. Overall, having some federal loans is better than taking out nothing but private loans as I will describe in the next category because you are saving money in the long run, both with the subsidized interest deferral and possibly a lower interest rate.

Overall, it is up to you whether or not you need to take out student loans. For those of you who would like to inquire about FAFSA, a quick Google search will give you everything you need. I ended up paying off all of my federal student loans first because the sum was less than the sum of the private loans. This technique of paying off the lesser debt amount first is called the "debt snowball" and it comes from Dave Ramsey. One quick note as well—there is also a similar technique called the "debt avalanche" which prioritizes paying off the highest interest rate loan first. Just to be clear, the "debt avalanche" is not one of Dave's methods; however, I just wanted to mention the two approaches here for you, the reader, to decide which one works best for you. At the end of the day, I am not mad about the fact that I took out loans to pay for college. It was a resource I needed at the time, but I was also aware of the responsibility I was undertaking as I signed my name for $27,000 worth of debt.

PRIVATE STUDENT LOANS: $35,760

Since federal student loans only provided so much money toward my college tuition, I needed to pay the rest that I owed with private student loans if I did not have enough other financial assistance. Upon graduation, I had taken out $35,760 in private student loans from Discover Bank. It was fairly easy to sign up for these loans. This is because banks want to lock customers into agreements so they can collect interest, and unfortunately this was my only option. Discover was nice because, at the time, they had a 1% cash back incentive where if you score above a 3.0 GPA, they will send you a check for 1% of the value of your loan. Another "positive" (if you want to even call it that because debt is still debt no matter how many incentives you have) is that when you file your taxes, you receive a Form 1098-E for both federal and private loans. This form reports the amount of student loan interest you paid during the year. You may be able to deduct a certain amount of that interest on your tax return, which can reduce your taxable income and potentially increase your refund.

As mentioned earlier, I came out with a surplus of $14,394 once I summed up all of my financial assistance versus cost of college. This was due to the fact that I took out too much in private loans. I gave a few examples as to why this occurred including the purchase of my car and my London study abroad trip. This was a calculated decision at the time. I was anticipating certain scenarios I needed additional money for to facilitate me getting through four years of college. Divide $14,394 by four years and you have an average of $3,598.50 in excess loans taken out per year, which isn't too drastic. Again, I caution anyone to only do this when absolutely necessary and to only take out what you need to facilitate your schooling because you will need to eventually pay it back. The other reason why this surplus occurred, again, was due to the fact that I won more scholarships as each semester progressed than I originally planned for at the start of the semester when the tuition bill was due. Bradley's financial aid office wrote me refund checks in the amount of the scholarship awards I won over the course of the semester because I had already paid off the full tuition using the student loan in the beginning. This is a good problem to have because who doesn't want to receive a $2,500 deposit into their bank account in the middle of the school year?

At the end of the day, student loans are unfortunately a by-product of a college education. It is up to you, the borrower, to be responsible with the loan and to pay it back promptly. Don't get too discouraged if you have to take out loans because they are allowing you to receive a college education which will better your future. Without the loan, that might not be possible. If you approach not only that idea, but all less-than-ideal things that happen in your life by trying to see the positives and the blessings or lessons behind why certain things are happening the way they are, you will be a happier person. *Don't look at bad situations and think "why is this happening to me?" Think "what is this situation trying to teach me?"* This ideology will change your life, and you will embrace and conquer conflict because of it. As it pertains to the lessons I was taught after taking out these loans, I learned to be responsible, fulfill promises (which in this case was to the bank), and do everything in my power in the future to avoid going into more debt!

BRADLEY GRANT (UNIVERSITY SCHOLARSHIP): $24,000

Every decision you make in the present will always affect your future. This was the case for how I received this grant totaling $24,000 from

Bradley University. When I attended Bradley, the university considered prospective students' ACT scores and high school GPAs during the admissions process. Based on those two factors, Bradley would award that student with some form of financial assistance package when they are accepted as an incentive for the student to choose to attend their institution. When I applied and was accepted to Bradley, they awarded me with what is called the "University Scholarship," which is a scholarship of $6,000 that is applied toward my tuition every year I am a student. Just to clarify some definitions: a grant is money given based primarily on financial need, while a scholarship is money given based on merit, talent, or other specific criteria. I know in this category's title, I labeled this amount of funding I received as a general "Bradley grant" when in reality it acts as a scholarship. I did this just to have consistency in the verbiage I used amongst all the other financial assistance categories since the other grants that will be introduced truly do function the way "grants" are supposed to. That being said, my high school non-weighted GPA of 3.334 (3.609 weighted) and ACT score of 24 earned me this academic scholarship.

There were different entry levels of academic scholarships you can earn at the time I enrolled at Bradley. The University Scholarship ranked second to last in regard to award amount. At the top was the "Presidential Scholarship," which was $12,000 of financial assistance toward tuition each year. Followed by the "Dean's Scholarship," which was $9,000 per year. Then the University Scholarship at $6,000 per year. Then there was the lowest award at $3,000 per year, though I've forgotten its name. To be honest, I was disappointed after I opened up my acceptance letter from the mail and saw my academic scholarship award. The other schools that I received acceptance letters from prior to Bradley granted me a lot more! Some of the highest academic scholarships I was offered were valued at $12,000 per year. Why couldn't Bradley meet this? This was all attributed to my ACT score of 24. Looking back, I can't blame them since I'm sure they have thousands of applicants every year. To make their application process as streamlined as possible, either you meet the eligibility for higher academic scholarships, or you don't. They don't have the time or resources to dig into every student's background to determine whether their ACT and GPA truly reflect their potential—me included. In the "Bradley Grant (Special Enhancement)" category, I explain how I made them invested in my personal story, but for now $6,000 per year is where I was at. Take it or leave it. Obviously, I ended up taking it because, again, I just couldn't see myself at any other school after I visited Bradley. This turned out to be a decision for the better, because not only did things straighten out for me financially, but attending Bradley also opened doors in my personal and professional life that I'm certain would not have been possible at another university. It was such an intimate, well-connected campus community, and that environment helped me take advantage of many resources and programs designed to set students up for success in the real world and distinguish them from graduates of other universities. Keep in mind, these opportunities only became available because *I took advantage of them*. I made a point to seek them out, ask questions, and put myself in the right situations at Bradley, and those choices shaped my success both in college and beyond. If you do not take those necessary steps for yourself, you will never move forward. All this to say if I were to have attended another institution solely based on the fact they offered me the most in financial assistance at the time of entry, I would not be where I am today. Weigh all your options and make calculated decisions on what you feel is best. Sometimes money is not always the answer.

Of course, I would not have even had to go through that headache if I had just scored higher on my ACT test and maybe had a slightly better GPA. If I scored 25 or 26, I would have qualified for better academic scholarships and been accepted into better schools. Please take this as a lesson for those of you still in high school. *Put in the work while you are in high school.* Your hard work and dedication toward your academics will only help you in the future, and in regard to college applications, give you better tuition assistance packages. It's not that I didn't try when I was in high school. As mentioned previously, at the end of my freshman year, I had around a 2.8 GPA. I saw I needed to make some improvements because I was quite surprised when I reviewed my report card. I knew this wasn't the real me nor did I want this to represent me. This motivated me to see what I was capable of, and I ended up graduating with a non-weighted GPA of 3.334 and a weighted GPA of 3.609. Regarding the ACT, I do not remember taking ACT preparation classes, but I do remember taking a few mock exams to simulate the actual test. I also had a lot of at-home practice books that were hand-me-downs from my older brother and sister. I had a good work ethic back then. I remember doing countless hours of preparation for the ACT, yet I only scored a 23 the first attempt, followed by a 24 (with a 10 out of 12 on the optional essay portion) on the retake despite my best efforts. At the end of the day, I tried my best, and although neither the ACT nor the academic scholarship awards were what I had hoped for, I am thankful and grateful that I scored what I did because it could have been a lot worse. Of course, I did not have the same mindset in high school as I do now, but I put in a solid effort toward my academics at the time and I encourage all of you with this same situation to do so as well. Your GPA and ACT are gateways in determining certain paths of your future. Do not take these—or high school in general, for that matter—lightly, because trying your best at this stage in life can translate to thousands saved if college is in your long-term plans.

BRADLEY GRANT (NORMAL): $8,500

There is nothing too extravagant about this category as the summary I provided on it earlier basically sums it up. I had no control over how much financial assistance this category ended up providing. Again, Bradley assessed my financial need by analyzing my FAFSA information to determine what state and federal aid I qualified for. After federal and state aid were taken into consideration as well as funding available from an institutional standpoint, Bradley had a good sense of my financial need and awarded additional funding in the form of grants to students such as I. In my case, my financial need was extremely great my freshman year which explains why I received $8,000. I did not have any additional financial assistance like scholarships at that time. Therefore, Bradley provided the funds I needed to help pay for tuition. The only other "normal" grant given from Bradley was $500 during my senior year. Since I had a good amount of scholarships applied to my senior year already, I cannot justify as to why I received this, but I cannot complain! Of course, $500 is fairly small, but any amount used to pay for tuition makes a huge impact and I was grateful regardless.

It is good to know that the university had my back during my freshman year when I was in dire need of extra financial aid, but it is best not to have to rely on the university for matters such as this. Sometimes money is not going to be available from the university for each and every student. That is why it is so important to take matters into your own hands and go out and get extra financial aid independent of any university handicap. *I encourage every student who reads this to frequent your respective college or university's financial aid office and ask what forms of financial aid are available to you as a student.* Ask questions about any and all scholarships, grants, or other forms of aid that can apply to you. You never know what is hiding in plain sight unless you ask!

BRADLEY GRANT (NEED-BASED): $10,222

Although this category is extremely identical to the previous category, Bradley Grant (Normal), it is important to note the differences. The first difference is in regard to the line items labeled "Bradley Grant (Need-Based)" in my financial assistance breakdown. Sophomore year there is a line item for $2,000 and junior year there is a line item for $2,160. These line items were funding through what Bradley called the "Stephens/Morgan/Richey Scholarship." When I was conducting my research and tracing back all my financial assistance, I saw this scholarship entry and could not remember winning any external scholarships with this title. After contacting the financial aid office, I found out Bradley has generous private donors that donate funds to the university. Bradley uses those donations to partially fund tuition for students who meet the same need-based qualifications they analyze in the Bradley Grant (Normal) category. Again, this is out of my control, and it is important to be independent of any reliance on university-granted financial assistance as there is no guarantee there will be funding available.

The second difference is in regard to the senior year line item labeled Bradley Grant (Need-Based) for $6,062. Part of what makes up this number is a grant from Bradley called the "Brighton Endowed

Scholarship" that was awarded to me in the amount of $1,500. This Brighton Endowed Scholarship has the exact same reasoning as the Stephens/Morgan/Richey Scholarship, only this has a different name and was awarded at a different time. What truly differentiates this line item, though, is that the other $4,562 came from funding known as the "State of Illinois MAP Grant." MAP stands for Monetary Award Program (MAP). This is a government program run through the State of Illinois in which eligible Illinois residents who attend approved Illinois colleges and who demonstrate financial need based on information provided on the FAFSA receive a MAP grant. I remember going into the financial aid office and inquiring about this when I saw it applied to my tuition bill. The synopsis I formed was that this was out of my control and that there are so many variables at play for when and who receives this award. This explains why I only saw this type of grant applied once. A MAP grant is roughly calculated the same way as the Bradley need-based scholarships, but it is through the Illinois state government instead of the university. I did not need to apply for this whatsoever because everything was taken care of through the Bradley financial aid office since they do a lot of financial reporting to the state. I wanted to include this point to encourage you to get informed about similar programs available where you live so you can be aware of what's at your disposal, use it to your advantage, and avoid missing out on these options for aid.

By adding the Bradley Grant (Need-Based) category with the Bradley Grant (Normal) category, it shows that I received $18,722 in grants that I do not have to pay back. This was all due to the fact that I met their need-based eligibility requirements. To give you a better idea why I qualified, I came from a middle-class family. In my eyes, I had a great upbringing. Not from the financial or material sense, but from the values and character my family holds themselves to and live by. My father is the owner of a small business called Specialty Welding. He puts a new meaning to the phrase "small business" because he is the only employee and has been for the majority of his career. His welding shop is about fifty feet from the house I grew up in. It is a small, modest operation with a fair amount of customers to provide for his family, but it is by no means a cash cow. My mother works part-time as a waitress. Together, my parents were able to raise four children with the standards they lived by. We always had just enough with a little extra to spare from time to time. There is no way that my family would have been able to pay for college alone. I know everyone's financial situation is different. Some are better and some are worse than mine. It is imperative to know that there is funding available for students that takes into consideration whatever your financial situation is. I was fortunate to have a lot of my need-based grants automatically applied to my financial assistance packages, *but you still need to take a proactive approach and understand what aid resources, both university-based and government-based, are available to you.* In any financial aid office, you will find experts who can answer all of your questions surrounding these need-based programs.

BRADLEY GRANT (SPECIAL ENHANCEMENT): $18,000

"Ask and you shall receive" is a phrase I like to use when talking about winning scholarships, and this category is a living testament of this phrase in action as well. The Bradley Grant (Special Enhancement) category is the most important out of all the grants I have covered thus far due to the action I took to be awarded it. When I was discussing my backstory of why I chose Bradley, it had a lot to do with what the university offered at the time and not so much the initial academic scholarship of $6,000 per year. In fact, this was one of the lowest offers from a school I had received. Even though I had made up my mind that I wanted to attend Bradley, the fact that I was still receiving such little financial aid bothered me. I still remember crunching the numbers of how much my first semester at Bradley would cost me the summer following my high school graduation. I had never handled money in the tens of thousands before, and knowing that my family and I would eventually be responsible for that bill was daunting. My initial thought was that there wasn't much I could do to change the number I was going to be charged. It really irritated me that I worked so hard to get my GPA up to meet so many higher academic scholarship prerequisites and that the only thing holding me back was my ACT score. Since I had already decided on attending Bradley, I figured I would send a letter to their financial aid office to plead my case. I really didn't have anything else to lose. This action turned out to be one of the best things I could have done to help my financial future.

Below is the first letter I sent to Bradley's financial aid office to request that they raise my academic scholarship during the summer of 2013 before I started Bradley in the fall of 2013. To maintain privacy, I have omitted the name of whom I addressed the original letter to and only included their title. You will see similar privacy measures taken for all other examples throughout this book as necessary. For the purposes of this book, I assigned a title to each paragraph in this letter so they can easily be referenced back to during later analysis.

SPECIAL ENHANCEMENT LETTER 1

May 20, 2013

[REMOVED NAME]
Director of Financial Assistance
[REMOVED ADDRESS]

Dear [REMOVED NAME],

PARAGRAPH 1

I am pleased to inform you that I am considering attending Bradley University this coming fall! Bradley University is one of my top choices because of its esteemed Engineering program that has affiliations with Caterpillar Inc.

PARAGRAPH 2

Unfortunately, Bradley is not at the top of my college list in terms of financial aid offered. In my acceptance letter, I was awarded the University Scholarship, which is $6,000 per year, verses other universities that offered me scholarships valued at $10,000-$12,000 per year. As a student who holds a GPA of 3.555 (as of 7th semester) and is involved in multiple extracurricular activities, I strongly believe that the University Scholarship is not reflective of my academic capabilities.

PARAGRAPH 3

Since both my brother and sister acquired great sums of student debt, I am aware of the financial struggle a college education can bring. Therefore, I request that the Office of Financial Assistance upgrade my scholarship to the Dean's Scholarship, which is $9,000 per year. Once I send in my final transcript around June 14th for proof of graduation, you may verify that my GPA exceeds the required GPA for the Dean's Scholarship.

PARAGRAPH 4

I urge the Office of Financial Assistance reevaluate their decision and offer me the Dean's Scholarship. If not, this issue may affect my decision to attend Bradley University. Thank you!

Sincerely,

Jeremy Kaszycki

Enclosure: Résumé

You may have noticed some differences to what I wrote so far in this book versus what I wrote in this letter. Trust me, there is a strategy behind it. There are two main points I want to elaborate on.

First of all, I originally told you that I had decided to attend Bradley despite their scholarship offering. This was absolutely true, but I did not want to tell this to Bradley just yet. *Remember, in life the strongest negotiating position is the ability for someone to walk away and mean it.* If I had told them that I was planning on attending their school yet still asking to raise my scholarship, they probably would have thrown out my letter as soon as I started asking for money. Why would the school offer a scholarship increase to a student they know is already committed to attending and paying the tuition as originally billed? That's like walking into a car dealership and telling them you would appreciate them reducing the price to $35,000 for a new car but you are fine with paying $40,000 and you are absolutely going to buy it anyways even if they do not lower it. Of course they are not going to lower it in that case! Same applies here. I recognized I could not immediately say I was sold on Bradley. That is why in the very last paragraph of the letter, I told them that if they do not raise my scholarship, it may affect my decision to attend Bradley. This gives them a little more reason to think about raising my scholarship to the next level. Now they have to weigh their options: either they award me an additional $3,000 per year, totaling $12,000, or they risk losing a student altogether and forfeiting four years of tuition revenue.

Notice how I did not ask for too much. I simply asked to be raised to the next level of scholarship aid, and I justified it through my GPA. This is a more logical approach that has a higher chance of you getting the result you want. *I was trying to create a win-win scenario between myself and the university.* I could have asked for the max scholarship aid, but I knew my GPA did not meet the requirement, thus throwing off my persuasive approach. When I wrote this letter, I felt that getting my scholarship increased from $6,000 to $9,000 would have been a huge win regardless.

Secondly, I addressed and mailed this letter to the head of the financial aid office at the time—the Director of Financial Assistance at Bradley University. I did not want to send the letter to the office without a specific name tied to it because it could end up on the wrong desk, in the wrong person's hands, or worse, in a pile of junk mail that never gets looked at promptly or that ends up in the trash. I wanted my letter to be read by a decision-maker in that office. Someone who has the power to actually make my scholarship increase a reality. I did some research prior to drafting this letter and found out who the head of the department that dealt with financial aid was. I wasted no time in addressing the letter to, in this case, the director, and sending it in the mail.

I do not remember receiving a response to this letter the summer I sent it. Also, I do not quite remember if I followed up with the financial aid office to see if they received the letter and to discuss about their thoughts regarding my request. My first instinct is to say I didn't because I would have remembered such an event. If I did not, this was a huge mistake on my part. I will go over the importance of why following up is so crucial in a moment. If I did, I must not have gotten very far because my message was not heard loud enough. At the end of the summer, I still had no response from Bradley about my letter, so I had to prepare for my freshman year with the financial aid I originally received.

I had a great freshman year experience, but my bank account did not with the financial hit it had taken. I ended my freshman year with a GPA of 3.34 and was involved in a lot of on-campus extracurricular activities. I recognized that with such a great year that I had at Bradley, it further strengthened my point that I was deserving of a higher academic scholarship award than the University Scholarship. Therefore, I decided to write a second letter addressed to the same Director of Financial Assistance the summer of 2014 in preparation for my sophomore year starting in fall of 2014. Although this time, I used a slightly different strategy.

SPECIAL ENHANCEMENT LETTER 2

June 5, 2014

[REMOVED NAME]
Director of Financial Assistance
[REMOVED ADDRESS]

Dear [REMOVED NAME],

PARAGRAPH 1
Finishing my freshman year at Bradley University was a milestone in my life. I am truly blessed to have met so many fascinating students and faculty that made my first year memorable. I have learned so much already about myself, others, and more importantly, my major of Manufacturing Engineering that I am excited to tackle whatever awaits me coming Fall Semester of 2014.

PARAGRAPH 2

There always seems to be a bump in the road and, in my case, is my family's financial situation.

After paying off living expenses and taxes, my family has little to contribute to my education. As represented in my 2014 FAFSA, my parents, in total, had less income than they did last year. That is why I have taken it upon myself to work as hard as I can to pay off Bradley's tuition. The past two summers I have worked as a lifeguard at Magic Waters Water Park. This summer, I have been blessed with a paid internship at a local manufacturing firm all while taking Calculus III at a local community college and participating in a 6-week scholarship competition through my local YMCA. On top of that, I plan on either learning to weld or finding another job to work on weekends.

PARAGRAPH 3

Even though it is fewer hours, I accepted an internship position because I believe getting a hands-on approach to my major early on will help me find a job in the near future. As a full-time student with a GPA of 3.34 and holding executive positions in both the Bradley "Red Sea" and Bradley SME, I believe I have shown great work ethic in trying to excel in becoming a Manufacturing Engineer. Whether it is watching videos online, getting help from peers, or attending professor's office hours, I really tried to benefit from all my resources and my grades exemplify such effort.

PARAGRAPH 4

I have been fortunate enough to be able to pay off my freshman year on my own but coming Fall Semester of 2014, I will be forced to take out a loan. Both my brother and sister currently have hefty sums of debt that they owe due to college loans that they have taken out and interest accumulated from them. Therefore, my parents are more focused on providing them with the funds to get out of debt which leaves me on my own. This worries me because I cannot afford to jeopardize my plans for the future just because of a few loans I have taken out and also I do not want to think it is up to them to get me out of debt.

PARAGRAPH 5

Out of the countless applications I have submitted, I was lucky enough to be selected to win a few scholarships. Unfortunately, even with the extra scholarship money factored into my tuition, I *fear that I will not be able to afford next semester's payment. This is partly due to the fact that Bradley now charges 2% interest on tuition payments via credit card. Also, my engineering department raised the price per credit hour on classes from $5 to $50. Therefore, I would love to work out something between the Office of Financial Assistance and my family to hopefully make ends meet. I want to be able to focus on school as much as I can without having to worry about not making payments on time and ultimately ending up having the same financial difficulties as my siblings.*

PARAGRAPH 6

I appreciate you taking the time to read this letter and hope that you find time to review my case. If you have any questions concerning my situation, please feel free to contact me via cell phone at [REMOVED PHONE NUMBER] or email at [REMOVED EMAIL]. Thank you.

Sincerely,

Jeremy Kaszycki

When I compare these two letters, it's clear that the second one offers much more substance to support my case for additional financial aid, even without saying so directly. I focus on the fact that I did not take out a private loan up until this point (I did have a federal loan taken out though) and certain financial events, both family and school-related, will be negatively impacting my ability to pay for next year's tuition. Before I get into too much explanation on the strategy behind the second letter, so you too can utilize this approach, I want to talk about the events that transpired next.

I explicitly remember following up with the financial aid office later that summer before the fall 2014 semester started. I asked if I could speak to the director and I ended up getting transferred to his office. He picked up the phone, and I explained that I was calling to follow up on the letter I had sent. The director said he personally read the letter. I do not recall how the exact conversation flowed but I do remember him saying that he recognized the hard work I was putting in. He also understood the financial burden the cost of tuition was having on myself and my family. One thing I do remember in vivid detail is how he described how the financial aid office was going to approach my situation. He said they were going to apply a "special enhancement" to my financial assistance package in the amount of $6,000 every year from sophomore to senior year. I can't tell you the relief I felt in this moment. I had butterflies in my stomach because I could not believe what I was hearing from the director himself. He said I did not have to do anything extra other than to keep up the good work and that the extra $6,000 in addition to my original $6,000 from the University Scholarship will be reflected on each tuition statement from then on. He said he would make a note on my file to finalize everything and make it official. I tried to express to him my appreciation over the phone as best I could but, due to the state of shock I was in, I probably did a terrible job at it. An extra $6,000 in an "enhancement grant" means I just solidified $18,000 extra of financial assistance over my next three years. That is $18,000 I did not have to pay back in loans with interest! Now that I have real bills to pay on top of other obligations that life throws at me, I cannot imagine being another $18,000 in debt. If that were the case, that translates to months of slow payback and putting my future plans on hold such as investing that money into income-producing assets. The earlier you start on investing, the quicker you will achieve financial freedom in your future if you manage your money accordingly. If you are stuck with debt, you cannot advance yourself and will miss major opportunity. This is the value of opportunity cost! As Dave Ramsey would say, "The borrower is slave to the lender!"

Writing these letters turned out to be one of the pillars of the financial assistance success I had. It was because I took this action that I got this result. At the end of the day, I wrote this letter to the Director of Financial Assistance because that was my only option on how I could change my situation since I did not initially agree with it. I asked myself, "What is the worst thing that could happen if I just ask them to raise my academic scholarship?" If I had never asked in the first place, this would have never happened. Again—ask and you shall receive. If I were too timid at this time and thought "Oh, they wouldn't even bother to read a letter from some insignificant incoming freshman," or other negative thoughts, this financial win would have never happened. Don't let thoughts like this stop you from taking action to better your future. The outcome could be exactly what you are looking for and all you have to do is take the first step forward! Remember, the first step in another direction changes your destination completely. *The point is this: don't be afraid to ask for what you want.* In life, no one is going to give you a handout. You need to go out and make things happen for yourself.

LETTER BREAKDOWNS

Now, I will dive into some specifics about each letter. I am sharing this strategy with you so that you may apply this technique to a similar situation you may be having. The main reason why I chose to write a letter is because I knew how to format it appropriately. By that I mean create what is known as a business letter format. This is very basic and I remember learning how to write a business letter in high school. There is also a myriad of resources online that give you the basics on this. I knew if I wrote my letter in a business letter format, they would take my request seriously. Also, writing a letter is a good idea because it is something physical that someone has to handle in their hands. It is better than, let's say, an email because the recipient will be more attentive toward a letter. One thing I learned now that I have been exposed to a corporate environment workplace is that if you are sending an email to a high-level executive, their email attention span is about ten seconds. This is because they are running multiple facets of an organization and have a constant bombardment of emails related to several projects going on simultaneously. The same thing would apply to the Director of Financial Assistance that I was addressing my letter to as well.

Below, I will break down and explain each letter using the following sequence: Structure Breakdown, Paragraph Breakdown, and Final Breakdown Comments. At any point during the breakdown, please flip back to the pages containing each respective letter or take a picture of the letter on your phone if you need to see first-hand what I am referring to when explaining the ideas within each letter.

LETTER 1 BREAKDOWN

When writing a letter of this nature, you cannot simply just dive in, list your demands, and expect the recipient to meet your every request at the snap of a finger. Although how I wrote my second letter uses that idea more so than my first letter, it is present in both to some degree.

STRUCTURE BREAKDOWN

Business letter style. I included a header on the top portion of the page to really elevate the look of my letter. The header usually is simple and includes your name, current address, and best methods of contact for you. When I was interviewing for jobs, I included the website address to my LinkedIn profile in my letter headers as well. It is up to you what you want to include, but just remember whatever you include helps you paint a picture of what you want your recipient to think of you. I wanted to give off as professional of a tone as I could.

I have stated this once but will state it again. Address this letter to whoever has the most power in order to help you get to where you need to be or accomplish what you want to accomplish. In my case, I went straight to the head of the financial aid department.

PARAGRAPH 1 BREAKDOWN

I start off in a light-hearted manner, and I bring excited energy because both the director and I have positive associations with Bradley University.

PARAGRAPH 2 BREAKDOWN

Here, I describe the problem, which is the lack of financial aid Bradley is offering compared to other schools. I also explain that the reason this is a problem is because, in my eyes, the financial aid offered is not proportionate to the level of student that I am due to my high GPA and extracurricular involvement.

PARAGRAPH 3 BREAKDOWN

I provide a legitimate connection of why I am worrying about the lack of financial aid through the example of my older brother and sister. As the author of a letter like this, this example is key because it shows that you are not requesting additional financial aid just for selfish reasons or through entitlement. It shows that you are conscious about the negative affect student loans can have upon young adults. It shows that you recognize the problems student loans bring and you want to do everything in your power to not fall victim to them. I then go to request the solution of increasing my financial assistance from the University Scholarship of $6,000 per year up to the Dean's Scholarship of $9,000 per year. Again, this is a very reasonable request due to the fact that my GPA met the requirement for the Dean's Scholarship despite my ACT score being below target. I am using my extracurricular activities earlier as leverage to make up for the fact that my ACT score is lacking.

PARAGRAPH 4 BREAKDOWN

I summarize the point of the letter very concisely here. The strongest part about this letter is how I state that this may affect my decision to attend Bradley if my request is not met. As mentioned earlier, this was a negotiating tactic I used. Remember, the strongest negotiating position is the ability for someone to walk away and mean it. I framed it this way because I thought Bradley would be more inclined to increase my aid rather than risk losing a student who planned to stay and pay tuition long-term.

FINAL BREAKDOWN COMMENTS

At the bottom, I left enough room so I could handwrite my signature to solidify the personal nature of the letter. I also enclosed a résumé within the letter when I sent it. I believed this was important considering how I spoke so highly of my extracurricular activities and how they presented me as a stand-out student. For anyone wanting to take this approach, adding attachments can be where you tailor your message to show your strengths. Maybe instead of a résumé, you print out your LinkedIn profile, or some project or portfolio-type document that exemplifies your strengths. Whatever will make your point stronger in this negotiation.

You see that the second letter seemed more from the heart than this first one did. That is because I did not have a lot to go off of for the first iteration. If you think about it, I am not even tied to the university yet, and I am making demands for more money when I do not meet standard academic scholarship criteria. That is why I decided to make it fairly cut and dry. Also, typically with business letters, it is best to keep them under one page. Despite this first iteration being fairly simple and to the point, you can see how I nearly ran out of space while still keeping appropriate format spacing. This letter overall did its job. It introduced myself professionally, stated the problem, requested a solution, and left the ball in their court with my statement that it may affect my decision of attendance. This letter started the conversation that no one was originally having. *That is why it is an absolute must to follow up.* You need to close the conversation.

Earlier I had mentioned I do not remember following up to see if the director read my letter. The only way I would have remembered following up is if he had given me a yes or no on whether Bradley would fulfill my request for more scholarship funding. Unlike with the second letter, I do not recall this happening with the first. If I had followed up earlier, I may have received the special enhancement grant earlier. This mistake may have cost me $6,000! I will go into more detail behind following up within the breakdown of the second letter.

One last note: if you do end up following up after a first iteration letter such as this, make sure that you talk with the person who you want to talk to. If you do not get through to them the first attempt—maybe your call was sent to voicemail, or you talk to the secretary—keep trying until you reach them. It's important to speak with the person who actually has the influence to get you where you need to go. Be persistent, but not to the point where your outreach becomes excessive or intrusive. When you're on the phone, always be polite and professional, but above all, be direct. Do not settle for relying on someone else to relay a message. If you absolutely have to, you can have someone else relay the message but then if a week goes by and you don't hear back, contact them again. Also, your default option for following up should be in person. The next best thing would be a phone call. Do not hide behind email or text. An in-person arrival or a phone call shows your recipient that you care about the matter, that you're confident and professional, and that you respect them enough to seek a personal interaction. It will make the other party appreciate and respect you more in return.

LETTER 2 BREAKDOWN

The second letter I wrote had more relatable subject matter to write about than compared to the first. I still was quite discontent with my financial assistance package after I completed my freshman year at Bradley which is the reason why I decided to write a second letter. I did not give up after the first attempt because I truly believed I had a convincing argument as to why I needed the extra financial aid. For the second letter's strategy, I did not mention a specific number in aid I would have liked. Rather, I explained my situation to Bradley—and more importantly to the same director I sent the first letter to—and hoped they would hear my plea and respond to my case appropriately. I focused on how I was exhausting every option to fund my college education despite several roadblocks—the most prominent being my family's financial situation. This letter was more heartfelt and gave the impression that I truly cared—and I did. That's why I went through this process in the first place; I believed in my cause and was passionate about it. My letter was the equivalent of me extending my hand out for help. Luckily, Bradley caught me before I fell.

STRUCTURE BREAKDOWN

Business letter style. Same overall style and formatting as the first letter.

PARAGRAPH 1 BREAKDOWN

I make the Bradley connection again to establish common ground, and I open in a light-hearted way by explaining how excited I was about everything I had going on at the time, starting the letter on a high note.

PARAGRAPH 2 BREAKDOWN

Be mindful of transitions. You want your letter to flow. The flow found in the second paragraph is that despite the high note of a great freshman year, there are always setbacks. This is where I briefly mention about the bigger problem at hand, which is my family's financial situation, but then immediately transition to what I am doing about it. Again, nobody just wants to give handouts in life. I will touch on this later in the book; however, they see that I am not simply complaining, asking for a handout, and calling it a day. I am doing my best with the circumstances provided to me in order to make ends meet, with those "ends" being the cost of school.

PARAGRAPH 3 BREAKDOWN

This paragraph is an extension to what I highlighted in the second. The second highlights what I am doing outside of college while the third highlights what I am doing related to college. Here, I am explaining how serious I am about my education and that I am not taking this opportunity lightly. I want to succeed in Manufacturing Engineering and the only way I will do that is to take action.

PARAGRAPH 4 BREAKDOWN

I introduce the main problem in the letter by explaining that I was being forced to start taking out student loans and why. The problem isn't simply that they're inconvenient; it's the long-term effects of debt and the fact that I alone am responsible for paying for school.

PARAGRAPH 5 BREAKDOWN

This paragraph is an extension of the problem stated in the fourth. Part of the reason why I felt so strongly I had a case for writing a letter was because it seemed at every financial turn I was getting knocked down. More specifically, on top of the hefty tuition price, Bradley increased its price per credit hour on all engineering classes. Also, if I were to pay tuition through credit card, which is what I was using to pay at the time, I would be charged a 2% fee. A 2% fee from a bill that is thousands of dollars adds up to hundreds of dollars of extra cost! This paragraph is very important because it gives concrete examples of how much these small changes have a big effect on students, especially students in financial situations such as mine. Therefore, you will evoke emotions of empathy in your target audience if you use this type of approach. After the main concern of me stating that I fear I will not be able to afford next semester's payment, I don't offer a solution like the first letter. Instead, I humbly suggest if the university would recognize my situation and further look into possible options to help.

PARAGRAPH 6 BREAKDOWN

I conclude with the best way to contact me. Plain and simple. You have already stated your case so any more explanation here would just be rambling. If they want to learn more about your situation, they will call you.

FINAL BREAKDOWN COMMENTS

No résumé enclosure this time as my track record described in the letter was evidence enough. *The biggest takeaway from this letter is the need to come from a place of humility and genuine concern.* For me, I was legitimately concerned about my ability to pay, and it showed by *how* I communicated that concern in the letter. Come from a place of logic, reason, and truth. I could justify everything I said in the letter, and it made sense why I was struggling. Therefore, my plea became more compelling.

LETTER BREAKDOWN ENDING NOTES

To conclude the discussion of the financial aid letters: the main idea is that if you have a legitimate financial struggle or concern, **do not be afraid to put it on the table and be up front about it**. By this, I mean do not be going on social media and posting about it or complaining about it to random people on the street. Instead, be aware that your situation is your reality. It does not define you by any means. It is simply a challenge that you must overcome, one that will make you stronger. So, when you bring up topics like this, make sure they are to the right individuals. Individuals who can help you include people such as the Director of Financial Assistance I addressed my letter to. In these instances, do not be ashamed or think, "Oh, no one even cares." Why? What is there to be ashamed about? Why would you assume the financial aid office doesn't care? These close-minded ideas can shut the door to opportunity the moment they enter your head. Even if you don't get as significant of a result as I got, maybe whoever you mentioned your story to can point you in a direction where you can get financial assistance, other help, or something even greater.

Another example of an appropriate time I talked about my financial situation and how it related to my ability to pay for my college education is as follows. It was the summer of 2013, and I had just completed my freshman year at Bradley University. As briefly mentioned in the second financial aid letter, I was involved in a six-week scholarship competition through my local Young Men's Christian Association (YMCA). The concept of this competition modeled itself off Donald Trump's reality show, "The Apprentice." The participants were broken up into two teams who, each week, worked on a different project related to local community businesses. The teams were presented with a problem and were tasked to come up with a solution by the end of the week. At the end of each week, winning teams would be declared and, based on the events that transpired over the course of each week, certain people were eliminated until there were three winners, each of whom won a scholarship amount. The competition was fun, competitive, and stressful. The summer I participated in this competition was the same summer that I sent the second financial aid letter and, up to that point, I did not hear a response back from them. The thought of me not having a definite way to pay my tuition subconsciously lingered in my mind throughout the competition. At one point, the Chief Executive Officer (CEO) of the YMCA, who was the main organizer for the competition, noticed I was off from my normal demeanor at one of the presentation events. We stepped to the side, and I told him about my college financial situation. I even started to tear up as I summoned the courage to tell him such a touchy and personal subject. Despite performing well in the competition, I worried that if I didn't place in the top three and win a scholarship, I would fall far behind in my goal of paying for college. Writing about this now, I should not have been so worried. Instead of focusing about whether I would be a finalist, I should have focused on performing even better at the competition. I was young at the time and emotion overcame me at that moment. The CEO understood where I was coming from and told me to continue to do the best I can. Nothing more came from the interaction. I am not sorry I had this conversation with him because, even though nothing came of it, this was still a person who was in a position to help if he chose to do so. I ended up finishing as a semi-finalist and was not awarded a scholarship. Still, I was grateful for the experience as it gave me a lot to write about on my résumé and future scholarship essays. The local YMCA CEO who I shared my story with had the ability to make a difference in my life and possibly grant me additional scholarship money. If I never even mentioned it to him and kept my situation bottled in, I would have never even given myself a chance to have something come out of it.

The bottom line is someone is bound to listen if you open up to them. Even if one person hears your story, that may be the one person you need to change your life. The idea of "ask and you shall receive" will be a consistent factor throughout this book. Even though the YMCA situation didn't work out, asking Bradley's financial aid office for assistance resulted in an extra $18,000 in financial aid. If you do not get the result you hoped for but believe you truly deserve it, do not give up—stay persistent. Remember how the success of the second financial aid letter followed the failure of the first. Use these tips, strategies, and concepts talked about in this category and apply them to your own situation. You can make something out of nothing. Once you recognize that, determine what you want, plan how to achieve it, and—most importantly—take action.

Step 2

IMPROVE YOURSELF

5

Get Involved

We've all seen successful people from a distance—on social media, in the news, or simply through what others say. "Successful" can mean many things, but for the purposes of this section, let's define it the way most people instinctively do: someone who is financially well off. I'm a huge basketball fan and one of my favorite players who embodies this aura of being successful is Kobe Bryant. If you know anything about him, you know he was a basketball legend who excelled not only on the court but also in business after he retired. He is a great example because his success spans multiple areas—athletics, business, discipline, mindset—making him relatable to a wide range of people. Even to someone unfamiliar with him, if they managed to come across him in passing, the outward markers alone—his attire, his vehicle, or his entourage—would clearly suggest success.

Whether you already knew of Kobe or were seeing him for the first time, both situations would lead you to the same thought: success. In either case, we need to analyze *why* the thought of being "successful" comes to mind. Even now as I am writing this, Kobe was so successful and had such an impact during his time on earth that I chose to write about him when there are thousands of other inspirational people I could have used as examples. Kobe did not have anything given to him that made him have that type of influence. He wasn't a child prodigy. As a teenager, before any fame, he wasn't offered any basketball contracts or million-dollar business deals. As a young man, he wasn't immediately glorified as one of the best to play the game when he entered the NBA his rookie season. Now, when we look at the end of his twenty-year, Hall-of-Fame career with the Los Angeles Lakers, we see the millions of dollars he amassed, properties he owns, businesses he is a part of, and kids everywhere shouting his name whenever they throw a crunched up piece of paper into a recycling bin. How did he get all that? Why did he get all that? The answer is simple. He deserved it.

Kobe Bryant approached his craft of basketball with tireless intensity. Countless hours of practice, drills, and rigorous exercise. Days spent studying his opponent's weaknesses to exploit them, studying his own weaknesses to improve them, and training his body and mind to endure the challenges that most tend to avoid. His relentless pursuit to become the greatest player to ever play the game of basketball etched his legend and story in human history. His relentless pursuit is what made all of his success possible. People paid him because of what he was able to do. The value he offered was better than some average NBA player that just sits on the bench and is the last string of the rotation. So is the same for any and every person that we see as "successful" in our eyes. **They did or are doing something that is deserving of whatever success they achieved.**

Being "successful" is scalable on any level, and the level we are most concerned with in this book is success through scholarships. When looking at high school and college students applying for scholarships, the successful applicants are those that display *why* they are deserving to win those scholarships. They demonstrate their value. They offer more over the average student who applied to the same scholarship. Winning scholarships is not something that will magically happen just because you read this book if you take no action. Plus, how fair would it be if scholarships were just given out to anybody and everybody who applied? You have to show the donor—whether it be an organization, business, or individual—why you are deserving of their scholarship fund. The main ideas that will be introduced next will help you to improve yourself if applied. By improving yourself, you are improving the person who is depicted on the application that the scholarship judge, who has never met you before and does not care how "nice of a person you are," reads about. All they care about is why you are deserving of the scholarship. So, you have to ask yourself, "Why do I deserve to win this scholarship—be it $500, $1,000, or $10,000—over someone else?" If you can't give solid, concrete, compelling answers to that question that would catch the scholarship selection committee's attention, then you have some work to do. Don't worry though. Step 2 is all about how you show them on the non-essay portion of the scholarship application that you deserve to win.

GRADE POINT AVERAGE

Before we even get into all the other fancy aspects of "getting involved," the most important thing you need to make sure you do first is to get involved in your *classes*! What I mean is you need to take your classes seriously so that you can maintain a competitive GPA. I can tell you right now that if you have a low GPA, you will not be taken seriously for scholarships. The *minimum* you should strive for is 3.0. Having a GPA that is in good standing tells a lot about an applicant. It gives off the impression that you try hard at school, you show up and perform, you are intelligent, and overall you are a good student that they do not need to worry about. A solid GPA eliminates GPA concerns altogether. Judges and employers see it, check the box, and move on to evaluating the rest of your strengths. It functions like a basic prerequisite you're expected to meet. On the contrary, if your GPA is lower than you would like, it opens up a number of problems. For one, you might not even be eligible to apply for the scholarship you are trying to get. The other issue is that it simply makes the person evaluating your credentials ask, "Why?" Once this question is asked, they can start to speculate all sorts of scenarios why your GPA is low and start fishing for reasons not to pick you for a scholarship, job, or other opportunity. Try to avoid this at all costs. I know it's frustrating, and scholarships should place more weight on a student's character, but that isn't always how the process works. Rather than complaining about it, you have to accept that your GPA needs to be maintained at a certain level—and then execute. Having a high GPA opens more doors than not. This is one of the easiest parts of a scholarship application to control, so take advantage of it. If your GPA is not where you want it at, don't worry. There are so many resources at your disposal to help you increase it. *The bottom line is that you need to put in the effort, stay locked in, and give your best so your GPA becomes a blessing instead of a curse.*

EXTRACURRICULAR ACTIVITIES

The idea of "getting involved" is a simple one, yet it makes all the difference. I am not trying to sound like a typical, overly enthusiastic college tour guide that constantly tells the prospective incoming freshman on tour to get involved in campus life. I am coming to you from the viewpoint of a student who has walked down the path you are currently on and has achieved success and I can tell you, with zero hesitation, the overly enthusiastic tour guide is not wrong. Scholarship donors are always looking for an applicant who goes the extra mile as a student and consistently does more than what's required. The reason why is because they want to know if the student they are going to award the scholarship to is an overachiever and someone who takes improving themselves seriously. If they see that you are involved in more than just being a standard student, it signals to them that you are someone who will keep striving to pursue meaningful goals long after college. Donors look for students who will continue on to make significant contributions to society, especially in disciplines aligned with the organization's focus, such as engineering or health. Funding those students indirectly allows the donor to contribute to that broader good. Think of it like an investment, only in this case the return on investment for the scholarship donor would be the student giving back to the world. If they see that an applicant only does the bare minimum, the donor will perceive that you are just going to continue to do the bare minimum after college. Later in this section I will show you what exactly I was involved in over the course of my time in high school and college, but first I want to elaborate on how one can "get involved."

Getting involved is extremely easy. Schools present a multitude of opportunities, so you're bound to find something you can not only participate in but truly thrive in while developing valuable skills. These opportunities include extracurricular activities such clubs, organizations, sports, student groups, and so on. Whatever school you are attending, they will have virtually unlimited options of what you can join to start to enhance your scholarship application.

When it comes to extracurriculars, you can choose to get involved in anything that interests you. If you have a hobby that you enjoy or there is an activity or subject you have always wanted to learn more about, joining a group related to that is a great decision. Even if it is unrelated to your college major, whatever you get involved in is not a bad idea. This will show that you are a well-rounded individual. The main point is that you are doing *something. One thing that I strongly encourage, though, is to make sure that at least some of your extracurriculars are in fact related to your college major or course of study.* A lot of the scholarships that you will be able to apply for will more than likely be related to the major you are studying. Being proactive within your primary field of interest by joining clubs or groups within that interest will show that you are serious about your field of study. If the scholarship donor had to pick between two identical scholarship applicants with membership in five different clubs and the only difference was that "Applicant A" participated in clubs that were all random versus "Applicant B" who participated in clubs that were mostly related to the donor's specific area of expertise, chances are they will pick Applicant B. They see that Applicant B has the highest chance of making an impact in the donor's field of interest because they see the drive Applicant B already has in being successful within that field through participation in related clubs, and they want to be a part of fueling that drive. That is the premise of why most scholarships were created: to fuel interest and careers within the industries that the donors, companies, and organizations are part of.

There is a strategy you can implement while getting involved that will guarantee you stand out among your peers. *That strategy is focusing on the titles of the clubs, groups, or organizations you are a part of.* Don't get me wrong, being a regular club member is valuable and can open a lot of doors. However, picture yourself as a scholarship judge reviewing dozens of average applications before finding one from a student who served as president, vice president, or co-founder. Now tell me, having a title such as "president" instead of "member" on an application sounds a lot more enticing, doesn't it? That's because it is. Having titles can take your application from ordinary to extraordinary. Even if it is not as influential as being president of something, any title is a good title. It highlights that you're actively engaged and serve as an essential part of the organization's team. It shows you are able to deal with responsibility, use leadership skills to achieve objectives, and genuinely care and want to contribute to the cause for which the group exists for.

I was inspired to get involved in this way since my older brother used to tell me stories of what he did when he was elected president of his dormitory building at his university. Being a high school student with little influence among my peers at the time, I was amazed at how he acquired such a lofty title. From that point on, I always aspired to hold a position like that and eventually I manifested my dream into reality sophomore year of college when I was voted president of my residence hall that had an occupancy of around five hundred students. After earning the role, I felt a real sense of pride in being president. It was a great experience that gave me insight into the importance of titles and using them as leverage on scholarship applications due to the weight they carry. Another key insight that I picked up on was that a title such as "president" may give the impression of a heavy workload, but in reality the real responsibilities can be much lighter. This was the case with my tenure as president of my residence hall. I had a great team that worked with me and helped to coordinate all of our hall events. All I had to do was be the face of the organization by talking and greeting everyone at all the events, providing a vision, making decisions at our hall council meetings, and delegating work. I'm sure there are positions within certain clubs that are a lot more strenuous in terms of effort needed, but you never know unless you find out. *The lesson here is I was able to acquire such a high-status position that I could put on my résumé or scholarship applications and in reality have it be, for the most part, a fairly easy role.* In the scholarship judge's eyes though, the title of "president" subconsciously holds a higher importance factor when reviewing scholarships and you will be perceived as being more deserving of a candidate because of it, even if being the president of the club you are in is not too difficult.

The bottom line is having a focus on any type of title or position of leadership within an extracurricular activity, not just being a member, can immensely raise your stock in the scholarship judge's eyes. Evaluate the organizations you're part of, and if a leadership title such as president or vice president carries manageable responsibilities, you should strongly consider pursuing it. By doing this for the majority of your involvement within extracurriculars, you will build an extremely unique and hard-to-beat application. At the end of this chapter, I provide a comprehensive list of my involvement that shows how I applied this strategy for myself.

Before moving on, it's important to acknowledge that overcommitment or taking on roles you're not prepared for can backfire. You don't want to join activities just for the sake of being involved if you're not actually contributing. Join whatever you will be able to handle because, at the end of the day, you are at school to complete your education, not to plan out the next event for your residence hall. It's never a good idea to spread yourself too thin. When you do, you make only a millimeter of progress in every direction and end up feeling like you're accomplishing nothing, versus making meaningful progress in the one direction you truly value. If you are worried about only having two or three clubs on your résumé during your four years, then don't be afraid to drop one club after two years in which you hold one position to join another club in which you hold a different position for two years. That way you have another title on your list of accomplishments to use on an application. There is no definitive number of activities required for a strong scholarship application. However, my involvement that I outline at the end of this chapter serves as a useful benchmark as it helped me secure thousands of dollars in scholarship awards.

Lastly, when talking about campus organizations that you can join or participate in, if there is no club that exists with a particular interest or idea of yours, *do not be afraid to create your own*! Do some research into what exactly you have to do to create a new club or organization and then make it happen. Any scholarship organization will love a little bit of entrepreneurial spirit! Plus, you can automatically make yourself honorary president and reap all the perks that the title comes with as discussed! One example of me putting this idea into practice actually comes from my father's welding shop. It's not the creation of a college club, but it does show how I created something out of nothing to improve my credentials. Around the time when I was a senior in high school up until around freshman or sophomore year of college, I was quite active on LinkedIn and other job search engines with the goal of finding summer engineering internships. Since my résumé was relatively empty and lacking virtually any professional experience other than my summer lifeguard job at the time, I decided to take matters into my own hands. My father owns a small welding shop. In addition to his welding services, he also offers new boat propeller sales. During those summers, I looked into how I can help his small business in areas he lacked. I focused in on the new propeller sales aspect of the business to see if I can give it a boost because the performance of those sales was not great. My involvement included making an all-encompassing business Facebook page, professional Craigslist advertisements for propeller sales, creating a detailed database of all in-house propeller inventory, facilitating all potential new propeller customer email and phone communication, and setting up meetings around my hometown to discuss advertising partnerships with local companies within the marine and boating industries. Originally I did this work out of sheer curiosity and willingness to improve my father's small business, and it wasn't until later that I realized I could leverage my self-created experience to my advantage by posting it as "professional experience" during my job searches. I called my title "business liaison." This was a great move because it gave my résumé a much-needed upgrade and filled in the blanks with relevant information. I used this self-created experience for a long time on job applications, scholarship applications, and in interviews, until my internships eventually gave me enough real experience that I no longer needed to include it.

Being a self-starter, like in the case with my father's welding shop, can open the door to greater opportunities in the future. Unfortunately, a lot of people either do not realize manufacturing your own experience is an option or are too afraid to do so because they are worried about failing. If you are reading this and you are in high school or college, it may be hard to realize it now, but failure can be a huge blessing in disguise. *Failure offers valuable lessons when you reflect on what went wrong and identify ways to prevent the same mistakes in the future.* Failing can prevent you from going down paths you were never meant to go down in the first place, despite how painful it may be. One failure I had when I was the self-proclaimed "business liaison" was that I did not notice until late that all of my messages to potential customers were not being received due to a technical glitch within the Craigslist anonymous messaging system I was utilizing. Not noticing this in a timely manner cost me so many potential sales! Despite this, the lesson I learned was to that validate every step of a process functions correctly before implementing. It hurt at the time, but

I still used the experience to my advantage and did not get discouraged. If you approach failure in this way, you will find that it gets easier overtime and it will make you more resilient for the future. Remember Murphy's Law: anything that can go wrong will go wrong. We cannot control what happens around our environment, but we can control how we respond and react to it.

VOLUNTEERING

Involvement doesn't stop at clubs, sports, student groups, or other standard extracurricular activities. One huge participation point that needs to be addressed is volunteering. This is a subject many people frequently mention, often with comments such as, "I'd love to volunteer, but I never have the time," and similar remarks. I know I was one of those people, but that was before I knew the importance of it when talking about scholarships. I'm not going to dive into the argument that you shouldn't volunteer solely to earn scholarships and should instead do it out of genuine goodwill. That is a separate issue that you, yourself, need to sort out internally. You are reading this book because you want to know how to win scholarships, and one of the key ingredients to accomplish this is by including volunteering as an experience on your applications. So, if that is the sole reason why you are volunteering, then so be it. Can't complain with winning a few thousand dollars and helping people on the side!

In all seriousness though, when I was relentlessly applying for any and every scholarship I could get my hands on, I noticed a trend of applications inquiring about volunteering experience. Volunteering matters to scholarship judges because it shows you're proactive, willing to give back, and engaged—just like extracurricular involvement does. It was so popular that I had to devote time and energy to actually attend volunteering events and keep track of what I did. Unlike involvement in school clubs, volunteering doesn't have to be related to anything specific such as your major. The important thing is to just complete the volunteer service or activity. Nowadays, I know some high schools require a certain amount of service hours you need to complete in order to graduate. This is a good thing because it gets you going in the right direction, so don't think of these required service hours as a burden because it will help you in the future.

When it comes to volunteering in high school or college, I recommend doing at least one volunteer activity each semester. When you are home for the summer, do one during the summer at least. Although I wasn't heavily involved in volunteering as a student, my participation was sufficient to complete the volunteer section on every application. When you volunteer, *keep track* of the date of service, the hours you volunteered, the organization you worked with, and what you did—I'll elaborate more on this concept later. Keeping a log is important because you do not want to forget information on applications that can make you stand out.

AWARDS

Increasing your involvement in school, extracurriculars, work, sports, and volunteer activities naturally leads to opportunities for recognition through various awards. Either the activity you're involved in will recognize you if your effort or participation merits it, or there will be times when an organization opens applications for awards. In the scholarship process, documented awards provide strong evidence of your merit and enhance your credibility. Not every scholarship has a section asking for a list of accomplishments or awards; however, I have come across plenty that have so it is important to be prepared when this topic comes up. *The main point here is that if there is any opportunity for you to be honored with a prize or award—regardless of what it's for—take it.*

I'll explain this more later, but the bottom line is that you shouldn't leave anything blank on scholarship applications. Give them as many reasons as possible to consider you. Does your awards section feel a bit empty? You need to find ways to increase your accomplishments. There are some easy awards that many students earn without even realizing it, the most common being making the Dean's List or Honor Roll for one or more semesters. Another easy one would be to earn a varsity letter for a sport if you are in high school. Other awards may not come as easy. Once you understand how awards can help you win scholarships, you'll feel more motivated to push yourself in the areas that will help you earn the awards you're aiming for. Having an award-focused mentality is not a bad thing. The harder you push to earn recognition through awards, the more you're investing in your future. For instance, these awards can be highlighted on LinkedIn and other platforms, incorporated into your résumé, contribute to skill development, facilitate networking, and offer additional benefits

This is one area, though, that is a little harder to come by because people aren't just handing out awards left and right. You need to be vigilant and when you hear of one, find out what it takes, and try to get it if it is relevant toward you and your goals. Don't think you'll get it? Apply anyways. What do you have to lose? One award in particular that I was recognized for happened because of an action that I took. At Bradley, there was an award called the "I Am Brave" Student Leadership Award that was advertised my sophomore year. It asked for all students to take a minute and think of any deserving students that they knew who showed leadership qualities on campus and to submit their name so those students can be recognized by the university. There was not just one winner. Anyone whose name was submitted received the small award. I asked some of my close friends if they could nominate my name, but they were too lazy at the time. So, I made them a deal. I explained why it was important to me and suggested I would take care of the whole application and submit it on their behalf so long as I had their permission to do so. They agreed, and I submitted around four or five applications that referred me to be recognized for the award. A few weeks later I was invited to a large banquet where I, along with several others, would be recognized to receive the "I Am Brave" Student Leadership Award. I happily accepted the award and also happily listed it on every single scholarship application thereafter!

Another example that did not have such a happy ending was when I applied to receive the Intern of the Year award through Bradley University, which recognized students that participated in outstanding work internships during the year. In my opinion at the time, my internships were not as intense or as value-added as some of my other colleagues'; however, I still applied and put forward my best application. Two consecutive years I applied for this award but did not get it. It was unfortunate because it was a very prestigious award, but I cut my losses and kept moving on. At least I submitted an application and gave myself a chance. Not applying at all because I thought my internship wasn't impressive enough would have been even worse. If I had done that, I would have lost something bigger than just losing out on winning the award. But I didn't, and I am glad that is the route I chose. *A life lesson here is to not get discouraged to do something when the odds are stacked against you. You never know what the result of something can be unless you try.*

To sum up the importance of awards: when you consistently give your best effort, you create stronger results—and those results often lead to recognition. Also, do not be afraid to put yourself in a position of success like with how I won the "I Am Brave" Student Leadership Award. Take every step you can to present yourself as a strong, deserving scholarship candidate on paper, particularly through the awards you highlight.

INTERNSHIPS

Another pillar of making you a deserving candidate to win scholarships is to have internships. Let's explore this idea with a hypothetical situation. If a random person who seems well put together and is not struggling financially asks you for $5.00 for no reason, will you give it to them? Chances are no. What is the incentive behind giving them $5.00? Now, imagine if that same person comes up to you and asks for $5.00 to benefit a local boy or girl scout group. Taking a closer look at the apparel they are wearing, you notice they are a volunteer scout leader. Now will you give it to them? The latter sounds a bit more convincing and has more incentive or reasoning behind it, correct? The same applies for scholarships. The person who is being asked for money is the scholarship donor or organization. You are the person requesting $5.00. Let's assume that there is an organization within the psychology industry that is offering a scholarship. If you just run up to them asking for money, and upon closer review of your application they see that, outside of your major, you really don't have any other ties to the values of their organization, it would be hard for them to justify why you deserve the scholarship over others. If you change the circumstances and let's say you volunteered at or completed a summer internship at a certified local psychologist's office and gained experience, they have a higher incentive and reasoning to consider you because they clearly see your interest in their primary field of interest.

I bring up the topic of getting an internship in a field related to your course of study because you're most likely going to be applying to scholarships in which the donor organization is related to that field as well. You will find that the majority of scholarships you are eligible to apply for will require a certain course of study. I bring up internships as one of the last things you can do to enhance your scholarship application because not a lot of applications ask for job experience such as internships. I have had some that required me to submit a résumé or answer a small question inquiring if I had ever worked in a certain position related to my field of manufacturing, but it was uncommon. This does not mean that internships are not vital to your scholarship success! On the contrary, they are one of the most vital parts of a scholarship journey because internships give you, the applicant, a lot of content to write about on the essay portion of scholarships. The essay portion, which will be covered in the last portion of Step 4, is usually where the winners get a chance to distinguish themselves from all other applicants and truly explain why they are deserving to win. Within the non-essay portion though, internships are less critical.

For those that do not know, let's quickly define what an internship is. An internship is a short-term, structured work experience that allows students or early-career individuals to gain practical skills, exposure, and insight in a specific field or industry. In my experience, the majority of internships for myself and my colleagues happened during summer breaks from college; however, the timing and length of internship programs can vary. It is worth noting about another program similar to internships that offers work experience exposure while in school called a "co-op," short for "cooperative education." A co-op is an extended, structured work experience in which students alternate between full-time academic study and full-time paid employment in their field. I never had one of these; however, I had colleagues of mine sign up for these. They usually involve taking a certain amount of time off from your regular schooling or postponing it temporarily in order for you to work at a company for a longer period of time than an internship. As with internships, the exact timing and length of co-op programs can also vary; however, it is worth pointing out as an option available to students. Over the course of this book, I will primarily focus on internships just because I have had the most experience with them and I see them as the more popular and practical option of the two for students. Both still offer the same valuable experience that you can apply to your scholarship journey, and it is up to you to decide which one is the best fit for you.

If you are able to secure an internship or co-op but it is not related to your field of study, that is okay although not ideal for reasons stated earlier. Something is better than nothing. In the same breath, if you are unable to secure one at all, at least apply for a regular job during your summer breaks and other times away from school. Being productive with your time is the best thing you can do. I have interviewed and hired interns during my professional roles, and I can tell you that we still look at non-major-related experiences and see if we can apply skills learned in random jobs to the actual internship position we are looking to fill. For example, there was an Industrial Engineering student candidate that we ended up hiring for a training and continuous improvement internship that had no previous manufacturing experience. They did, however, have a lot of videography and customer service experience with the jobs they listed on their résumé. With their customer service experience, we knew they would be able to integrate well with the new hires we were training at the company, and with their videography experience, we knew they would be able to help create training videos for us. They presented themselves well in their interview and that led to us offering them the position which they excelled at during the summer. It was a win-win for both parties and was a great example of why still being productive during your away from school time and doing *something* is important. *Still though, for the best odds at winning as many scholarships as you can, try to aim to get an internship that is related to your college major as quick as you can.*

Internships and co-ops are just like professional full-time jobs in terms of getting hired for them. You need to find a job listing posted either online or somewhere else, submit a résumé, and complete an interview process. This method of securing employment is acceptable, well-established, and remains the standard practice in today's workforce. For some internships, the level of competition is so high that securing your first or even fifth choice may not be possible. When this occurs, notice everyone's pattern of thinking. When everyone is doing something one way, like the routine process I explained in the beginning of this paragraph, there may be an opening or an opportunity that a lot of people are missing. It's kind of like herd mentality—this hiring process works, which is why many people follow it—but is it the only way? Sometimes you have to turn left when everyone else is turning right. In other words, think outside the box if you cannot get your foot into the door of a certain place or certain type of internship right away.

I know there is a different way of thinking and process of finding internships because I was able to acquire an internship after my freshman year of college the unconventional way. Going into summer of 2014, the summer after I completed my freshman year at Bradley, I was still fixated on the idea that I would be a lifeguard for a third consecutive year. In the back of my mind though, I knew I needed to start getting into jobs associated with engineering. Although I searched, I found very few opportunities in my hometown appropriate for someone with my limited experience in engineering or manufacturing. What I do remember vividly, though, is recalling a manufacturing company that was about five minutes away from where I grew up and currently lived. I used to drive by their company every day when I attended elementary and middle school. Despite them not having any official internship job posting listed at all, I did some research, found the contact to their human resources department, and sent them an email. In the email, I stated who I was and that I was studying Manufacturing Engineering. I stated that my intentions were to seek employment as a summer intern at their facility to gain hands-on learning experience working within the manufacturing industry. Much to my surprise, a few days later I received an email back asking when I was available for an interview. I attended the interview and spoke exclusively with the engineering manager. He asked why I wanted to work there and about the engineering-related classes and skills I've developed so far. I did not have much to offer in my favor, but I told him I had some experience in AutoCAD, 3D modeling, and working with industrial tools at my father's welding shop. At the end of the interview, he offered me the job and asked when I could start. I was so thrilled at that point! The next day, I immediately resigned from lifeguarding and began my dive into the world of engineering through my first internship.

This experience is so powerful because *again* you see the power of creating something out of nothing, just like in the "business liaison" role I developed or the "I Am Brave" Student Leadership Award I earned. By proactively emailing a company with no advertised openings, I created an opportunity that led to an internship. It wasn't the greatest pay at the time, but it was an upgrade. I went from $8.72 per hour as a lifeguard to $11.00 per hour. It wasn't the money that was the important win here. It was the knowledge that I gained from this internship. The knowledge alone was worth far more than whatever I was getting paid at the time. Also, the doors that opened for me *because* I had this experience so early on in my college career was what made this such a profound experience. If there's one thing to take away from this book, it's that even when you feel stuck or believe there are no opportunities during your high school or college journey, that is absolutely not the case.

Being persistent in finding new ways to get your foot in the door to achieve your goals, being resilient in adapting to situations if your initial plan falls apart, and being proactive in actually taking the steps to advance your life and situation is a guaranteed equation to find new opportunities that will lead you where you want to go.

Persistence + Resilience + Proactiveness
= Opportunity

Even by reading this book, this shows you are a person who has these traits because you are being persistent in accomplishing your goal of paying off college the right way! Having this type of understanding as you go through life's challenges during and after high school or college is truly powerful. Again, this experience of creating my own internship is related to the mantra of "ask and you shall receive," which is a main theme present in this book. I encourage you to look for similar, unconventional, creative actions you can take in your life today that will not only improve your chances at receiving scholarships, but also help you both in your personal and professional life!

LIST OF INVOLVEMENT

The above examples described so far in Step 2 show the key areas to develop first, since most scholarship applications will ask about them in some form. However, this does not suggest that the list of how to improve your qualifications to win scholarships stops there. I'll reiterate: include anything you deem worthwhile that adds to your value in your scholarship application. You could be taking night classes to gain a new skill, running an online business, getting certified in a certain trade or task, and the list goes on. So long as you are making strides to improve yourself and how you are perceived on paper in your scholarship applications, you will have success. *Your willingness to go beyond the average effort or comfort zone of students, the greater edge you will gain over your competition who are also competing for the same scholarships.*

Now I will go into a full list of what I was involved in during high school and college to give you a good sense of what I did that made me more deserving to win $92,322 in total grants and scholarships. Before going too deep, there are some key points to remember when you are managing all of your involvement activities to include on the non-essay portion of each scholarship application you submit.

SAVE EVERYTHING

Save every participation ribbon, awards large and small, projects you complete during an internship, relevant school materials, and even your class record such as your honors and AP courses that you take. One of the biggest factors on an application is filling out as much as you can and leaving nothing blank. By saving everything significant that happens to you or that you do, no matter how little it may seem, you are making a timeline of your validation for winning scholarships that you can reference later. You may not remember what you did three or five years in the past. This could lead to leaving certain bits of information out of a scholarship application that may be the deciding factor of whether you win or not. Do not leave any cards on the table.

MAKE A PARTICIPATION LOG

This is very closely tied into the first point of save everything, only that this point focuses more on every single event that you participate in. Write down what volunteering you did, what sports you played, what clubs you were in, what conferences or trade shows you attended, special events or seminars, and all other extracurricular involvement you were a part of. Making a participation log will help you for the same reasons that are described in the save everything point. You will not miss any key information.

BE VERY DETAILED

It's not enough that you know you did something. During my scholarship journey, there was a very professional, prominent scholarship organization in my local area that I used to send a lot of applications through. Within their application format, they wanted me to include the following information for each activity I was involved in.

- Name of the program/event/club/activity
- Name of the organization/organizer of that program/event/club/activity
- Time frame when I participated in that program/event/club/activity
- Time commitment of that program/event/club/activity
- Title or participation role of that program/event/club/activity

Using this approach to break down your involvement history will allow you to keep track of every single detail you need to know when you need it. You will not have to go digging for information and get frustrated when you don't find it or don't remember. Recording information this way will make applications easier, less stressful, and more accurate. Having this information saved and readily available will give you the confidence that your application is accurate and help it stand out. Are you starting out late and have not made one of these participation logs yet? No worries, it's never too late to start putting one together. Initially, you'll need to do some digging to document your past experiences, but once it's organized, you won't have to repeatedly search for the same information with each application.

Volunteer Involvement:				
Description:	**Organization:**	**Date:**	**Duration:**	**Title / Role:**
Polish Fest	St. Stanislaus Kostka Parish	2009-2017 (summers)	6 hours	Volunteer (ticket booths and game tables)
Senior Retreat Team	Boylan Catholic High School	2013	10 hours	Small Group Leader
"Service on Saturday" Program	Bradley University	2013	15 hours	Volunteer ("Worldwide Day of Play" with Peoria Park District)
YMCA Big Brothers Big Sisters Program	YMCA of Rock River Valley	2014	5 hours	Volunteer (Back-to-School Picnic)
Methodist Medical Center Gift-Show	Bradley University - Delta Upsilon Fraternity	2014	4 hours	Volunteer (set-up tables & exhibits)
Bake Sale for St. Jude Children's Hospital	Bradley University - Delta Upsilon Fraternity	2014	15 hours	Organized & implemented the whole program
Collecting Donations for St. Jude Children's Hospital	Bradley University - Delta Upsilon Fraternity	2014	4 hours	Volunteer (accepted donations outside Kroger in Peoria)
Collecting Donations for St. Jude Children's Hospital	Bradley University - Delta Upsilon Fraternity	2014	4 hours	Volunteer (wrote 100 letters to ask for donations)
Collecting Donations for St. Jude Children's Hospital	Bradley University - Delta Upsilon Fraternity	2015	2 hours	Volunteer (occupy table selling wristbands/accepting donations during Philanthropy Week)
Hall Township's Echo Bluff Park - Haunted Halloween Trail	Bradley University - Delta Upsilon Fraternity	2015	4 hours	Volunteer (setup prior to event)

Clubs / Other Involvement:				
Description:	**Organization:**	**Date:**	**Duration:**	**Title / Role:**
Ultimate Frisbee Club	Boylan Catholic High School	2009-2013	5 hours/week	President (2013)
Society of Manufacturing Engineers (SME): Bradley Chapter	Bradley University	2013-2015	7 hours/week	Secretary (2013) Vice-President (2014)
"Red Sea" Executive Board	Bradley University	2013	3 hours/week	Student Fan Section Coordinator
Williams Residence Hall Council	Bradley University	2014	7 hours/week	President
YMCA "Intern Challenge" Participant	YMCA of Rock River Valley	2014	25 hours/week for 9 weeks of summer	Semi-Finalist (Project Manager for 2 separate weeks)
Delta Upsilon Fraternity	Bradley University	2014-2015	10 hours/week	Philanthropy Representative for 2014 Pledge Class

Association of Residence Halls (ARH)	Bradley University	2015	3 hours/week	Event Coordinator
National Society of Leadership & Success (NSLS): Bradley Chapter	Bradley University	2015	2 hours/week	Associate Member
Professional Organization	Association for Manufacturing Excellence (AME)	2015	1 hour/week	Student Membership
Professional Organization	Fabrication & Manufacturers Association, International (FMA)	2015	1 hour/week	Student Membership
Association of Residence Halls (ARH)	Bradley University	2016	2 hours/week	Executive Board
Teacher's Assistant	Bradley University - IMET Department	2017	10 hours/week	Part-Time Job
Study Abroad Program: London, England - January Interim	Bradley University	2017	16 days	Student (completed travel writing class)

Sports Involvement:				
Description:	**Organization:**	**Date:**	**Duration:**	**Title / Role:**
Men's Track & Field	Boylan Catholic High School	2009-2010	10 hours/week	Sprinter
Men's Swimming & Diving	Boylan Catholic High School	2010-2013	15 hours/week	Varsity Swimmer
Intramural Racquetball	Bradley University	2013	4 hours	Semi-Finalist
Women's Basketball (Division I) Male Practice Player	Bradley University	2013	135 hours	Volunteer Practice Player
Intramural Ultimate Frisbee	Bradley University	2013-2014	6 hours	Champion (2013)
Intramural Basketball	Bradley University	2013-2017	4 hours/week for 9 weeks	Team Captain (2014) Champion (2017)

Awards:		
Description:	**Organization:**	**Date Awarded:**
Special Mention in Industrial Technology	Boylan Catholic High School - Fine Arts Fair	04/17/2012
Exceed Ellis & Associates Audit	Magic Waters Water Park	07/22/2012
Varsity Letter (Swimming)	Boylan Catholic High School	02/25/2013
NIC-10 Scholar Athlete Award	Boylan Catholic High School	03/01/2013
Excellence in Architecture	Boylan Catholic High School	05/01/2013
Excellence in CADD	Boylan Catholic High School	05/01/2013
Excellence in Web Design	Boylan Catholic High School	05/01/2013
Honor Roll	Boylan Catholic High School	2012-2013
"I Am Brave" Student Leadership Award	Bradley University	02/14/2015

Anonymously nominated to receive Student Recognition Award [Did Not Win]	Bradley University	05/04/2015
Dean's List - Engineering	Bradley University	Spring 2015
Dean's List - Engineering	Bradley University	Spring 2016
Dean's List - Engineering	Bradley University	Spring 2017
Manufacturing Outstanding Senior Award	Bradley University - IMET Department	2017
Graduated Cum Laude	Bradley University	2017

Getting involved has many other benefits too other than just being good for scholarship applications. The more you get out there, open yourself up to new people and new opportunities, and explore your interests, the more answers you will find about who you are, what you like to do, and you will gain many great relationships and experiences along the way. I am a living testament to this fact. My roommates whom I met in college will be my lifelong friends. We are always going to look back at those moments and experiences we shared together doing certain events and activities. They are moments that I will cherish and would never have happened if we chose not to do something because a little bit of insecurity, laziness, or anxiety that we were feeling at the time. My hope is that by getting involved, you not only earn scholarships but also gain a deeper appreciation for the opportunities around you—ones that can shape your growth and set you ahead in life.

Step 3

FIND SCHOLARSHIPS

6

Executing Step 3

Life in some respects is a game of hide-and-seek. The majority of the time, it feels like we are doing a lot more of the seeking. If we want answers to our questions, we are going to seek them out. More often than not, we tend not to know where to look. When we look for answers in the wrong places, not only will we not make progress, but we will also get frustrated and sometimes give up entirely. Other times we stumble upon exactly what we've been looking for when we least expect it. The point is, some answers come easier than others. I have heard it said that people come into your life for two reasons: either you are there to help them, or they are there to help you. My goal with this book is to serve the latter by guiding you through the scholarship process and helping you avoid frustration or burnout. You could be the most deserving candidate in the world, yet do not know your first step toward finding a scholarship. Thankfully, we live in a world today where scholarships are abundant. They are easy to seek out and win if you choose to put in the effort. I want to walk you through the approach I used to uncover the scholarship opportunities that opened up for me. Not to say that my way is the *only* way. Rather, this is the method I used when I was trying to figure out where to find scholarships to pay for college—and it worked, which is why I'm sharing it with you today. I strongly encourage you to use these methods as a stepping-stone to begin your scholarship journey, but also to think creatively about other places you can look for additional opportunities, since everyone's situation and environment is different. Opportunities presented to one student may not necessarily be available to another. For example, a student in a coastal community may qualify for scholarships tied to ocean-conservation work, whereas a student in a major city might find scholarships centered on solving urban pollution problems. Scholarships are hidden everywhere and it is your job to seek them out.

Our world is forever changing. It seems like every day there is a new trend or way to do something that we have never thought of before. The same applies for scholarships. As I'm writing this, I'm already several years removed from a university setting. I'm sure in that span of time there have been new scholarship techniques or resources that have come out, and there always will be more to follow. That is great and gives you even more options, so I really hope that is the case! For the purposes of this book, however, I will be explaining what my proven methods were of finding scholarships to apply to. These tips are what I always forward to people when they ask me how I did it. Even as new scholarship-search tools appear, these core strategies will always hold true. So, without further ado, let's get into it.

COMMUNITY FOUNDATIONS

In today's society, there are community organizations and foundations that are centered around providing scholarships and financial aid for deserving students. These organizations receive contributions from donors who wish to establish scholarship funds, often to memorialize loved ones, promote their company while making community impact, or simply sharing their generosity with others. The purpose of these types of organizations or foundations is to streamline all of these different scholarships into one. Their goal is to provide a professional structure through which donors can establish scholarship funds, knowing the awards will reach the appropriate recipients.

These entities have thousands of dollars in collective scholarships that are aimed to be distributed among students from all different backgrounds, majors, schools, skill sets, talents, geographic locations, and the list goes on. Rest assured, you are sure to find a scholarship in which you meet the eligibility requirements to apply for. Often, these scholarship entities can be found not only on the national level, but on the local level which can be overlooked or underrated. For me in particular, there was an organization called the Community Foundation of Northern Illinois (CFNIL) who, at the time, provided over $200,000 annually in scholarships to students. Years later, that number has climbed to over $500,000 and is poised to keep rising. Here, I searched through their catalog of scholarships offered, found the ones that I met eligibility requirements for, and applied to all of them. The nice thing about their system was that it made the application process very easy in that a lot of information I filled out for one scholarship would be carried over to others, thus cutting down the time I had to spend on each individual application. Also, there were support staff available to answer any questions I may have had when filling out applications. I won $3,000 in total from CFNIL which turned out to be the same scholarship for $1,000 from sophomore to senior year.

PROFESSIONAL ORGANIZATIONS

Professional organizations are occasionally affiliated with community foundations that support them in administering and awarding scholarship funds. Although in my experience, the professional organizations that go through a community foundation of some sorts are often small and do not have the resources to manage the scholarship-donor process themselves, thus outsourcing these tasks to third-party community foundations. Once you stumble upon bigger professional organizations, they often have a dedicated charity branch or section of their organization that is focused on giving back to the community. A lot of their "giving back" involves offering scholarship awards within their primary field of interest or expertise. Now, when talking about professional organizations, I am often referring to worldwide groups, societies, and membership-only type entities that specialize in a certain primary field of interest or expertise. For example, since I am an engineer, there are several societies that exist within different fields of the engineering sciences such as the Society of Automotive Engineers (SAE), the American Society of Civil Engineers (ASCE), or the Society of Manufacturing Engineers (SME). These types of professional organizations have global influence and exist for a diverse range of job backgrounds. So, whatever your major or course of study, chances are you will have some type of professional organization that applies to you.

Professional organizations often fund and manage their own scholarships, supported by private donors within the organization and awarded through an application process they oversee. They are often on a national scale, and their scholarships usually come with more detailed criteria, including the specific majors they want applicants to pursue. All of the $26,500 in external scholarships I won came from professional organizations, both local and national. Of that amount, $22,000 came from organizations connected to the manufacturing industry, which aligned with my field of study.

One example of these professional organizations that I utilized during my scholarship journey was the Society of Manufacturing Engineers (SME). Their organization had a division called the Society of Manufacturing Engineers Education Foundation (SME-EF) where they offered a multitude of scholarships totaling $500,000 at the time I was applying. I came across their foundation when I got involved with my engineering department's SME chapter. I won a total of $5,000 from SME-EF, which consisted of $2,500 junior year and $2,500 senior year of college. Along with the scholarship winnings, I secured free SME membership for every year I won. Having a membership in a professional organization also built my résumé, my professional network, and gave me access to unique job opportunities only posted on their society's site.

ONLINE RESEARCH

As cliché as this sounds, finding scholarships is as easy as looking them up! In today's digital age, we have unprecedented access to information at our fingertips through the internet. Use this technologic breakthrough to your advantage when searching for scholarships. This was my main resource when finding potential scholarships to apply to. By using search engines like Google, I found the Community Foundation of Northern Illinois (CFNIL) and other community and professional organizations. I would be reading ten to fifteen pages deep of search results that came up from my scholarship query to make sure I exhausted all potential scholarship leads for that specific search term or phrase.

Whether you're using Google or another search engine, the keywords you type make a big difference. Of course, if you just search for "college student scholarships," you will be led to some pretty general websites that are on a national scale. Do not get me wrong, this type of search is completely fine, and I encourage this to be one of your search queries. Very generalized searches will yield generalized results. Take a look at these results, search the scholarships on there, filter out the scholarships you meet the application requirements for, and apply. One drawback of these broad search results and generalized websites is the sheer amount of traffic they get, which lowers your chances of success because you're competing with so many other applicants.

One of the best ways for finding scholarships that best fit you is to refine your search criteria. This means tailoring your search terms to include things like your major, background, interests, talents, or any other characteristics that describe you as an applicant. The more targeted your search is, the easier it becomes to find scholarships that are actually a good fit for you. This approach will help you uncover scholarships that are more localized and narrowly tailored to your profile, thereby reducing the applicant pool and offering better odds at winning.

Here are some search queries I used to yield specific scholarship results that applied to me:

- Rockford Illinois scholarships
- Scholarships in Rockford Illinois
- Manufacturing scholarships Illinois
- Engineering scholarships Illinois
- Engineering scholarships Winnebago county
- Manufacturing engineering scholarships

- Manufacturing engineering scholarships Rockford
- High school scholarships Illinois
- College scholarships Illinois

Since I live in Illinois and my major is Manufacturing Engineering, the majority of my searches were centered around keywords such as those shown above. Using this technique, you will start to find that most scholarships applicable to you will be somewhat local. Through my experience, I have found that a lot of scholarships require you to be a resident of whatever state you permanently reside in, or you have to be living within a certain county of a state. That is why using your location within your search queries is important. However, don't let that prevent you from searching across state lines because some scholarships may lift that restriction.

These types of searches frequently reveal smaller professional organizations that provide scholarship opportunities. Do not discredit these as being any less important than the national professional organization's scholarships talked about earlier. In fact, these are better because you will have less competition yet roughly the same potential monetary award amounts available. Almost all organizations I found that offered external scholarships were from my Google searches.

Ultimately, the majority of your scholarship research should take place online. Also, utilize internet search tools powered by artificial intelligence (AI) to speed up your search results. Don't rely exclusively on AI tools though. It's still important to manually review the first few pages of search results to avoid missing smaller or local scholarships that AI may not surface. The more you search, the better you will get at finding scholarships.

SCHOOL COUNSELORS

If you are in either high school or college, chances are you are paired with a school counselor whose main job is to ensure you are meeting the correct graduation requirement criteria. Though both apply here, I used my high school counselor more when looking for potential scholarship opportunities. These counselors get sent information on scholarships all the time, but they do not always advertise them. Make a habit of asking whether they've come across any new scholarship information or postings. Mutual friends of mine have noted that high school counselors often juggle many responsibilities, which can limit how much scholarship guidance they're able to provide. For that reason, you may need to seek out additional scholarship information elsewhere. Take a proactive approach and inquire about scholarship opportunities you can apply for at the main office or other related office. If you ask questions, you will get answers. This was one resource that did not create many opportunities for me; however, you will still need to exhaust every option—no matter how small—if you want to be successful in locating scholarships. This is called **abundance mentality**—more on that shortly.

LOCAL PUBLIC LIBRARY

Check your local library if they have any sort of scholarship database for your area. This is a more unconventional way of finding scholarships. The more unconventional the better, because not a lot of people may know this resource exists thus lowering your competition. I did not think of this resource at first until a librarian pointed it out to me. My local library offered different classes as part of their services and, in addition, created a scholarship database to assist those seeking further education outside of the library. The majority of listings within my library's scholarship database focused more within the local area. Personally, I did not have a lot of scholarship opportunities generate from this resource, but I still would check it frequently to see if it would produce any potential leads.

ABUNDANCE MENTALITY

The last method of how to find scholarships is to have abundance mentality when approaching your search. It was hard not to dive too much into this subject for any of the previous scholarship finding tips because the concept of abundance mentality can be applied to all of them. As discussed earlier, when searching for scholarships, there are several ways to filter your results so you can find the opportunities that relate most to you. However, paying for school is likely going to take more than just one or two scholarships where you are the perfect applicant. If you are that *hungry* for scholarship funds, you are going to apply to *every* scholarship you can. Put simply: no matter how unusual or obscure the scholarship is, if you qualify, submit the application. The strength is in the numbers. For each scholarship you find and apply for, you give yourself one more opportunity at receiving extra financial aid. Why wouldn't you take as many opportunities as you can?

I applied for some very weird scholarships during my time in high school and college. One involved sending an application to the local sheriff's office where I had to write an essay on the dangers of illicit substances. Another was when I had to make a thirty-second video of me explaining why I chose my major and why I deserve to win the scholarship. Unfortunately, I didn't win either of these scholarships mentioned, but I am still glad I put in the effort. This type of effort is needed if you truly want to use your opportunity of being a college student to the fullest. Think about it. The majority of scholarships are only available to students. Rarely do you get a chance to apply for *free money* when you are out of school.

Anything goes when you are searching for scholarships. Look at the different traits that make up your life and your identity, and then search for scholarships tied to those qualities. For example, my heritage is Polish. Therefore, I found and applied to a certain Polish scholarship where I actually won $1,000 from every year from sophomore to senior year. This particular scholarship came from a Polish life insurance company that my parents were a part of which helped me with eligibility. Still though, if it hadn't been for our heritage, I would never have received these funds. There are so many scholarships available today that chances are you will be able to find a couple unique ones to apply to.

The first of two concluding points on abundance mentality is to remain observant and ask questions. Leverage your social media platforms by posting inquiries and seeking information about available scholarship opportunities. Ask teachers, professors, employers, friends, and family about potential scholarships. When you are in school, you need to be in a constant search mode. Always be aware and mindful of opportunities. The worst thing is when you find out about something too late and you can no longer apply to it. If that does happen though, keep a record of that scholarship so you don't lose track of it and when enough time passes you can apply when the application window opens once more.

The second point is to start as early as possible with your scholarship search. If you are in high school or college and reading this book is your first attempt at acquiring scholarships, then I suggest as soon as you're done reading for today, get on a computer and start searching immediately. *The point being you do not want to prolong your scholarship search.* Start searching and applying for scholarships as early as possible so you don't miss deadlines and can maximize your window of receiving financial aid. Do not delay because your procrastination or deliberation on whether you're "ready" or "deserving enough" could cost you thousands of dollars.

Step 4

APPLY

7

General Application

At this point in the book, you now have a good understanding of the different variables that surround the topic of scholarships. The information covered in Steps 1 through 3 acts as the outer layer of the fruit. Step 4, the application process, is the seed of the fruit because it contains the core ideas behind the process of winning scholarships. If you have a healthy core, you will taste the sweet, juicy rewards that the scholarship fruit can offer! If the core is rotten and is not taken seriously, your fruit won't taste good and your success with scholarships will not be as sweet. Don't let this scare you though. How do you think I started? I didn't have a step-by-step manual of someone who had won $92,322 in grants and scholarships. I simply started with one scholarship application and then built from there. This brings me back to a topic we just covered: abundance mentality.

We already know having an abundance mentality is crucial when finding scholarships; however, *it is also a key component when carrying out the full application process*. You could find one hundred scholarships to apply for but if you are picky about which to actually pursue or if you just don't feel like going through the process one hundred times then your success rate will reflect that. You simply will not have as much success as you can have. Give yourself as many chances as possible to win scholarships. When you're a student at any level, you're in a rare position where people and organizations are willing to give you *free money with no strings attached.* Obviously there are some ethics at play here. Remember, their contribution is an investment into you where their return on investment is when you go out and make change in the world through your education. Therefore, at this point in your life, right here, right now, if you are a student reading this book who wants to win scholarships, your primary focus outside of actually graduating is finding scholarship funding.

This means time is of the essence. In order to be successful at anything in life, you have to put the time in. When I was in college, I used every single break from school to do research on finding new scholarships to apply to, writing essays, networking with professional references who were writing me letters of recommendation, doing side projects to help build my résumé and scholarship application strength, mailing applications, following up with existing applications that I did not hear back from, and so on. The hours stack up, and if you are unwilling to put in the work toward what you want to achieve, then this book may not be for you. My advice is to please not waste time on the non-essentials in life, like video games for example. Don't get me wrong, we all need leisure time. I'm not saying quit everything you find enjoyable and become a robot. If you do that, then you miss the whole point of life. What I'm really saying is to avoid spending days, weeks, or years on non-essential tasks that don't advance your life in any meaningful way. I heard a great quote recently of someone who was just turning thirty. He said that he wished he spent his time leveling up in real life rather than leveling up in video games. That put things into perspective for me. We all have vices that add no value to our lives, and it is up to us to limit those occurrences to truly be our best selves every day. Don't let those vices be the reason you do not win scholarships. Use your breaks to be proactive and productive, and it will pay off. Hard work works. Period.

That said, your scholarship efforts shouldn't be limited to just breaks during the school year. I did scholarship side work during the course of the whole school year because I had to. Sometimes deadlines for applications have to be met while school is in session. Breaks were simply opportunities for me to focus more intentionally and put in extra effort to move my scholarship goals forward.

With this understanding of the importance of time, having an abundance mentality in relation to applying for scholarships becomes easy! Like I said, I started with one application my senior year of high school and learned from there. I won second place and received a $500 scholarship from a veteran's association in Rockford, IL. Eligibility required me to be related to someone who had served in any branch of the military. Thankfully my father served in the Air Force for four years. I do not recall how many applications I sent out during my overall journey until I graduated, but I know for a fact that the rate of my applications increased exponentially over time. I began with just a couple of applications my senior year of high school, increased that number freshman and sophomore year, and eventually hit my peak during my junior and senior years of college. The more you apply, the easier the process becomes, the more experienced you will be, and ultimately the more scholarships you will win. During my journey, I actually found it fun hunting these opportunities down. It was sort of like hitting a miniature lottery! For example, if I found some random organization that I had never heard of that I met all eligibility requirements for a scholarship that they offered, I would apply and would wait to hear back from them. A good portion of the applications I sent out never got back to me, even after I followed up. When good news finally did arrive—like winning $1,000—it was incredibly rewarding. I was excited to be outputting these applications because I never knew when I would receive good news about being selected as the winner, and when I did it was exhilarating! The anticipation of it made it fun. You will find this to be true for yourself if you follow what is in this book. Now, scholarships have given me a new outlet to get excited about: giving back what I have learned to you, the reader. As stated previously, the application process gets easier once you go through it a few times. By going through the upcoming sections of Step 4, you will have an even easier path because I will teach you what took me up until junior and senior year of college to grasp. Hopefully this will accelerate your success, sparing you the delay I experienced. Now, let's set the daydreaming aside and get to work.

From my experience, we can break down a scholarship application into two main sections:

- General Application
- Essay Portion

To begin, I will go over all the details that go into the "general application" section of a scholarship. Meaning, the non-essay portion. This is the portion that asks for your general information, school information, your credentials, involvement, some short-answer questions, and other miscellaneous information that make up the first half of a scholarship application.

WHAT MAKES A GOOD GENERAL APPLICATION

TAKE PRIDE IN YOUR WORK

There is a famous saying that goes something like, "If you want something done right, do it yourself." When you think of doing something yourself in order to do it right, how do you think you will approach that "something?" Most likely, you will want to do a good job in whatever it is you need to get done. So, you will take pride in your work. You will be mindful of the details. You will see to it that "something" gets done in its entirety. This is exactly how you need to approach applying for scholarships, and it's the first step in What Makes a Good General Application: taking pride in your work.

Taking pride in your application means submitting an application you can be proud of. A lot of scholarships that I applied for usually had an application Portable Document File (PDF) that I would need to print out, handwrite in all the details, and then mail to a specific address. I approached these handwritten applications with meticulous detail. I would make sure I did not wrinkle the paper or stain it. I used a smooth, bold pen when writing down my information. I made sure not to make any mistakes that would force me to cross something out or use correction fluid. I would make sure my handwriting is completely legible. I usually defaulted to not using cursive and instead print all my letters as capital. In my opinion, I thought that was the cleanest and most concise way to fill out applications that required a manually written submission. I wanted to make it as easy as possible for the scholarship judge to go through my application.

Think about it. If you include typos in a job résumé, or the résumé overall just has a sloppy look to it, the person reading your résumé is going to get the perception that this candidate also performs sloppy work at their job and therefore will take them out of consideration. The same applies to your scholarship application. Don't give them any reason to second-guess whether you deserve to win. Your application is like your résumé. Just like in Step 2 where it was mentioned that you want to give scholarship judges multiple reasons to pick you through getting involved, the opposite holds true here. Your goal is to give them as few reasons as possible to rule you out. Making sure your overall application is clean, neat, and tidy is a small step in the application process but it has a big impact.

The same goes for when you have to mail the handwritten application to a specific address. Use a professional 9" × 12" yellow business envelope to send your documents in. I never liked folding up any scholarship materials into smaller envelopes. I wanted to give the scholarship organization the impression that I was serious about this application. Even down to the address on the 9" × 12" envelope, your handwriting should be clear and consistent with the image you want to project. Be mindful of the details!

If you come across applications that allow you to type everything and submit all documents electronically, the process will be much easier. One thing to remember is to keep your formatting the same for all typed answers and information. Everything still applies to electronic submissions the same as it does with handwritten submissions. This leads me to my next point which is being consistent throughout your application.

CONSISTENCY IN FORMATTING

Being consistent throughout your application means applying the same formatting, sizing, style, and structure to both handwritten and electronic submissions. From my experience, there are usually two main areas in which you need to make sure to have consistent formatting in a way that is easy for the reader to decipher the information you are filling out:

- Short-answer sections where you have to provide some sort of list
- Additional reference materials you are asked to provide outside of the general application

When talking about the first bullet point, Figure 1 below shows an example of an application in which I had to provide lists of my organizational (extracurricular) involvement and a list of any recognitions (awards) I may have received. This was an electronic application that I submitted in October 2015, when I was a first semester junior at Bradley. In question seven, I had to think of the best way to include as much relevant information as possible without making the response look cluttered or disorganized. First, I organized my organizational involvement from the most recent to the oldest related experience. I separated the dates of all involvement into brackets, so they don't distract from the role's title. Since I had too much information for a simple top-down list, I then had to find a more creative way to space out my entries. You can see how adding enough space along with a " -- " symbol effectively separated each entry.

In question eight, I used a similar styling, only the big differentiator here was college versus high school awards. I didn't have as much information compared to question seven, but I used a similar dividing approach and organized the information in a way that could be understood. I ended up being one of twenty recipients of this $1,500 scholarship.

7.	***Organizations:*** Please list any organizations where you have volunteered in which you are now active or have been active. Note leadership roles and dates. Program Coordinator for the Association of Residence Halls (ARH) [Fall 2015] -- Member of National Society for Leadership & Success [Fall 2015] -- President of Williams Residence Hall Council [Fall 2014-Spring 2015] -- Marketing Chair of Society of Manufacturing Engineers (SME) (previous: VP & Secretary) [Fall 2013-Fall 2015] -- Member of Delta Upsilon Fraternity - Bradley Chapter (previous: Pledge Class Philanthropy Representative in 2014 Pledging year) [Fall 2014-Fall 2015] -- Male Practice Player for Bradley Women's Division 1 Basketball Team [Fall 2013-Spring 2014] -- Captain of Intramural A-League Basketball Team [Fall 2013-Fall 2015] -- "Red Sea" Student Fan Section Event Coordinator [Fall 2013-Spring 2014] -- Corporate Intern/Mentor to new interns/consistent volunteer for YMCA of Rock River Valley [Summer 2014 & 2015]
8.	***Recognitions:*** Please list important awards and recognitions received. Note organizations presenting the honor and dates. Dean's List - Engineering Department [Bradley - Spring 2015], "I Am Brave" Student Leadership Award [Bradley - 2/14/2015] Anonymous Nomination for Student Recognition Award (DID NOT WIN) [5/4/2015] HIGH SCHOOL: Varsity Letter [2/25/2013], Honor Roll Junior & Senior Year, NIC-10 Scholar Athlete Award [3/1/2013] Excellence in Architecture, CADD, & Web Design [5/1/2013], Special Mention in Industrial Tech. at Fine Arts Fair [4/17/12] Exceed Ellis and Associates Audit [7/22/2012] (when previously employed as lifeguard)

Figure 1. Snippet from application requesting information on involvement and awards

When talking about the second bullet point, the additional reference material they could ask for could include a separate written essay, letter of recommendation, current résumé, professional reference, and so on. When I encountered situations such as this, it usually involved attaching an essay. We will cover more on essays toward the end of Step 4; however, the point I want to make here is that I always typed out and printed my essays, as well as all other supporting material, if I had to mail my application. The only thing I ever filled out by hand was the general application form when typing wasn't an option. So, one thing to ensure a clean, neat, and consistent application is to always opt to use a computer to type out and print any materials you need to submit by mail. Obviously if the application and supporting materials are being submitted online, you do not have to worry about this.

You're only as strong as the content you put within your additional reference material. However, one way to elevate your reference material even further is to go above and beyond with polished formatting if you want to make a stronger impression. As you format your documents, keep the same style consistent across any additional material you submit. If you want to go the simple route and keep your attachments modest and straight to the point, then make sure all other attachments have that theme. If you want to dress up your documents with fancy headers and other add-ons, then follow that same theme throughout. Whatever formatting you choose, at the end of the day do not dwell on it too much because the content of your reference material is what matters most.

Below I include examples of documents that had simple, straight-forward formatting as well as how I would format a fancy document with a detailed, professional header. The only times I used a professional header were on résumés, professional reference lists, and business letters. All other documents I ever submitted had a simple formatting approach.

Figure 2 shows an example of a document in which the scholarship application asked me for "supporting information." This is what I provided them. Again, I was focused on the content rather than the overall look of the document, though I made sure that the document itself had consistent simple formatting throughout. The figure below shows two separate pages of a Microsoft Word document that I merged together into one picture for better viewing clarity.

12. Other College Activities, hobbies, awards, etc.

- Society Of Manufacturing Engineers (SME) - Bradley University Chapter
  Present: *Marketing Chair;* Past: *Secretary, Vice-President*
  - Years Active: 2013 - Present
- Williams Residence Hall Council
  President
  - Years Active: 2014
- Male Practice Player for Bradley Women's Division I Basketball Team
  - Years Active: 2013
- Delta Upsilon Fraternity - Bradley University Chapter
  2014 Pledge Class Philanthropy Representative
  - Years Active: 2014 - 2015 (1st Semester Junior Year)
- "Red Sea" Student Fan Section Executive Board
  Event Coordinator
  - Years Active: 2013
- Intramural Basketball
  Co-Captain
  - Years Active: 2013 - Present
- Intramural Ultimate Frisbee
  Captain
  - Years Active: 2013
- Intramural Racquetball
  - Years Active: 2013
- National Society of Leadership and Success
  - Years Active: 2015 - Present
- Association of Residence Halls (ARH)
  Program Coordinator
  - Years Active: 2015 - Present
- Association for Manufacturing Excellence (AME)*
  - Years Active: 2015 - Present
- Fabrication & Manufacturers Association, International (FMA)*
  - Years Active: 2015 - Present

*Not affiliated with Bradley University, joined professional organization with student membership

Awards:

- Dean's List – Engineering (Spring Semester 2015, Fall Semester 2015)
- "I Am Brave" Student Leadership Award (2/14/2015)
- Anonymously nominated to receive Student Recognition Award (5/4/2015) [did not win]

13. Voluntary Community Services.

- YMCA Big Brothers Big Sisters Program - Back to School Picnic
  - Total Hours: 5
- Delta Upsilon Men's Fraternity - Bradley University Chapter: Fundraising for St. Jude Children's Hospital
  - Events included: Collecting donations outside local grocery stores, writing letters asking for donations, selling baked goods/items around campus as fundraisers.
  - Total Hours: 25.5
- Delta Upsilon Men's Fraternity - Bradley University Chapter: Volunteer for miscellaneous events happening around Peoria, IL involving different organizations
  - Total Hours: 18.5
- "Service on Saturday" program at Bradley University
  - Total Hours: 15

Figure 2. Additional reference material showcasing consistency in simple formatting

Figure 3 shows an example of a simple header attached to one of my additional reference materials which was a typed essay.

Jeremy Kaszycki
Dr. Sherrie Ford – Manufacturing as a career path 2015-2016 Scholarship
Winter/Spring Term application: Essay Question

Growing up having had two older siblings already attend college, I was able to learn a lot from their accomplishments as well as their mistakes that really made me ponder what it is I

Figure 3. Additional reference material showcasing simple header

Figure 4 shows an example of a fancy header I would use. Again, I would only include anything fancy such as this on résumés, professional reference lists, and business letters. The contact information shown in the fancy header has been changed to reflect confidentiality.

Jeremy J. Kaszycki

1234 ADDRESS ST | CITY, STATE 12345 | EMAIL@EMAIL.COM | 123.456.7890

Figure 4. Additional reference material showcasing fancy header

FULLY FILLED APPLICATION

The next point in What Makes a Good General Application is filling out as much of the application as you can. This point ties in very close to Step 2: Improve Yourself. If you take Step 2 seriously, you will have no problem filling out scholarship applications because you will already be involved in so much. *You want to strive to leave as little blank in the application because you want to give them as many reasons as possible to select you the winner.* If you were the scholarship judge and saw two applications—one only 30% complete and another 90% complete and packed with involvement—which one would you assume belonged to the stronger candidate? Obviously it would be the candidate with the 90% full application.

If you're including a significant quantity of information, it's important to maintain quality by listing only what's truly *relevant*. Avoid listing minor, one-off actions as experience, such as helping someone cross the street once and calling that legitimate volunteering. If you do that, the selection committee will not take you seriously. Be sure to include only legitimate activities and events you've participated in, and if you need a reminder of what a quality experience is, refer back to Step 2. That being said, once you get to the point where you have a lot of experience, don't sacrifice quality or neatness just to fill space in these sections. If you have a lot to include with not enough space, either get clever with your formatting or remove the least essential listings. This goes back to taking pride in your application, as discussed earlier. Lastly, if you don't have enough, just list what you have and work toward getting something to eventually fill in your missing gaps to truly make a fully filled out application.

INSPECTION BEFORE SUBMISSION

There is a funny scene in the movie *The Pursuit of Happyness* when Will Smith's character, Chris Gardener, had just finished the final exam of his stockbroker internship program—a program with about fifty highly qualified participants all competing for a job at an exclusive New York brokerage firm. Chris completes and submits his exam and then exits the floor he is on by walking into an elevator where he is joined by a much younger program participant who walks in right after. Chris and the other individual discuss certain parts of the exam. Chris then states that he struggled on the essay portion of the exam and asks the individual what he wrote for it. Surprised, the other participant immediately gets off the elevator. That other person did not realize there was an essay portion and went back to finish it, which more than likely they will not give him a second chance.

This movie scene highlights the next important point in What Makes a Good General Application: *you must triple-check everything before you submit it.* During my school breaks working at home on my dining room table, my workspace would be flooded with all sorts of papers from countless scholarship applications that I would be working on. It would be easy for me to miss a certain section of an application or forget to submit a certain piece of reference material an application requests and end up like the person that ran out of the elevator to clean up their mistake. Luckily, I didn't fall victim to that fate for any application because I was obsessive about making sure I put the right scholarship materials in the right envelope before I mailed it out or submitted it electronically. Triple-checking if you have all required documentation included, all sections filled out, all addresses correct, no typos, no misspellings, all names accurate, and so on, can save you from forfeiting a few thousand dollars in scholarship funds all due to an unforeseen error. Some of these applications can ask for a lot. In addition to multi-page general application pages, they may want you to include high school or college transcripts, essays, and other pages of supporting material. It's easy to get overwhelmed by the paperwork, particularly when managing several scholarships at once, and either forget to include something or accidentally place the wrong documents in the wrong application. The more scholarships you start to apply for, the more organized you have to be. Stay on top of your game. Right before you submit any application, triple-check if you have every single piece of information that the scholarship application asks for.

One thing in particular that you need to be especially fond of is eligibility requirements. Before even going through the trouble of filling out an application, triple-check the scholarship's eligibility requirements before moving forward. You can have the best application in the world, laced in gold and served on a silver platter, but if you do not meet the applicant eligibility criteria to even submit it, then that is the epitome of not having a good application. If you have a question about whether you meet certain eligibility criteria for an application, do not hesitate to get in contact with whomever is hosting that scholarship to find out the answers. Do your due diligence upfront and it will pay off in the long term.

INFORMATION ACCURACY

When you start filling out each section of the general application, aim to be as accurate as possible with the questions or information they are requesting from you. For example, if they ask you to provide a list of your extracurricular involvement in high school or college, make sure you are listing out the exact dates or time periods of involvement. If they ask you for tax or family income information, do your research and provide as accurate of financial information as you can. You get the idea here. The more transparent you are about your answers, the better your application will be. Your application will be better because you will be submitting a document that you are confident of, and if the scholarship donor contacts you requesting more information or asks you to elaborate on a specific point, you will be prepared. Also, if you have false or misleading information on your application to make yourself look better in the eyes of the scholarship judges, it may lead to severe repercussions. I'm not a lawyer, and I haven't dealt with a situation like that personally, but some reminders are worth reiterating, even when they feel obvious. That said, I never had a scholarship organization contact me asking for more information or to clarify something within my application. For me, the process has always been simple: send in the application and then wait to hear whether I was selected.

Providing as accurate answers as possible is related to another theme regarding the process of winning scholarships just like the "ask and you shall receive" mentality, and that is to save everything! We talked about this point earlier with saving all information related to extracurricular activities. If you save key information on significant events that happen to you during your time as a student and make a participation log, then providing accurate answers on your scholarships should be quick, easy, and simple. If you do not quite remember certain dates for example, try your best to research that information to fill in the blank, otherwise use your best judgment. The reason why I am bringing up to save everything again is because this time it applies to your actual answers within the general application. As you continue to fill out scholarship applications, you will come across very similar sounding questions and sections. There were multiple times where I remember writing a great answer to a short-answer question on one scholarship but forgot what I had put down. When I ran into another similar question on a different application, I remembered writing a perfectly phrased answer but could not recall how exactly I had written it. Therefore, I wasted time trying to rewrite that same answer to the best of my ability but in the end it did not come out as good as my original forgotten answer. *I highly encourage getting in the habit of saving all of your short-answer questions, and frankly any information within the applications you submit.* As you continue to apply, you can reuse these same answers over and over again, adjusting them when necessary. This will make applying much more efficient, freeing up time so you can submit even more applications. Also, the more you save your applications, you will begin to see patterns to your work and find areas of improvement in order to make your answers even stronger. You might notice patterns—like how most short-answer questions or lists are fully filled out, but the volunteering section, for example, is often only half completed, if at all. You now can see that volunteering may be an area you need to strengthen in your application.

MEET ALL DEADLINES

One final point in What Makes a Good General Application is making sure it's submitted on time. This should go without saying, but deadlines for submitting scholarship applications are a part of the scholarship process and cannot be overlooked. You should already be familiar with deadlines through regular school. If you struggle with deadlines, strengthening that habit is crucial to being successful with scholarships. The more scholarships you apply for, the more you will be juggling deadlines and the easier it will be to forget about one. There is no secret to getting good at this. Either you are organized and on top of your responsibilities or not. You cannot have a successful application without meeting the scholarship deadline. *One tip that I will provide is that the earlier you start preparing an application, the better.* That way you will not be rushed. If you are rushing to finish an application, you may make a mistake that will jeopardize your chance at winning. Give yourself sufficient buffers of time to prepare all the necessary documentation. When you are finding scholarships and you come across potential applications that are several months away from being due, do not brush them off to the side. Keep track of them, apply whenever the submission period is open, and always note when you can reapply to the same scholarships the following year.

GENERAL APPLICATION ENDING NOTES

At the end of the day, no two scholarships are the same. Saving your general application answers is a good start, but you most likely will need to get creative with how to rephrase them if you plan to use them on new applications. Be mindful that different scholarships require different answers. A lot of this differentiation is based on the scholarship organization. Some may want to focus more on questions that align with their organization's values. Some may want to strictly focus on your area of study. Some may ask questions that appear random or unrelated, but they're actually meant to assess an applicant's character. Regardless of the application, if you use the tools and strategies talked about in this section of What Makes a Good General Application, you are well on your way to structuring a winning application.

8

Key Points When Executing Step 4

KEY POINT 1: FOLLOWING UP

Humans are forgetful by nature. In today's society we are surrounded by so much new information, constant headlines, daily distractions, or interruptions from social media. It's easy to get pulled in another direction and not complete what you wanted to do by the end of the day. As you're reading this, you can probably think of times when you forgot to do something and faced a consequence—whether it slipped your mind because it felt unimportant at the time or simply fell off your radar until someone reminded you. When I lived with my family for a short time after college, this was a constant occurrence for me. I was so caught up in writing this book, for example, that my mom would tell me before she left for work do to something around the house. A few hours later, she'd come home from work and ask if I had completed the task. I would realize I had forgotten, and that usually ended with her being pretty upset! The moral of the story is if forgetfulness can happen to me or you, then it can happen to whomever you submitted a scholarship application to.

Following up is a powerful tool whenever you're waiting on a response or have something unresolved. Take a job for example. After an interview, the employer said they would get back to you but never do. In cases like this, it is best practice to follow up with them to understand your application status. Treat following up on scholarship applications with the same urgency you would a job interview. They are different situations, but both involve compensating you in some way, and it's important to approach that with intention. Before you follow up with scholarships that you have not heard from in a while, do your own research to see if they posted a date when winners will be announced either on their website, application, or other form of communication. The majority of time the more legitimate and established scholarships will have this information. For scholarships such as this, you may not need to contact them. If they said they would announce winners by a certain date and you don't hear anything back from them, chances are you probably were not selected as a winner. However, I emphasize you *may not* need to contact them because there could have been an issue with the scholarship winner selection. Let's say they needed to delay the announcement of winners for some odd reason. These are scenarios in which a follow up would be helpful and save you some anxiety as you wait in anticipation. Of course, this situation is an outlier. I have never had this happen to me. Still though, it is good practice to always follow up with scholarships in which you do not hear any feedback from regarding the status of your application. Who knows? Maybe your name *was* selected but never communicated to you by mistake, thus having you forfeit the scholarship due to not claiming the prize.

Like I said, most applications will have some date on which to expect to be notified if you have won or not. In my experience, there are other scholarships that did not have a defined date on which I would receive feedback. For me, these tended to be the less established scholarships that I may have stumbled upon buried in the fifteenth page of a Google search result, barely met the criteria, and found just in time before the application deadline expired. When I submitted these types of applications, I would usually never hear from them and did not know any better at the time, so I cut my losses and didn't follow up. That was a mistake I made because I would always have that in the back of my mind. I would be waiting in anticipation if I were to wake up to an email from that particular scholarship saying that I won, or that I would receive a letter in the mail or something. In reality, I wasted energy worrying about the scholarships that were caught in limbo rather than being focused on the present moment and what I needed to do *now* to win more scholarships.

I do not have a concrete timing of how long you should wait before you contact a scholarship about an application. What you can do, however, is look at the notification timelines listed by more established scholarships to get a sense of their typical waiting period. If the established scholarships can review, select winners, and issue out feedback within a certain amount of time, so should the less established scholarships.

When you are going to follow up after submitting your application and essay, *stay professional and keep it brief*. Again, this is different than if you are following up for a job. In a job setting, the employer may still be in the process of making their hiring decision. Therefore, if you come across as too desperate or convey a negative persona when following up for the job, that may affect your chances at receiving an offer. Every contact you have with individuals at a company during your interview process matters. When you follow up on a scholarship application, you'll probably reach an administrative staff member who handles the donor organization's day-to-day tasks but isn't part of the selection committee. The follow up may seem more relaxed with less chance to affect your pending scholarship result; however, this does not excuse you from taking the encounter seriously. It is important to be professional and well-mannered in any follow up you do.

As far as actually conducting a follow up, the most effective ways are either through email or phone call. Refer back to the scholarship's contact information listed on the application or on their website. *The main tip here is that it helps to have a structured follow-up script the more that you make these follow ups.* Plan out what you are going to send in the email or say on a phone call. Just as you save and reuse strong scholarship answers, you can also save an effective follow-up message and update the names and details as needed. For myself, I only remember following up with one scholarship organization at the time. I talked earlier in the book about a thirty-second video I did as part of a scholarship submission. I was very proud of the video but after not hearing anything back in quite a few months, I contacted the organization with a phone call. They ended up telling me that if I was selected as a winner I would have received a notice. Since I never received any such notice, I was safe to assume I was not a winner. In the moment I was disappointed but, as I keep emphasizing, I needed to cut my losses and move on using my abundance mentality.

A quick side note here is that if you have followed the necessary steps to validate why you deserve to win scholarships through continuous improvement on yourself, yet you find yourself still not winning scholarships, it is important to ask "why." From asking that question, you can find further insight into how you can improve your scholarship approach strategy. In the case with the video, this did not warrant enough reason to change my scholarship strategy because I rarely applied to applications which required video submissions. If the majority of my scholarship submissions were video entries and I kept getting rejected, then I would have asked "why" to understand how I can fine-tune my approach. Since the majority of my scholarships aligned with the process I describe in this book and produced strong results, I had no reason to make any significant adjustments to my strategy. This point is important because I guarantee scholarship winnings if you use the process I go through in this book. If you are not winning and you have been using this process, then there is an area within your application that is inhibiting your success. *You will need to identify these areas for yourself and improve them as necessary.* Use the essays, involvement examples, formatting, and all other topics in this book as a baseline for what your application should include to maximize your odds of success.

To conclude, make sure following up is a habit you get into when appropriate. Imagine if I never followed up with the second business letter I sent to the Director of Financial Assistance when I was asking for an increase in my financial assistance package. I would have lost out on $18,000. That said, following up during your scholarship journey involves more than just asking about the status of your applications. It can apply to a business letter reply you're waiting on, someone who hasn't responded about a letter of recommendation, or even a person you contacted to ask about potential scholarship leads. Following up in a general sense is a key professional skill that you should have as you progress in the world, and there is no better time to learn how to do it than while you're winning scholarship money. Keep in mind, if after one or two attempts at following up and still not hearing anything back, then cut your losses and move on. At that point, whomever you are contacting is not professional enough to manage their own time accordingly and is not someone or something that you should involve yourself with anyways. Self-respect in life is key. If others cannot value your time and effort, then find people who do and surround yourself with them. Likewise, you should also respect the time of anyone you interact with and treat others how you wish to be treated.

KEY POINT 2: THANK YOU LETTERS

I remember as a kid, the earliest form of manners my parents instilled in me was to always say "please" and "thank you." At that time there was really no substance in those words since I was still learning about life and really only cared about my Beanie Baby stuffed animals, Legos, Pokémon cards, and Nintendo video games. As an adult, those words play a bigger role than ever before because of the positive effects they have when used consistently—especially "thank you." Saying "thank you" shows a level of gratefulness for the things you have. *The more you are thankful for, the more you will appreciate and be satisfied with what you have versus with what you don't.* If you think about it, no matter what possessions you have in life, I guarantee you can always find more things you can have. When would it stop? When you own everything in the world? It's a never-ending cycle. Being grateful is a skill in life. Not only being grateful for possessions, but for opportunities, people, health, and countless other examples. The more you are grateful, the happier you will be in life.

Also, the more scholarships you win, the happier you will be in life! No matter how small the scholarship is, being grateful is an important step in succeeding in scholarships for a number of reasons. For one, being grateful about any amount that you win will fuel your drive to apply and win even more. Second, it is more money than you had in the beginning, so what is there to complain about? Third, if you apply for the same scholarship or to the same organization multiple years in a row, then it increases your chances of winning again because the scholarship organization knows that the funds they are providing to you mean something to you and you aren't just taking advantage of their generosity.

For every single dollar of scholarship funds I won, I sent a thank you letter. Sticking with the theme of saving everything, I mainly used one common thank you letter structure and reused it multiple times to save time and energy. Sending a thank you in a business letter format is sufficient and will provide the right amount of professionalism to your gesture. The first example below gives a great idea of how my thank you letters were constructed:

THANK YOU LETTER 1

Chapter 31 - Peoria Scholarship
SME Education Foundation
[REMOVED ADDRESS]

To whom it may concern,

I wanted to take the time to show my appreciation for awarding me with the Chapter 31 - Peoria Scholarship in the amount of $1,500. I am very glad that my hard work and dedication in searching for extra financial aid outside of my university is finally paying off. My parents are extremely proud of what I have accomplished over the years, not only with my academics, but also with my diligence in finding scholarships so that it may ease the burden on them so they do not have to pay for my college. I can show them I am responsible for handling my own debts and finding ways to *conquer such obstacles, and it can only be done through scholarships like these.*

Over their college years, both my older brother and sister have accumulated hefty sums of student loans that will take years to pay off. That is why I am truly thankful for the scholarship you have granted to me because not only will it help pay off my student debt, it will help speed up my plans for the future as a Manufacturing Engineer. I am excited as to where this major will take me and what new ideas and innovations I can bring to the world of manufacturing after graduation. Again, thank you very much for awarding me with the Chapter 31 - Peoria Scholarship. Incentives like this definitely will motivate me to work harder in school in order to have a successful career in the future.

Sincerely,

Jeremy Kaszycki

This thank you letter took a little less formal of an approach but overall gives the professional impression I was aiming for within a loose business letter context. In the first paragraph, I focused on immediately showing gratitude to the specific award I received. When writing thank you letters, always make sure to use full names of donors, organizations, actual titles of the scholarship, and the specific award amount. The detail here is critical because it leaves the interaction between you and the scholarship organization on a high note. This level of specificity reassures the donor who selected you that they made the right decision. Moving on, I touched on *why* I am so appreciative of the award. I explain that my long search for additional funding is finally bearing fruit, and their scholarship is a meaningful part of that. Don't be afraid to be personal here. The donor is doing you a huge favor. Imagine like you are writing this thank you letter to a dear family member that just gave you a scholarship—put some heart into it!

In the second paragraph, I give them a little snippet of what I plan to use the scholarship for. As you can see, I phrased my future plans quite vaguely because that was the truth. I knew I wanted to become a manufacturing engineer, but I didn't yet understand how the major's skill set would translate into future ideas and innovations. So, I kept my answer simple, and that honesty is what made it personal. I took the time to go through the whole scholarship application process, so it was nothing to invest a little bit more time in creating a heartfelt thank you letter.

I worked smarter, not harder, by reusing this general structure for all thank you letters to come. There will be times when you need to rephrase portions. I am not saying the "save everything" strategy is something where you only write one piece of content and that you are done. Rather, you write the main idea, and edit as necessary. While you may occasionally reuse your material as-is, you'll often need to revise the wording, phrasing, or even full paragraphs so they align with the theme of each individual scholarship.

That being said, the following thank you letter illustrates exactly what reuse looks like in practice. This scholarship was the most money I ever won in one single award—$5,000 for one year split into two semester payouts of $2,500. The scholarship organization that awarded me this scholarship instructed me to write thank you letters to eight individual donors, and I chose to use a more formal tone and structure. Here is the result of one, which I just replicated seven other times by changing names and addresses:

THANK YOU LETTER 2

April 20th, 2016

[REMOVED NAME]
[REMOVED ADDRESS]

Dear [REMOVED NAME],

I would like to take the time to show you my appreciation for your generous monetary contributions in being a donor for the Howard Bernstein Scholarship through the Material Handling Education Foundation, Inc. Recently, I was fortunate enough to be selected to receive this scholarship in the amount of $5,000. I cannot begin to thank you, MHEFI, and all respective donors of this scholarship enough for providing students with a means of financial aid in order to help defray the cost of receiving a college education. Incentives like this continually motivate me to work as hard as I can in school in order to learn about Manufacturing Engineering so that I may have a positive impact on the industry in my future career. In fact, I am pleased to inform you that this semester (Spring 2016), I am on track to receive straight A's in all of my classes, making it my best semester at Bradley University so far!

Having had two older siblings attend college before me, I was well aware of the financial obligation college demands. That is why I have made it a point to seek out as much additional financial aid during my college career as possible so that my plans for the future may not be delayed due to hefty student loan debt. I am excited to finish out my last couple years at Bradley and am anxious of where my major will take me. Again, thank you for being a part of my Howard Bernstein Scholarship award and rest assured I will make the most of it!

Sincerely,

Jeremy Kaszycki

By reading the second letter, you can see the differences, but the main idea stays the same. One final point when sending thank you letters, and frankly any piece of documentation, is to send them in a PDF file format if sending electronically. Do not send a Microsoft Word file because the formatting of the letter could be broken when it is opened on a different computer. Microsoft Word files should primarily be used for editing the initial document before saving into a PDF. A PDF file allows the recipient to view the exact same file in a cleaner form, eliminating a lot of unnecessary hassle that comes with sending Microsoft Word files. Overall, thank you letters are a small but necessary step in any successful scholarship process.

KEY POINT 3: LETTERS OF RECOMMENDATION

People most commonly attribute letters of recommendation to job applications. Well, if you treat finding scholarships like a part time job—which you should—then they are right! I was caught off-guard at first when I saw I needed to have someone write me a letter of recommendation for a scholarship, but the more applications I submitted, the more common it became for that requirement to appear. Contrary to what you might think, a recommendation letter is the easiest part of the application process. Why? For once you are not the one doing the writing! However, do not take these letters lightly. Although it is the easiest part of the process, it can take a very long time in preparation work before you are able to acquire a sincere and authentic letter—one that will sway a scholarship judge when your application is up against someone with similar credentials

If you've never handled letters of recommendation before, don't be intimidated. First of all, a letter of recommendation is a document written by someone you've asked to evaluate your qualities, characteristics, and capabilities as they relate to a specific task, role, or opportunity. They are validating why you're the best candidate for whatever you're applying to. *Preparation starts very early with letters of recommendation because it is all about the relationship that you have built with your recommender.* For example, a common individual you might pick to write you one of these documents will be a teacher or professor. This is where the kids who actually listened, participated in class, and received good grades have an advantage because they built rapport with that teacher or professor. They will see you in a good light and they will be happy to write you a letter of recommendation when you ask. Now, coming from the opposite spectrum—if you are a kid who slacks off in class, disturbs the lecture, and has bad grades because of your classroom antics, chances are they will not write you a recommendation because they do not respect you.

I'm not suggesting that you overly flatter your teachers or try to become their favorite. All you have to do is have a cordial, professional relationship with them. Ask some genuine questions in class, go to some office hours, maybe stay after and chat with them on occasion. Students who take this approach will have no problem receiving permission for a recommendation letter in this case. Teachers and professors want to help you out! Act accordingly and everything will fall in your favor.

This approach is how you should interact with all people in your network that you'd eventually want to request a letter of recommendation from. Do not restrict it to school faculty either. Anyone who is a professional—whether it be a co-worker, manager, supervisor, mentor, or spiritual guide—can write you a letter of recommendation. It's ultimately your decision, so choose someone with whom you have a strong relationship and who you know will speak positively about you. In my experience, not every scholarship asked for a document like this, but when they did, it was typically a manufacturing-related scholarship. In this case, I would pick people to write letters of recommendation for me who were within the manufacturing industry because they could speak to my industry knowledge and experience, thus validating why I was deserving of a manufacturing scholarship. This does not necessarily have to be the exact model you follow though. For example, I had the CEO of my local YMCA at the time write me a few recommendation letters for scholarships in which some were manufacturing related. I knew the CEO through the previously mentioned YMCA scholarship competition I participated in. Pick who you feel would best represent you for that particular scholarship you are applying for, but make sure they are a legitimate reference. You do not want to have any random stranger, family member, or friend recommend you because it is important to strategically portray the best image of yourself through the eyes of the scholarship committee. You want to give them the perception that you are surrounded by the right people in the business or industry, and are respected in those circles. Let me clarify "friend." You can have friends at work who are your professional colleagues that can write you letters. All I am saying is you want to avoid asking the person you only play basketball with on the weekends, for example, because they will not be able to validate your professional experience first-hand. When I sought out people to write my recommendation letters, I generally sought out people who were in a higher position than me with whatever I was doing professionally at the time. I would make sure they were well-established professionals, and were people who I looked up to. During my scholarship journey, I received recommendation letters from multiple professors, senior-level co-workers, work managers and supervisors, the CEO of the YMCA, and the dean of the IMET department at Bradley.

As you apply to more scholarships, you will eventually run out of relevant people to ask letters of recommendation from. When this happens, do not be afraid to reach out to the same people who had already written you a letter once before. Sometimes, just like how you can recycle scholarship answers, *you can work with your recommender to use one letter they wrote and send it to multiple scholarships by just switching a few names or titles, thus saving both of you time*. There were times when I asked the same person three or four times. Again, it depends on your relationship with that person. If you decide to rely on the same person for multiple recommendations, keep two principles in mind: always express sincere gratitude for their help, and be respectful of their time by spacing out your requests and giving them ample notice.

In regard to the first principle, always thank them for using their precious time to help you. Do not take it for granted. As a small gesture of thanks, buy them a gift card or a small coffee without them knowing. This will enhance your relationship and build your character because, who knows, you may use this person for a job recommendation in the future too!

In regard to the second principle, you do not want to overwhelm the particular person you are asking because you want them to always be willing to write you a recommendation without feeling taken advantage of. Personally, I tried to reach out to all of my professional contacts before going back to anyone a second time for a recommendation. When I reached out a second time, I made sure to explain that I had already contacted all my other professional references, so they understood I wasn't relying on them by default. I would also keep track of what scholarships I asked them to help me out with so I didn't get any of my references mixed up. It got to the point that after asking a few people multiple times, some of them asked me to draft the letter myself so they could simply review and sign it. This was great for me because I had free reign to hype myself up as much as possible!

Lastly, save all the letters of recommendation you receive. It's a good idea to carry past letters in case a recommender needs an example to guide their draft. Also, when you ask someone for a recommendation a second time after a year or so, they may suggest reusing the letter they wrote for you previously. This happened to me on occasion, and by saving every single document associated with my scholarship applications, I saved both of us a lot of stress because I just reused what was written in the past. Make the process easy for both you and your recommender.

Below are two examples of letters of recommendation that were written for me. The first is from the YMCA and the second is from the dean of my manufacturing engineering department as well as academic advisor at Bradley University. There is no "best way" for your recommender to write a recommendation letter. This will just give you an idea of something you can expect to be written:

LETTER OF RECOMMENDATION 1

To Whom It May Concern:

I am writing in enthusiastic support of Jeremy Kaszycki for an opportunity for scholarship through your organization. I have known Jeremy since he was involved in our YMCA Intern Challenge in 2014. Jeremy distinguished himself in the internship by becoming a semi-finalist in our city-wide competition and also returning the next year to mentor other interns.

During his time here, he helped create unique marketing campaigns for various companies in the Rockford area that include social media plans, promotional videos, and ideas for various community events.

He also began implementation of strategic procedures for several agencies, which helped advance their reputation and services for the next generation.

The teams he led collected over 5,000 books, 500 canned goods, 1,200 articles of clothing, and $7,500 for local charitable organizations around Rockford in 2014.

In short, Jeremy's high caliber of character, drive, and passion set him as a cut above the rest. I warmly recommend him for a scholarship.

[REMOVED NAME]
President & CEO
Rock River Valley YMCA

LETTER OF RECOMMENDATION 2

Dear SME Scholarship Review Committee,

Being an academia advisor and faculty advisor of the SME student chapter at Bradley University, I strongly recommend Mr. Jeremy Kaszycki, a sophomore in our Manufacturing Engineering program at Bradley University and current Vice President of SME student chapter, for being considered to receive the 2015 Ford Motor Company STEM Scholarship from SME Education Foundation Scholarship.

Jeremy has served as the Secretary of SME student chapter at Bradley University since he was a freshman and he has demonstrated great leadership skill and excellent passion with the manufacturing engineering program. He was elected as Vice President for the student chapter and continues to demonstrate his leadership for many chapter activities.

As a freshman, he was able to secure a paid internship position in Rockford, IL to work on facility design, lean projects, and manufacturing planning. He has gained much industrial experience by assisting the company to re-design a tool used by more than 20 plus operators. The tool he designed was able to reduce injuries for operators and enhance his or her job performance. He was able to design the tool, conduct manufacturing processes plan, and produce a prototype. He conducted a presentation to the managers about the approach of design and cost benefit of the design.

Upon his return from his summer internship, he volunteered to speak to freshman engineers at Bradley about SME and has shared his abovementioned internship experience with students. He has also volunteered to speak with high school students during their visits to Bradley University. His story has even inspired some students to become interested in the manufacturing program. In addition to his recruitment support, he has conducted many activities, such as, plant tours, and welding workshops during his time as vice president of the chapter. His academia record remains at 3.35 out of a 4.0 GPA. He has also demonstrated to be a role model for many Manufacturing Engineering students at Bradley University.

I am very proud of Jeremy that he is able to accomplish so much as a sophomore. It is my belief that he will accomplish much more when he receives his BS MFE degree from Bradley University two plus years from now. I am sure he will be able to secure an excellent manufacturing engineering career to enable him to contribute with his talent and leadership in manufacturing to impact the local and regional economy. He will also continue to volunteer his time and efforts speaking to many young students about manufacturing engineer being an excellent career fit. He will be always a leader in SME.

Because of the above mentioned evidences of his outstanding records and much more, I wholeheartedly recommend Jeremy Kaszycki for the 2015 Ford Motor Company STEM Scholarship. Should you wish to further discuss his attributes as a leader in Manufacturing Engineering, please don't hesitate to call me at [PHONE NUMBER REMOVED] or email [EMAIL REMOVED]. Thank you.

Sincerely yours,

[REMOVED NAME], Ph.D. & P.E.
Faculty Advisor, S110, Bradley University
Professor and Department Chair

KEY POINT 4: DO WHATEVER IT TAKES

Before we transition to the essay portion of the scholarship process, I need to teach you about one more key trait that you need in order to make a good general application. This trait applies both for the general application and the essay portion. This trait, at the end of the day, separates the winners from the losers. Imagine if you are a cheetah in the African savannah. You are alone. You are hungry. You are thirsty. The blistering heat forces you to squint as the dry savannah breeze pelts your face with sand, but you can just make out a wildebeest far off in the hazy distance. You manage to hobble closer to reveal that this wildebeest is very youthful and in prime health and strength. You perk up because you finally have found your long overdue meal, but the growls in your stomach snap you back to reality to remind you that you haven't had a meal in over seven days which has depleted your own strength and speed. The likelihood of you being able to catch your prey is slim to none because you know you are in no condition to catch such a healthy, strong, agile wildebeest. It will surely outrun you. You have two choices: you can either have a defeatist mentality, give up, and convince yourself that you wouldn't be able to muster up the strength to catch the wildebeest so why waste precious energy and risk waiting another seven days before finding another prey that you may have better odds at catching, or you can seize the opportunity that is right in front of you because you know you may not last another seven days of starvation before you find your next target. The choice is yours.

In life, your choices drive your outcomes. You can choose to eat healthily or not. You can choose to put in your best effort or not. You can choose to go after the wildebeest now or wait in the hopes you will stumble upon something else. There is an interesting idea on suffering that I recently stumbled upon. Undoubtedly we are going to experience suffering in our lives. You can choose to postpone the suffering that comes from living a healthy lifestyle by using your youth as an excuse to neglect your health and other life decisions. It may feel good in the moment because it is easy and there is no immediate suffering, but once you get older and your negative choices start to come back to haunt you, the suffering you have so desperately tried to avoid starts to creep in. Your body starts to shut down prematurely due to negligence, you are nowhere of significance in your professional career, you haven't experienced the things you've always dreamed of, and so on. This is what is described as "bad suffering." The other side of the coin would be good suffering. You realize that suffering breeds results. You suffer in the gym by working out and pushing your body in order to advance your physical health. You suffer in the library by studying hours on topics and pushing your mind in order to maximize your mental capabilities. You suffer by saying "no" to a diet of triple chocolate fudge volcano ice cream cakes you crave in order to prevent long-term bodily diseases. This type of "good suffering" may not feel good in the moment, but over the years the sacrifices you make now will help you reach new heights your bad-suffering self never could have imagined. You will be happier, healthier, stronger, more resilient, and have an overall better life so that you will age with grace, dignity, and will have built a character in which people will forever admire. As you get older, the suffering will not feel as bad. On the contrary, it will feel natural. You've already handled the hard stuff, and you have your past self to thank for that. Suffering is imminent. It's our everyday choices that will dictate our futures. Easy choices now, hard life later. Hard choices now, easy life later. Life doesn't get easier; you just get stronger.

With the importance of making the right choices in mind, the final trait for a successful scholarship application is to **do whatever it takes**. No excuses. A big emphasis was put earlier in the book on capitalizing as much as you can while you are a student in order to give yourself as many opportunities to win scholarships as physically possible. Think of the wildebeest you saw out in the distance as a $10,000 check. Are you going to wait and let that opportunity pass you by just because the application requires you to write two one-thousand-word essays instead of one, and you don't feel like writing them? That would be pathetic. You need to have the mental fortitude, work ethic, eagerness, grit, perseverance, and resilience to do whatever it takes to apply to whatever scholarships you can. If you know your "why," this becomes easy and is absolutely possible! Take my experience for example. I created a thirty-second video application when I had no video experience just so I can give myself a chance to win a few thousand dollars in scholarship money. I wore a suit, wrote and memorized a script, had my brother follow me around as he took video footage of me on the manufacturing floor of my engineering internship to make a collage, added background music, and made sure the lighting and capture angles were perfect, all for the sake of winning a scholarship. Why? Because I was doing whatever it takes! I knew I needed to make a legitimate video that would be competitive, not just sloppily throwing a quick video together expecting to win. I joined the scholarship competition at the YMCA that took up my whole freshman year summer! Why? Because I was doing whatever it takes! I knew that the winner of that competition was going to get $5,000 in scholarship money. I didn't even win a scholarship through that because I finished a semi-finalist, not a finalist. You know what though? That still was one of the best decisions I made in my young career because that competition gave me a vast amount of experience that I leveraged on my other scholarship applications and job interviews. I may not have won at the time, but I won ten times as much with what doors opened for me by participating in that competition.

I'm writing this section with great passion because you need to realize that what happened to me can happen to you! *It starts by taking action!* Whatever you do in your scholarship journey, no matter how small, rest assured it's better than doing absolutely nothing. You must recognize what can happen if you maximize your scholarship effort to the fullest. The possibilities are endless when you do whatever it takes to win these scholarships. Put in the time, have abundance mentality, and apply to as many as you can. Apply to the easy scholarships. Apply to the hard scholarships. Apply to the weird scholarships. Apply to the boring scholarships. Do whatever the submission criteria say to do. Write as many essays as you can. Brag and gloat about yourself as much as possible on these applications. I'm telling you—once you start winning, you will fall in love with the journey and want to continue to win and reap the rewards of your hard work. Do whatever it takes to apply!

9

Essay Portion | Connection Types

WHAT MAKES A GOOD ESSAY PORTION

The second section of a scholarship application is the essay portion. I consider this the most important part of the application process. Writing an essay allows you to separate yourself from all other candidates in unique ways that the general application cannot capture. Within an essay, you can communicate certain traits such as how passionate you are about a certain subject, how creative you are, how educated and well-spoken you are, what makes you unique, or who you are as a person. What an essay also allows you to do is connect with whomever is judging your essay in a way that the general application cannot. If you connect with them in the right ways where your written essay aligns with the organization's and the scholarship's values, that is the recipe of a winning scholarship essay and that is what we will be covering in this section. We will first dive into what type of information you need to include in an essay, along with the reasoning of why it's important. Then, I will start to share examples of whole essays that were part of my winning applications, breaking down each part as we go.

In my opinion, I think the reason why a lot of students do not put a great deal of emphasis on winning scholarships is because the majority of applications require an essay portion. Their mindset is that they already write enough research papers in school, so why should they tack more on their to-do lists? Well, if you have gotten this far in the book, you know exactly why! To be honest, the more people that have this negative mindset and do not change it makes it better for you, the reader, because that means there is less competition standing between you and winning scholarships!

Many students assume that the difference between a school essay and a scholarship essay is that scholarship essays must read like they were written by a Pulitzer-winning author, while school essays only need to meet the teacher's basic content requirements. I thought the same thing at first, but once I started writing essays and learning from the ones that didn't win, I realized that assumption just isn't true. In summary, here is the gist of writing scholarship essays: *a lot of the writing techniques that you learn in your regular English classes in high school or college are the same writing techniques that you use with scholarship essays, the only thing you have to add is to creatively tie in an emotional, personal, and passionate connection to the subject you are writing about in a way that strongly aligns with the essay prompt you are given.*

Emotional / Personal / Passionate Connections
\+ Proper Essay Structure
= Winning Scholarship Essay

The way in which you present these emotional, personal, and passionate connections is the creative part. These ideas can be molded into any part of the essay—introduction, body, or conclusion. Individually, they are powerful in their own right, but if combined, they make for a very strong essay. This idea will be explained more as we move on.

Do not worry if writing is not your biggest strength. With anything, practice makes perfect. Trust me, you will be getting tons of writing practice if you follow exactly what I teach in this book. Everyone has to start from somewhere. For me, I was your typical high school student when I wrote my first scholarship essay my senior year. I'm not a naturally gifted writer. I was never in any creative writing or AP English classes. To be honest, earlier when I mentioned how I received a 10 out of 12 on the essay portion of the ACT, I was surprised! I remember preparing for that part of the ACT by writing numerous practice essays, but I didn't think I would score that high. This was before I ever applied to any scholarships, so you could say this was a sign of what was to come! A funny thing in life is that you don't realize you're good at something until you find a particular interest that causes that undiscovered skill or talent to finally emerge. Traditional school writing assignments never truly engaged me, but once I discovered that mastering essays could help me win thousands of dollars in scholarships, my interest in writing surged. Also, writing in general is a great life skill so there is no losing scenario here. No matter where your writing skills are right now, you're in a good place. The more you write scholarship essays, the better you will become and the better your results at winning will be so long as you follow what is described in this section. By reading this book, you're already farther ahead than from where I started. So don't stress and don't overthink. Simply write—and before you know it, the skill you once struggled with will become one of your strongest.

CONNECTION TYPES

In Step 2, we talked about how scholarship organizations that are providing financial aid to students consider their money an investment, with their return on investment being the student's impact to society. General application sections allow judges to spot character traits in applicants, like being hardworking, smart, talented, or outgoing. These are great traits to have and certainly play a vital role in your success with scholarships. However, the general application section does not tell the whole story of who a person truly is. The organization wants to always pick the most deserving candidate. They want to make sure that the person who wins a significant lump sum of their money uses it for what it is intended for, is wholeheartedly grateful for the award, and trust that they will positively represent the scholarship organization's values. Representation is especially important because organizations may post the winners of their scholarship on some form of public media. To mitigate the risk of selecting the wrong candidate, the majority of scholarship applications will require submission of some form of written essay or short-answer section. An essay lets judges look beyond the basic, black-and-white profile shown in the general application section. Sure, you can be the smartest, most talented, or hardest working, but do you care about the future of the industry that the scholarship organization is representing? Are you wanting to drive change in the world because you see a bigger picture, or do you just want to sit back and rely on other people to fix the world's pressing problems? Do you care? Are you passionate about your course of study, beliefs, ideas, or values that make up who you are, or are you still uncertain and might shift from what you're telling the scholarship organization about yourself in three to five years? Are you a good leader? Are you able to influence others positively? These, and so many more questions can be answered through an essay portion, which is why it is such a big part of scholarships. They do not want to just grant a scholarship to the smartest applicant without getting a sense of who they are. If they did, the student could take the money for granted, use it improperly, or fail to create the impact the organization expects, resulting in no real return on their investment. The scholarship organization wants to impact the student's life just as much as they want the student to impact the world. If it means more to one student than the other, chances are the more passionate student will not take their award for granted and go on to do great things. This is precisely why the essay portion is so critical. *When writing your essay, it is up to you to show why you are different, why you care, how you care, and how you will use their money for a greater purpose.* The way to show them is by executing the first part of the winning scholarship essay formula—develop emotional, personal, and passionate connections to the subject you are writing about in a way that strongly aligns with the essay prompt you are given. Let's start by defining these connection types, starting with emotional.

EMOTIONAL CONNECTION

Emotion *(noun)*
An affective state of consciousness in which joy, sorrow, fear, hate, or the like, is experienced, as distinguished from cognitive and volitional states of consciousness;

–Dictionary.com

To establish an emotional connection in your essay, strive to evoke moods that your reader—such as a scholarship judge—can genuinely feel, visualize, and relate to, as though the emotion extends beyond the page itself. It will be something the reader will remember you by after reading the dozens of other applications they have in their queue. Often in relationships, when someone who was close to you or that you loved is gone, it is not what they said or did that you remember. Rather, it is how that person made you feel that sticks with you. The same applies for the information you put in your essay. Creating emotional connections moves you away from the flat, surface-level answers that far too many students rely on. You need to go deeper than the surface by asking yourself questions of "how," "why," or "what" when writing and elaborating on your answers. Are you excited about your ideas? Then convey that excitement in your writing. Are you saddened by a certain world issue? Then convey that sadness. You have an entire spectrum of emotions you can incorporate here. Your goal is to make them feel what you are feeling.

Let's say you are applying for an aeronautical scholarship to study plane mechanics, and part of the essay prompt asks you why you want to go into this field. An example of a surface-level answer would be something like the following:

> *"I am extremely interested in exploring all there is to know about planes so that I may become an expert in plane mechanics one day. Traveling is one of my biggest passions. With this course of study, I hope to achieve my lifelong goal of traveling to every country in the world."*

There are several reasons as to why there isn't much substance to these three sentences. First, there is no flow between the sentences. In the first sentence, I would ask "why" are you so interested in planes that it is making you want to become an expert? "What" specifically do you want to learn about, or find to be so appealing? In the second sentence, I would ask "why" is traveling one of your biggest passions, or "how" did traveling become a passion? In the third sentence, I would ask "why" is it your lifelong goal? Here, you have an opportunity to use imagery by describing what achieving that lifelong goal would look like and what feelings would be associated with it. Also, it is fine to have lifelong goals, and I advocate for that. However, when making an emotional connection, there has to be a deeper meaning to go along with the content you are writing. It can't all be about you. You want to connect this hypothetical lifelong goal with, for example, how you can use your experience in service of others, or to help people in some way.

Now, here is an example of how I would rephrase that answer to include an emotional connection:

> *"My fondest memories of childhood involved playing with toy planes. Now as a young professional, I channel that same childlike curiosity in studying to become an expert in the field of plane mechanics. Each subject in my curriculum acts as a piece of the puzzle for my future which in the end will display a picture of me not only achieving my lifelong goals of traveling to each country in the world, but also helping other people have those same experiences in life by continuing to improve the safety, reliability, and comfort of planes today."*

Notice a few things here, starting with flow. The first sentence easily flows to the second with the connection of childhood. You can see the same from the second to third sentence with studying plane mechanics to forming the puzzle pieces of the future. As a side note, not every sentence you write in an essay has to flow all the time so don't get too tripped up over your words. Another point I want to make is about the creativity aspect of this rephrased answer. Using a phrase such as "piece of the puzzle" to then say everything will come together to create a beautiful picture is an example of the extra step you should take to incorporate creativity into your writing. Creativity grabs the attention of your reader, and the connections you make help the reader's retention of your essay's ideas. More details regarding flow, creativity, and other techniques will be included when talking about an essay's structure.

I provided answers to the key questions I raised when critiquing the original surface-level answer. I answered "why" I was so interested by explaining that it stems from childhood, and used imagery to help them picture a little child playing with toy planes and how that translates into how the curriculum is approached. I also addressed that same "why" by explaining that my purpose is to help others gain the opportunity to travel the world through aviation. I posed a lot of questions in my critique. Do not think that you need to answer all of them when writing. Take my critique questions as opportunities to elaborate on your essay in order to make a point—an emotional connection. If you tried answering all of my rhetorical questions, your ideas would become too fragmented and the writing wouldn't flow. With essays, the majority of time you will have a certain word number requirement. That's why you should focus on quality over quantity and build around one or two major points rather than attempting to cover everything. Otherwise, you will end up with too many words that do not fit within the word requirement.

The rephrased answer centers on emotions of joy, empathy, and kindness. Joy is brought forth when talking about childhood. Usually everyone has happy memories from childhood that they can look back and reflect on. When I say that I approach learning about airplanes with childlike curiosity, it helps them picture my excitement about plane mechanics because it brings them back to the curiosity and enthusiasm they felt in childhood. Empathy and kindness come into play when talking about helping others. The essay suggests a higher purpose greater than oneself by helping others travel the world. You are advocating the reader to recognize and get behind this cause of greater good. The reader will look from the viewpoint of one of the people who will be helped by your efforts as you go on to improve the safety, reliability, and comfort of planes as suggested in the essay. They will *feel* the kindness and empathy that you are genuinely wanting to put out into the world as they read your essay. Therefore, they will remember you, your essay, and your application for these feelings which is exactly what an emotional connection strives to accomplish.

PERSONAL CONNECTION

> ***Personal*** *(adjective)*
> *Relating to, directed to, or intended for a particular person; pertaining to or characteristic of a person or self-conscious being*
>
> *–Dictionary.com*

Take for example the financial aid letter that I wrote requesting Bradley to provide more financial assistance toward my tuition. That letter is a perfect example of making a personal connection in writing. *A personal connection makes it known to the reader that you have external means and motivations that are driving you to win extra funding through scholarships.* It shows that you have a personal attachment outside of just wanting money. You are letting the reader know that you have bigger reasons outside of yourself for why you are applying to their scholarship. Think of it as a chip-on-your-shoulder mindset. Certain things happened in your past which are motivating you to win these scholarships. You are not applying for the sake of applying and hopefully winning. You are applying because **you need this**. Looking back at the financial aid letter, I talk about my siblings having immense sums of student loan debt. Their student loan debt was crippling my parent's financial foundation and retirement options because they were forced to help with loan payments, so I knew for a fact I *cannot* let that happen to me too. If it did, I would be putting my family at risk. I was forced to find a new way to pay for school. That was my personal reasoning.

In the next example, I will be using a snippet from a past essay of mine that talks about my own personal connection as to why I should win this scholarship. The below prompt had five bullet points of information I needed to address in the essay. I am only going to include the one bullet point that relates to the example snippet. The remaining four bullet points were addressed in other areas of the essay. Also just to give come context, the personal connection I make below was located in the conclusion:

> **Prompt:** *How will this scholarship help you achieve your objectives?*
>
> *"Being a first-generation college student, I am faced with a lot of pressure to succeed. However, realizing just how great of an opportunity I have, I plan to work tirelessly until I have achieved my objectives. Having had two older siblings already graduate college, I am aware of the hefty sums of student loans they have accumulated throughout the years that put their plans on hold.*

Therefore, winning this scholarship through SME-EF will help me to keep on track so that my future plans are not delayed."

Here, the personal connection I make is in regard to my first-generation college student status and my siblings' struggles with college debt. As it pertains to my student status, using "first-generation" as an adjective is a very powerful word combination because of the meaning typically associated with it. "First-generation" implies that you are the first in your immediate family to go to college. Unless explicitly described, using this term can make the reader think of a variety of scenarios. It can paint a picture of how your parents, or other family members, grew up with far fewer opportunities, yet pushed through their own struggles so their children could have the chances they never did. Their hardships can further be expanded upon—whether they grew up in poverty, faced geopolitical turmoil, or lived in communities with few resources—circumstances that left them without a path to college, or a better life in general, and forced them to concentrate on getting by. All of these thoughts are created just by adding this simple adjective. It tells a story of a student who is beating the odds despite the adversity their family has faced in the past, thus creating a personal motivation to show them their struggle was not in vain.

When talking about my siblings' finances, I explain how their future progress is slowed by the weight of their debt. As the younger sibling, I found it unsettling because I didn't yet grasp the impact of money, and what should have been a celebratory graduation was overshadowed by my family's worry about the looming loan payments. It's essential to make that clear in the essay because it helps the reader, who is also judging the scholarship, see that my motivations are genuine. Among all the reasons I have explained why scholarships are given out by generous organizations, one of the reasons is simply because they want to help those in need, and who have a legitimate reason for the extra financial aid. Your activities are important, yes. Your grades are important, yes. However, behind the virtual walls of a scholarship application on a computer is a human being who is reading your essay—your story. They have a heart and feel empathy. That is the key to personal connections. *You need to understand that the very things you're struggling with—family issues, financial pressure, health challenges—can become the strengths that set you apart.* Now, before you look too deep into that statement, writing personal connections in essays this way is by no means praising the issues in people's lives. As I said in the very beginning of this book, I am here to help people with the information I learned throughout my college years. The way to understand personal connections is to see them as expressions of vulnerability. That, if you win this scholarship, you are only going to better yourself and whatever situation you may be dealing with. I'm helping you learn how to communicate these struggles in a way that not only strengthens your application, but also opens the door to improving your situation. You want to use your struggles to your advantage in your essays. You want the reader to genuinely understand your pain and feel the sympathy, or even the pity, that naturally arises from the challenges that led you to seek additional financial aid. There is no reason to feel bad for using this strategy either. Think of the commercials you see asking for donations to feed hungry children, or wanting you to adopt formerly abused animals from animal shelters. They pull on your heartstrings to make you want to take an action. You are doing the same thing when using your struggles as personal connections in your scholarship essays. You are pulling on the heartstrings of the scholarship judge to have them take the action of granting you financial aid.

One last angle that you can take when making personal connections deals with others' struggles instead of your own. We all know the pain and suffering that we have felt in our personal lives which is what makes us able to relate to other people and their situations. One way I have included the use of personal connections in my writing is instead of being motivated from my own struggles, I "personally" would draw motivation from the opportunity to give back to individuals, communities, or whole networks. Highlighting the positive impact I could make through my major became a strong, natural talking point in my essays, and resonated with judges in the same way my own personal stories of hardship and triumph did. These examples centered on *why I* wanted to give back, thus making it a personal connection. If I were to have rephrased the giving back example to focus on making the reader *feel something* about giving back, it would be more along the lines of an emotional connection. When it comes to connections such as this, sometimes it is not what you say but rather how you say it. So, I just wanted to include this brief note on how I made these distinctions between emotional and personal connections since talking about struggles can be an emotional topic. To give you a better idea, you will see these distinctions in action later when we actually breakdown winning essays of mine. Ultimately, everyone loves a comeback story. Whether the struggle is your own or one faced by the community you serve, showing how you rise above limitations speaks volumes about who you are—which is why capturing it in your essay is so important.

PASSIONATE CONNECTION

Passionate *(adjective)*
having, compelled by, or ruled by intense emotion or strong feeling; expressing, showing, or marked by intense or strong feeling

–Dictionary.com

What do you enjoy doing most in life? Do you have a hobby that you cannot live without? What are some things you love? If you can answer these questions, you're likely passionate about whatever you named. *You can talk for hours about it. Describe it in vivid detail. Know every single thing there is to know about it. This same enthusiasm is at the heart of the third connection type—the passionate connection.* Most scholarships you're eligible for will most likely include a prompt asking about your major or course of study, such as: "Why did you choose to study *[insert major]*?" When making passionate connections, you need to be able to express everything that enthralls you about your major or course of study. What do you absolutely find fascinating about it? For me, I absolutely love playing basketball. I am a huge fan of the game, and I will keep aiming at getting better as long as I am able to stand on two feet. If I had basketball taken away from me, my life would not be the same. That is how passionate I am about the sport. I took the same energy that I felt about basketball and applied it to the way I thought about Manufacturing Engineering. Don't get me wrong, if I had the choice of either being a National Basketball Association (NBA) player or a manufacturing engineer for a career, without question I would pick NBA player because it is closer to my heart. Obviously though, that is not how things played out for me, and instead I had to enter the corporate world. If you remember in my backstory, I got into how I picked studying manufacturing. I love manufacturing because of the vast amount of amazing pieces of machinery, technology, systems, and processes that make up the industry. A lot of that same energy that sparks my interest in basketball exists for manufacturing too. Yet when I am writing essays about why I chose to study Manufacturing Engineering, I make it sound like I never even picked up a basketball before and that manufacturing is all I know, eat, breathe, and sleep. I really try to bring out, through creative wording and specific detail, how much I love my major in manufacturing, and that is what you have to do too. When talking about passionate connections, you really need to put your passion, your heart, and your soul behind what you are writing in your essay. You need to make it known to the scholarship judge that you really mean what you say and you are not just going through the motions.

Let's take a look at an example of a passionate connection in action. A little bit of explanation is needed about the essay that the below prompt and answer are from. This essay had a multi-question format with the below prompt being one of the main questions. There was no word-count restriction. Also, I make some references that may not make sense, but rest assured that is part of the flow of the whole essay. What we are focusing on here, though, is not the flow, but rather how I express genuine passion and desire for my major of Manufacturing Engineering. Do not worry if this snippet does not answer the full prompt. Again, it is only a part of the answer:

> **Prompt:** *What type of work do you see yourself doing after you graduate and what motivates you to pursue this specific career?*
>
> *"After my undergraduate studies, one area of manufacturing that I hope to work with is lean implementation in a manufacturing*

system. I am currently in a class taught by [REMOVED NAME] that looks at many ways a manufacturing system can be converted from a standard job shop into a lean, linked-cell manufacturing system that outputs products using one-piece-flow. I think it is absolutely fascinating how a manufacturing engineer can go into a factory floor, pinpoint where waste is being produced that does not add value to the company, and provide solutions using Kaizen methodologies and lean strategies in order to convert a system from mass production to just-in-time manufacturing. Some of these strategies include development of U-shaped manufacturing cells, setup reduction, integration of production, quality and inventory control systems, and improvement of manufacturing and assembly processes, which I hope to be a part of. I am interested in this type of work because it will allow me to collaborate, not only with other engineers, but also with the workers and operators on the shop floor in order to involve them in implementing lean since the internal customer is the company's most important asset."

This answer, though only part of the full answer, provides a lot of substance when answering the prompt. You can easily see why I am passionate about manufacturing through the specific examples and details I provide. I avoided any type of vague or surface-level answer here because I am passionate about the subject. The class that was mentioned in the second sentence was truly my favorite class out of my whole manufacturing engineering curriculum. Something about the material in that class genuinely captured my interest, so much so that I paid close attention during classes and even read the entire textbook cover to cover on my own time. I never did that for any other class I attended! That shows how passionate I was not only to learn the material, but also to retain it and eventually specialize in it. The power of passionate connections comes from the fact that the judge deciding the winners is often personally connected to the scholarship in some way. So for example, in my prompt I was given, the scholarship centered around the manufacturing industry. Therefore, it is highly likely that the people judging the applications are in some way, shape, or form related to the manufacturing industry. Maybe they are business owners, engineers, designers, managers, or other roles who have spent years in a manufacturing setting. As they read the essays of each application, they will be able to pinpoint those who truly have a genuine, authentic interest for manufacturing versus those who aren't taking their major or essay too seriously and aren't as passionate of an applicant. So, when the judges read my example, they could feel the depth and detail I brought by channeling the same energy I use in basketball into expressing my passion for manufacturing. They picked up on that—which is why this snippet comes from an application that earned me $2,500 during the second semester of my junior year.

A second way you can make passionate connections in your essay is to actually write about the experiences you had in the particular industry you are studying. If the prompt is non-major specific, like volunteering for example, talk about your experiences in volunteering. You get the point. There is nothing more you can do to convince somebody that you like to do something than to actually physically go out and do it. Let's say you are studying computer science. You should be doing everything in your power to get involved in the world of computer science. Whatever your major, getting involved in internships, apprenticeships, volunteer opportunities, seminars, conferences, or self-started side projects is the best thing you can do to show that you are passionate about your major of choice. The earlier you can start to build up your résumé relevant to your major of choice, the easier writing scholarships will be because you will have content to elaborate on. Scholarship judges want to see you get involved, and they especially love it when you have real-world examples to back up your claims of being as "passionate" as you say you are in your essay. It's one thing to say something, but it's another to actually do something.

Let's take a look at an example. Again, do not look too much into what the prompt is saying because I do not answer it fully here. Instead, pay attention to how I am making a passionate connection by simply explaining what I did while at an internship:

> **Prompt:** *How will your coursework help you to impact manufacturing technology in the Boone, Ogle, Stephenson, Winnebago, and Rock County regions?*
>
> *"For the past two summers, I was fortunate enough to work as a Manufacturing Engineering Intern at Rockford Products LLC, a manufacturing facility that specializes in the making of cold-formed products. During the summer of 2014, I was assigned various projects including the design and implementation of an ergonomic rake in response to a workplace incident that happened on the shop floor, the integration of a procedure to help reduce the likelihood of mixing burnished and non-burnished parts together during the part's routing, and the revision of forklift lane layouts on the shipping dock.*
>
> *Now as a second-year intern during the summer of 2015, I was tasked to work closely with the Quality Engineering Department in order to tackle a massive quality control project. Rockford Products is in the process of transitioning to using a different data collection system, known as InfinityQS that machine operators use in order to input data from dimensional checks they carry out. The first step was to update numerous control plan documents that list which processes the raw material must pass through in order to become a finished product. Most revisions included pinpointing different dimensions from each part by looking at the engineering prints and labeling the frequency of how often those dimensions would be measured when the part undergoes each process in the routing. Once revisions for a part are complete, that part must then be programmed into InfinityQS."*

This example works for the same reason as the first: a judge connected to manufacturing will appreciate the value of real industry experience, giving me an edge over applicants without it. The more experience you gain, the easier writing becomes because you now have something relevant to write about and elaborate on. The example given here makes up about half of the essay that it came from. I did not have to force words or insert fluff to meet the minimum word requirement of the essay. On the contrary, I had too much to write about because I did a lot at my internship, so I had to cut out all the unnecessary information and only leave the most significant points. Trust me, that is a good problem to have.

CONNECTION TYPE ENDING NOTES

Making emotional, personal, and passionate connections will make up the majority of the content you write within your scholarship essays. This is because of how you can use multiple connection types simultaneously. They can be used in your introductions, bodies, and conclusions—you just need to tailor them toward whatever it is the prompt is telling you to write about. Also, as you go deeper and explain your points in such a way that it creates an emotional, personal, or passionate connection, you will find yourself with a good chunk of meaningful content. The rest of the content will be filled in with the techniques in the next section titled Essay Portion | Proper Essay Structure.

Since the majority of content will involve these connections, your mindset when writing these connections should be focused on what the scholarship judge wants to hear. If you do not remember what the judge wants to hear, read through the connection types again because I explain why scholarship judges respond so well to them. *That said, when you're writing your connections, you want to highlight the values and experiences that resonate most with the judges.* Take the plane mechanic example that was brought up in the Emotional Connection section. Really make an effort to present yourself as someone who is genuinely enthusiastic about plane mechanics. Another example would be if you are writing a personal connection that is tied to your family not being financially stable and that is your motivation for winning scholarships, then try to make that situation sound as bad as possible. Make them feel pity for you. It may seem weird to say, but authentic struggle leaves the deepest impression. Of course, be fully honest and truthful in your writing, but the more you extrapolate on your points and highlight truly what it is that you are struggling with, the higher the chance of you winning the scholarship. Also, most scholarships require you to attach tax and financial documents, so lying about your need won't work.

To wrap up this section on connection types, I've included one of my essays below that showcases them in action. This essay was written for the Society of Manufacturing Engineers - Education Foundation on January 2nd, 2015. It was one of the earliest essays I wrote, and it turned out to be one of the most important. Although it was not selected as a scholarship winner, I used parts of this essay in twelve other essays that followed, the majority of which did go on to win. We will discuss how and why I was able to use portions of this essay to form other essays later in the book. You will find each sentence numbered at its beginning to make it easier to refer back to during the explanation.

Prompt:

- *Why do you want to enter this field of study?*
- *Career Objectives: What are your near and long-term career objectives?*
- *If you have selected "Engineering" as your major, please describe how your educational plans relate to manufacturing engineering or manufacturing technology?*
- *Educational Objectives: What are your near and long-term educational objectives?*
- *How will this scholarship help you achieve your objectives?*
- *Word Count: No more than 300 words all on one page.*

*" **1**Every day, people are exposed to endless opportunities around every corner but lack the ambition to pursue them in hopes of a better life. **2**Fortunately, I was blessed with the opportunity to receive a college education in order to fully exploit my potential, both as a student and as a person. **3**Manufacturing is used in just about every industry of the world in order to accompany the world's continuous population growth. **4**Seeing how this can have such an impact on society, I decided to study Manufacturing Engineering at Bradley University. **5**The numerous processes for product development and distribution that exist can truly be considered an art. **6**That is why I am excited to learn about how to improve upon these processes and eventually implement my solutions in the real-world. **7**Knowing that I have a chance, for example, to improve a food production operation that results in feeding hungry families that are in need faster is truly well worth the cost of a college education. **8**Also, with my newfound knowledge after graduation, I aim to work within my community of Rockford, Illinois in order to give back what has been given to me all these years; a chance at a new life and new opportunities for the residents, and especially the younger generation. **9**Being a first-generation college student, I am faced with a lot of pressure to succeed. **10**However, realizing just how great of an opportunity I have, I plan to work tirelessly until I have achieved my objectives. **11**Having had two older siblings already graduate college, I am aware of the hefty sums of student loans they have accumulated throughout the years that put their*

> *plans on hold.* [12]*Therefore, winning this scholarship through SME-EF will help me to keep on track so that my future plans are not delayed."*

After reading this essay, can you identify what connection types I used?

Sentences 3 through 6 create a passionate connection. Here, I answer why I want to enter this field of study (prompt bullet point 1). I clearly articulate why manufacturing resonates with me personally. It's not about how others see it; it's about my own fascination with the field. That makes the statement authentic.

Sentences 7 and 8 create an emotional connection. Here, I give insight into my near and long-term career and educational objectives (prompt bullet points 2, 3, and 4). I do not focus too much on the educational part due limiting my content to abide by the word-count restriction. The judge can imagine the hungry families that I talk about which makes them feel a sense of sadness and empathy for those families. They can picture the younger generation—or even their own younger selves—when I talk about giving back, and that sparks a feeling of hope and joy. These connections communicate to the scholarship judge that I am in manufacturing for the right reasons: to serve others and make an impact in the world, which is what the scholarship organizations are looking for.

Sentences 9 through 12 create a personal connection. Here, I answer how this scholarship will help me achieve my objectives (prompt bullet point 5). This part of my essay may sound familiar. That is because it is the same section that I used as the example in the Personal Connection section earlier. As explained in that section, I use the struggles of being a first-generation college student and the fact that student loans continue to haunt my siblings as motivation for myself to look for other means to pay for college. It gives a deeper meaning why I need and deserve this scholarship.

Now that you are an expert in identifying and creating emotional, personal, and passionate connections in your essay, you may be asking, "That's great that I know these connections, but where do I start? How do I connect them all together to create a competitive scholarship essay?" To answer this, we need to revisit our winning scholarship essay equation.

10

Essay Portion | Proper Essay Structure

It may not seem very obvious, but believe it or not the essay to SME-EF that was just shared in the previous section has structure built into it. Granted, it wasn't your typical essay structure due to its word-count restriction, but it contained structure, nonetheless. For now, it may just seem like a giant paragraph that was thrown onto a page, but once you go through this section you will understand how that essay turned out the way it did. Let's first revisit the equation for a winning scholarship essay:

Emotional / Personal / Passionate Connections
+ Proper Essay Structure
= Winning Scholarship Essay

The second part of this equation is proper essay structure. In order for your essay to be strong and provide meaning, you must have a structure. The good news is that you already understand structure more than you probably think. The proper structure I am talking about is the same structure that you learned about in your standard English class in high school. Didn't pay attention in English? Not to worry! You will get to know all you need to know as you keep reading. Disliked your English class in school? Don't fear! This is not going to be a regurgitation of your monotone teacher's voice teaching you about past, present, and future participles. You will, however, be receiving either a passing or failing grade. A failing grade is when you do not win a scholarship and a passing grade is when you win a scholarship!

Back when I started writing my first essays I knew nothing about winning scholarships or writing winning essays. At that time, I was still testing the waters to see what worked and what didn't. When it came time for me to write my first essay, I didn't have anything else to rely on other than what I learned in my regular English classes. I was taught a standard, general method for how to put together pieces of writing in a way that was universally acceptable. So, I started writing the way I was taught. The more I won, the more I relied on the same style and structure that helped me succeed in the first place. Using proper structure was a huge part of my success and it is proven to help win scholarships. Here is how that proper structure is broken down:

- Introduction
- Body
- Conclusion

What I just listed out is probably underwhelming. What did I tell you? I told you that you'd know more than you thought! Although, it is not as much about what you know as it is about how you *apply* that knowledge. There are key ideas within each of the points I just listed that will allow you to apply these points correctly toward a scholarship.

Again, do not think too much into it. These key ideas are still very similar to what is taught in English class, but the small tips that we will discuss make all the difference. Also, there are additional key points you need to know that are secondary to properly structuring your essay that will be covered later after explaining the introduction, body, and conclusion as they pertain to scholarship essays. So if you want that passing grade I suggest you keep reading.

INTRODUCTION

An introduction is just as it sounds—it introduces the reader to your essay. There are two parts that make up an introduction in standard writing: the attention-getter and the thesis statement.

ATTENTION-GETTER

There is no crazy science behind an attention-getter. Its main purpose is exactly that—*to get the attention of your audience or reader so that they will keep wanting to read on*. When I was writing the very first sentences of my introductions to my essays for scholarships, I would typically focus on a broader, higher-level idea that was related to the essay prompt. I would build up this idea in a way that was interesting and surprising. Then, I would have this broader, higher-level idea that is related to the subject I am talking about flow into the main idea—the thesis statement—of the prompt. It was a way for me to begin the essay by laying the groundwork for how I would introduce the thesis statement. The moment where the attention of my audience is captured is when I connect these high-level introductory sentences with the thesis statement, using one or two sentences that would flow in between the two entities. Connecting the opening sentences to the thesis statement would give the reader that classic "aha moment." As they begin to read the opening sentences, they are thinking, "I wonder how this relates to our scholarship." Once they read the sentences where the initial attention-getter connects to the thesis statement, they are thinking, "Okay, I see where they are answering what the scholarship asked for in the prompt. They built up their idea so now I am locked in and excited to read what they have to say that answers our prompt as I move on to the body paragraphs." Obviously this is a very specific line of thinking, but for explanation purposes I needed to describe the logic behind how the attention-getter works in the introduction in that way.

Whatever scholarship you will be writing an essay for, it will always have a theme. For me, the majority of "themes" I encountered were related to manufacturing, engineering, or technology because these were the scholarships that I met the most eligibility criteria of. However, there were other scholarships I applied to where the theme was centered around community service, swimming, creativity, texting and driving, and so on. Therefore, when starting to write the initial sentences of my introduction which are meant to be my attention-getter, *I would focus on that particular theme*. I would write about what makes the theme compelling.

For example, let's revisit one of the prompts that was brought up when we were talking about passionate connections. The below attention-getter was part of an essay that I first wrote the spring of my junior year that won $1,000 which applied to the fall of my senior year. I ended up using this same section in seven other different scholarships, several of them also being winners:

> **Prompt:** *How will your coursework help you to impact manufacturing technology in the Boone, Ogle, Stephenson, Winnebago, and Rock County regions?*
>
> *"In recent years, manufacturing has come to be one of the most pivotal industries in today's economy, accounting for a significant percentage of employment as well as global gross domestic product. In the U.S. alone, the drive for innovation, competitiveness, and constant improvement that comes from our ever-changing manufacturing environment has kept our nation's spot as a worldwide leader in quality and cutting-edge technology. The numerous methods of product development and distribution that exist provide endless opportunities for improving the everyday lives of a world population that continues to grow. Having the ability to contribute to this wave of innovation in which the end result is a better tomorrow is why I have decided to study Manufacturing Engineering at Bradley University."*

In the prompt, the theme is about manufacturing technology. So, to setup the essay and gain the attention of my reader, I expand on the theme of manufacturing technology by talking about higher-level ideas such as how the United States is a global leader due to its manufacturing efforts and how manufacturing is basically an art form through its technology's ability to push the boundaries of what can be created. The reason this works as an attention-getter is because I am talking about **interesting ideas** that are **related to the theme**. What makes the theme interesting is what the audience finds interesting. Why? As described earlier in the Passionate Connection section, the judge who will be deciding the winners of the scholarship will be related to the scholarship in some way. In the case of this prompt, the people judging the applications are in some way, shape, or form related to the manufacturing industry. Like mentioned before, they could be business owners, engineers, designers, managers, or other roles who have spent years in a manufacturing setting. Therefore, because I am expanding on interesting topics related to manufacturing technology to start off my essay, they will be intrigued at what I have to say but still questioning how it relates to the prompt. The last sentence of the attention-getter example starts to answer their question. The last sentence starts to connect the attention-getter to the main idea—the thesis statement. The actual thesis statement was left out of the above example. It was really supposed to be the last sentence of the example. Here it is:

> *"I am ecstatic to have found a college major I can apply my creative and ambitious personality to in the hopes of implementing my own solutions to the world of manufacturing so that I may have a positive impact, not only on society, but manufacturing technology in the Boone, Ogle, Stephenson, Winnebago, and Rock County regions as well."*

THESIS STATEMENT

As was hinted in the attention-getter portion, *a thesis statement is the main idea of your piece of writing and is a fundamental part of any introduction*. It is fundamental because, without a thesis statement, the reader will not know the point of what you are writing about in the essay. A thesis statement gives a direction for the essay. Thesis statements, as they relate to scholarships, are quite easy. Your thesis statement will generally be about the prompt that you are given and includes *how* you are addressing that prompt. In the attention-getter example, the prompt asks about how my coursework will help me to impact manufacturing technology in the Boone, Ogle, Stephenson, Winnebago, and Rock County regions. In my connection to the thesis statement (the last two sentences), as well as my thesis statement, I answer the prompt. My answer is that my coursework will help me impact manufacturing technology in the listed regions by *preparing me to be able to contribute to the wave of innovation* in manufacturing technology in which the end result is a better tomorrow. The thesis statement would not be as powerful if I had not highlighted exactly *how* my coursework would help me impact manufacturing technology. I further strengthen this answer by stating in the thesis statement itself how I aim to *implement my own solutions to the world of manufacturing*. To summarize: the coursework side of the prompt was answered in last two connecting sentences before the thesis statement, and then what results from my coursework is answered in the thesis statement itself. It is important to give the answer to the prompt in the thesis statement as I did here because you are explicitly introducing your main idea. My main idea then will be expanded on later in the essay stating *how* I will get prepared and *how* I will implement my solutions. You can see part of the prompt's answer extended prior to the actual thesis statement itself. That was all to establish flow within the introduction to ultimately connect the ideas together to give the reader a full direction. The thesis statement is a broad summary for what is to come further along in the essay. The body, as we will explain following this section, is meant to answer the *details* of how.

It helps to have specificity in your thesis statement as well. If you reiterate the prompt to a certain extent as I did in the given example, it lets the scholarship judges know that you understand the prompt and are going to address the exact concerns they want addressed. It gives them a direction. As you direct them through your scholarship essay, the next portion they will run into is the body.

BODY

The body of your essay is where you provide information that supports the main points of your thesis statement. This is where you will add value and substance to your essay through the use of examples, facts, experiences, and other pieces of information. The body of a scholarship essay tends to differ from a regular essay or research paper at school that you would encounter for the following reason. Let's say you have to write an essay for school on the following given topic:

> **Prompt:** *How can humanity reduce the risk pollution has on our planet and species?*

Your thesis statement might look something like this:

> *"Humans can reduce and even eliminate pollution around our world by investing in the clean energy solutions that utilize the elements of wind, water, and solar."*

The three main points brought up in your thesis statement are clean energy through wind, water, and solar. Now, to support your thesis statement, you will have three paragraphs in the body of your essay each discussing one of the clean energy solutions in greater depth. The main difference between scholarship prompts and school prompts is that the majority of time your scholarship prompt will be personally asking about you, the author, whereas a prompt for school will ask about some external topic in which you can conduct research for and provide hard evidence on. There are scholarships out there that have prompts like the example above, so if you encounter one just treat the content as a research paper while still following the overall structure highlighted in this book. Outside of these occurrences, you will be asked to write about yourself.

Below is an example of an essay prompt for a scholarship I applied to my freshman year in college. Note that the "background and criteria of this scholarship" they are talking about was manufacturing related:

> ***Prompt:*** *Considering the background and criteria of this scholarship, why are you the best candidate? Your response should demonstrate your interest in pursuing a career in business or engineering.*

The prompt is asking to write about why I am the best candidate. When you are asked to write about yourself, there is no real research or hard evidence that can mimic the subjects you would typically write about in the body of a research paper for school. You can't Google why you are the best candidate. Rather, when asked to write about yourself, the body should further elaborate and expand on the points that are mentioned in the thesis statement through the use of examples, facts, experiences, and other pieces of personal information.

The biggest thing that I can tell you with the body section of a scholarship essay is that you are going to have to freestyle what content you write about. The prompt will dictate whether you should write about prior experiences you had, what your future plans are, why you find the topic the prompt is asking for interesting, and so on. There is no one-size-fits-all solution for exactly what to write in your body paragraphs, and that goes for the whole structure of scholarship essays at the end of the day. There are a lot of variables at play that, despite what is taught in this book, you still may need to tweak certain parts of an essay to make it work. This idea as to why there is no one-size-fits-all solution will be highlighted in multiple key points after we finish the Conclusion portion of Essay Portion | Proper Essay Structure.

That said, it's up to you to decide what to include in your body paragraphs, as long as the content provides strong support for your thesis and directly addresses the prompt. You will see this at play in the full essay breakdowns that are given toward the end of this book. For me, the supporting information in the bodies of my scholarship essays varied. However, a common theme I found was that about 60% of the scholarship essays I wrote were about personal experiences I had. By personal experiences, I am talking about volunteering events, internships, school projects, extracurricular involvement, and other actual events, groups, classes, clubs, or roles that I participated in. I used these experiences as supporting information to connect to the thesis statement and prompt. *It's easier to write about real experiences than to force ideas around an abstract or less tangible topic.* That is why it is so important to get involved early! You will find it so much easier to write essays in general, because having past experiences gives you relevant information to write about if you cannot think of any other way to support your essay.

There are situations where your past experiences won't be the best approach, and you'll have to develop content that goes beyond your own background. This is where emotional, personal, and passionate connections are useful. In most of my essays where the body paragraphs weren't based on my past experiences, I used a connection type to support the thesis instead. As stated earlier, the majority of content you write will be using some form of connection type. The reason why connection types are so powerful and useful is that they can make a large impact to your reader without a lot of words or explanation. With most essays having word-count restrictions, you have to learn how to condense your ideas so you can make your point within the allotted space—and connection types are perfect for this. Remember, they can be applied anywhere in an essay.

Overall, if you're stuck on how to approach the body portion of your scholarship essay, keep reviewing the prompt. The prompt is a great starting point and will give you a general direction of how to write your essay. You will be able to tell whether or not to write about your past experiences, non-experience content, or a mixture of both. Regardless of the combination, you need a way to bring together the main ideas from the body to form a clear, unified answer to the prompt. The conclusion is where you make this happen.

CONCLUSION

The conclusion is the beginning of the end of an essay. In a standard essay written for school or other reasons, the conclusion normally begins with repeating or rephrasing your thesis statement followed by a summary of the main supporting points in the body that support the thesis statement. When I was in school, I would put a little twist at the very last sentence or two of the conclusion once I summarized the thesis and the content of the body. I would ensure my conclusion included a thoughtful closing line that drove home my point and gave the essay a confident finish. To give you a better understanding of how I approached writing my conclusions for both standard and scholarship essays, let's step back and take a wholistic view of an essay I would write. My introductions are mostly high-level ideas and concepts that introduce the topic in a way that captures the reader's interest. They usually hover at a 30,000-foot-view thought level. When I talk about being at a 30,000-foot view, I mean stepping far enough back from the details so the reader can see the entire landscape of the situation—the overall theme, the main ideas at play, and the overall direction the essay is moving. Think of the view out of a plane window at 30,000 feet in the air. Then, when I start to connect to the thesis and the body, this is where you will find all of the fine details that answer the specifics of the topic being written about. At this point, the essay hovers around a 300-foot-view thought level. A 300-foot view is like standing at the base of the landscape instead of above it—the reader sees the supporting facts, personal experiences, and all the granular details that give substance to the essay's overall direction. Think of that same plane window view, only this time at 300 feet in the air. Then, when the conclusion comes around and it is time to end the essay, I gradually lift back up to higher-level thought patterns. It eases out of the trenches of the body and ends up back at a 30,000-foot view. In those final one or two sentences of the conclusion, I try to bring the reader back to the high-level perspective where the essay began. By following this structure, you take the reader on a journey that leaves them more informed about your topic than when they first began. Figure 5 provides a visual representation of this journey, illustrating the expected flow of your essay, the progression of your content, and the points where you should shift between detailed and broad perspectives.

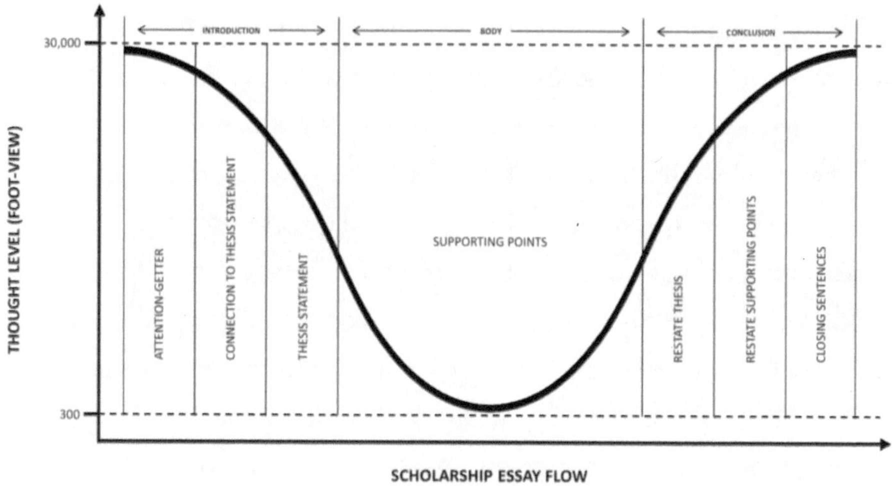

Figure 5. Relationship between the sequence of scholarship essay sections and the fluctuation of the thought level reflected within the content of each section

The good news is that the elements that make up an effective conclusion in a standard essay written for school or other reasons are virtually the same as in a scholarship essay outside of two limiting factors—both of which will be broken down more in Chapter 11. The first factor is *word-count restrictions*. Word-count restrictions force you to shape every part of your essay, including your conclusion. In cases where limits to word count exist, there is no way you will be able to follow a standard method of restating your thesis statement and then nicely summarizing the supporting points in your body. You will simply not have enough room in the essay. The second factor that shapes a conclusion is *creativity*. What I mean is you do not want to just regurgitate your exact thesis statement and supporting points word-for-word when you are restating them in your conclusion. Just like with the creative aspect of an introduction, you want to reword, rephrase, and reintroduce the main ideas of your essay in a new way. The reason is that it's boring if you just use the exact same phrasing that you have been using throughout the essay. This phenomenon explains why essays written for school seem boring. Also, you need to be conscious of the fact that essays, especially those with word-count restrictions, have limited space available. This means that the words you write are like prime real estate, and if you spend that real estate on exact or close-to-exact repetitions, you may not be extracting all the value you could. This value could, for example, take the shape of a new connection type that you include in your conclusion that both summarize the main idea and make another strong point toward your case to win the scholarship. Readers, in general, have short attention spans. Why do you think you need an attention-getter in your introduction? So, if you use the exact or close-to-exact phrasing for your thesis statement and main points in your conclusion, your reader will get bored. It's fine to do that in standard school essays, but the reason they teach you that standard structure in school is so you can understand the fundamentals of writing. I only care about scholarship essays in this book, and to write a scholarship essay that works, you need to diverge from the norm. Like I said, your conclusion in a scholarship essay will still hold the same *elements* as a standard essay, just not in the conventional way. If you think about it, the standard essay structure of a conclusion teaches you a guaranteed way to accomplish what a conclusion is meant to do—reiterate the main idea, summarize the talking points, and end the essay. What better way to accomplish this than simply repeating what was stated earlier. It works, right? *The scholarship essay conclusion still accomplishes what a regular conclusion accomplishes, just in a different way. It still centers around the idea and premise of summarizing what the essay is about, but it is executed differently.*

Here is what that execution looks like. *Introduce new high-level ideas that are still related to the core of what your essay prompt is about. You can also use any connection type to make up the majority of your conclusion.*

When looking back at your thesis statement and supporting points, you can still use them as building blocks, but try hard not to copy and paste them directly. Hover around those **ideas**, but use a different way to get to those **ideas**. The reason why standard essays simply repeat what is stated earlier word-for-word is because it is the easiest way to summarize the **ideas** that are talked about in the essay. Take a look back to how I explained how I wrote my introduction and thesis statement for the prompt I use in the Introduction section. Let's revisit that prompt:

> **Prompt:** *How will your coursework help you to impact manufacturing technology in the Boone, Ogle, Stephenson, Winnebago, and Rock County regions?*

Now, let's revisit not the whole introduction, but instead the very *last sentence* which brings up the thesis statement:

> *"I am ecstatic to have found a college major I can apply my creative and ambitious personality to in the hopes of implementing my own solutions to the world of manufacturing so that I may have a positive impact, not only on society, but manufacturing technology in the Boone, Ogle, Stephenson, Winnebago, and Rock County regions as well."*

Now that our minds our refreshed, let's look at the conclusion of the same winning essay that this prompt and thesis statement came from:

> *"As I enter my third year in the Manufacturing Engineering curriculum at Bradley University, it is hard to believe how far I have come both as a student and as a person when looking back to when*

> *I was just a freshman. I am confident that after graduation I will have all the necessary skills in order to succeed in my field of engineering, not only because of my courses completed at school, but because of the experience I gained through my internship as well. I cannot wait to apply my knowledge in order to help companies, especially those in Boone, Ogle, Stephenson, Winnebago, and Rock County regions, achieve their goals so that I too may continue to grow and learn how to improve upon manufacturing technology and processes in order to better the community I serve."*

Before analyzing this conclusion, it will help to be reminded of what direction the essay took thus far. The thesis statement gives the main idea that I will *implement my own solutions to the world of manufacturing*. Also, if you remember in the Introduction section, there was a connecting sentence before the main thesis statement also feeding into the thesis itself which detailed how my coursework was *preparing me to be able to contribute to the wave of innovation* in manufacturing technology. It is not pictured; however, the essay body's supporting points for this thesis centered on *preparation*—specifically, examples from my internships that my coursework helped make possible.

Now, look closely at the conclusion. In the first sentence, I am starting the gradual transition into a 30,000-foot-view **idea** from the 300-foot view of exact specific projects I did at my internships. The **idea** is *school* and how it has acted as a vessel for personal growth over the years. In the second sentence, you can see I am reintroducing the *main idea*—the *thesis statement*—but in a different light. The second sentence takes a 30,000-foot-view approach as it summarizes the **ideas** of the *preparation* aspect behind my coursework addressed in the thesis statement, as well as *experiences* from my internships which were the supporting points. It is a

30,000-foot view because I'm not going into specifics—instead I'm using phrases such as "necessary skills" and "experience gained." See how this approach takes no exact repetition, yet brings the essay back to the original main ideas in a different and creative way.

The reason why I used this particular conclusion as an example is because of the third sentence. Remember how I said that you need to hover around your high-level ideas and to use them as building blocks? This is true for generating different wording for your conclusion to avoid directly repeating your introduction. However, if the prompt gives you a "building block" like specific phrasing such as "Boone, Ogle, Stephenson, Winnebago, and Rock County regions," then it is perfectly acceptable to include this phrasing as an "exact repeat" in your conclusion just like you would when including this type of specificity in your thesis statement. This is because including this detail shows the scholarship judge you've had their exact prompt inquiry in-mind the entire essay. It shows you had a direction and knew exactly how to answer what they were asking. Lastly, including this type of specificity is a way to further summarize the content. Keep in mind, exact repeats—names, titles, locations, or other scholarship organization specifics—used in this manner are permissible. It's only when the full lead up of your thesis and supporting points are copied directly that it becomes problematic and takes away from the essay's message. The entire essay ends on both a high-note and 30,000-foot view by finishing this third sentence with a slight personal connection—expressing my desire to keep learning and growing so I can better support the community I serve.

This example puts into perspective how I approached writing conclusions during my scholarship journey. The majority of the essays I wrote followed this format and way of thinking. The introduction, body, and conclusion make up about 90% of the structure of your scholarship essay. However, there are several key points that make up the remaining 10% and will influence how your scholarship essay is created. By being aware of these key points, you will turn your essay from good to great, and give yourself the highest possible odds to win the scholarship you are applying for. Despite being a small part of the essay, these key points make a big difference. The upcoming chapter focuses exclusively on these key points. Be mindful that these key points are in no particular order because they all play an equally vital role in the success of your essay.

11

Key Points in Proper Essay Structure

KEY POINT 1: TRANSITIONS & FLOW

I talked briefly about flow when covering emotional connections and when picking apart a surface-level answer versus a rephrased emotional connection answer. Transitions and flow are sentences you use to help segue into different ideas over the course of your essay. Including transitions creates a flow of ideas that help guide your reader through your work. You do not want to spew all of your ideas on a page and assume the reader can understand where you're coming from or trying to go with what you are writing. Transitions and flow help the reader smoothly follow along with the ideas in your essay so they can build understanding as they read. This understanding develops as the reader connects your ideas and topics, recognizing how they relate to one another and, ultimately, how they work together to answer your prompt. When you think about it, the proper essay structure we've discussed up to this point establishes a broader, overarching flow on its own. Transitions help for a finishing touch to this broader flow to ensure a truly seamless reading experience. Although similar, it is important to note the differences between transitions and flow.

TRANSITIONS

I categorize transitions as the sentences that help switch from one main paragraph to the next main paragraph. They lead you into the second paragraph by relating ideas from the first paragraph. When I use a transition to connect two paragraphs, I typically either include it as the last sentence of the first paragraph or the first sentence of the second paragraph. I shy away from doing both because that would create too much non-essential information. The transition needs to be subtle because you want the reader to focus on your paragraph's main ideas, not the transitions themselves. The following example below goes over three paragraphs that formed the body of an essay that I wrote my second semester freshman year. The prompt asked why I was the best candidate and why I had interest in business and engineering. I did not end up winning this scholarship; however, the transitions between these paragraphs provide a good example to learn from:

> *"Having had two older siblings graduate college, I am aware of the financial debt that they have accumulated throughout the years. Both my siblings' plans for the future were slowed down due to several loans that they must repay. That is why I have made it a priority to receive as much assistance as possible. Being a first-generation college student, I realize there are many expectations that I have to live up to. Therefore, I cannot afford to put my plans on hold for the sake of paying college debt. Education, I believe, should not have a price tag because it is such a valuable asset in life, everyone deserves to receive it. I am truly blessed to be attending Bradley University and it would be a shame if money were to prevent me from achieving my goals.*
>
> *One goal in particular that I have set for myself is to give back to my community just as much as it has given to me. I cannot begin to thank my local community of Rockford in Winnebago County enough for making me the person I am today. One way I show my*

appreciation is volunteering annually for the St. Stanislaus Polish Fest held every summer. Also, by joining my high school's Senior Retreat Team, I was able to lead multiple underclassmen retreats, mentoring the future leaders of the school. Helping out the local Peoria community down by Bradley is important to me as well. From participating in multiple Service on Saturday programs to volunteering to help practice with the Bradley Women's Basketball Team, I help the community of Peoria grow as one.

Although participating in service is great, I believe my studies will have the greatest impact on my local community. Caterpillar Inc. helps fund Bradley's pristine Manufacturing Engineering program by donating money toward scholarships and state-of-the-art equipment. As a student, using this equipment will give me an opportunity to design and conduct various experiments that relate to different manufacturing processes and systems. Analyzing and interpreting the data collected will help me understand each component in the particular system as well as give me a hands-on approach to the world of manufacturing. This hands-on approach allows me to be aware of the constraints, benefits, costs, and materials associated with several manufacturing processes. I will also learn how to pinpoint what needs to be changed in a procedure that will allow it to operate with greater efficiency. Ultimately, I will have the ability to take these factors into effect to formulate the best possible solution for a problem."

When looking at the end of the first paragraph, I mention that money issues may prevent me from achieving the goals I have. I use this idea of "goals" to help me transition to my second paragraph by having its first sentence state that community service is one of my goals. For the whole second paragraph, community service was the primary supporting point. I used this supporting point of community service to transition into my third body paragraph. In the first sentence of the third paragraph, I imply that community service has a strong impact on my local community, but that my studies have an even greater one—studies being the supporting point of the third paragraph. Transitions can take a variety of forms. The point of including it in this book is to highlight that using transitions can further enhance your reader's experience and ultimately the strength of your essay.

FLOW

Think of transitions as achieving flow in between paragraphs. However, *flow itself is how your sentences and ideas tie together within those paragraphs. Flow is a steady stream of sentences that build up to connect to a bigger idea.* By using flow, you give the reader a logical pathway to follow through your ideas. They know why you are jumping from one sentence to the next. Imagine a transition between paragraphs, only this time it is a transition from one *sentence* to the next. The two sentences have something written in them that connect them together. For a great example, refer back to the Emotional Connection section where the plane mechanics answer was rephrased.

Just as with transitions, flow also needs to be subtle because you do not want to deviate from your paragraph's main ideas. Don't overthink flow. Not every sentence needs to perfectly feed into the next. It's more about the flow of ideas, imagery, and understanding what your paragraph's sentences are forming for the reader. You do not need to relate every actual sentence to one another in order to create that flow of ideas, imagery, and understanding. Rather, use it at your own discretion. This point on flow is merely meant to make you aware to what techniques are at your disposal in order to write a winning essay.

KEY POINT 2: WORD-COUNT RESTRICTIONS

This key point is something that I was eager to explain because this is a huge item that can influence what you write in your essay. It kept getting brought up as we talked about each section of the essay structure because it can apply to and manipulate each part. When we talk about word-count restrictions, we are talking about when you are told that your scholarship essay must be at or under a certain word count. For example, an essay must contain 300 words or less. The reason why I did not explain this in detail earlier is because I wanted you to concentrate on the core of the introduction, body, and conclusion without being clouded with worrying about word count. *When you're working with a word-count restriction, you have to be selective about what you include because you don't have the space to cover every idea or explore topics as deeply as you could in an unrestricted essay.* Your essay structuring will be roughly the same as discussed up until this point, but you will need to get to the point quicker. That means you need to have a shorter introduction, body, conclusion, or a mixture of all three. Your introductions and conclusions may be as short as one or two sentences. You may only be able to fit in one or two connection types. You may not have any paragraphs. These are all things that I have experienced. This will force you to be more intentional with your words and open up the opportunity to create more meaning with less space. This is where creativity comes into play. Figure out a way to make it work. At the end of the day, you still need to answer what the scholarship is asking for in the essay prompt. The entire section of What Makes a Good Essay Portion is meant to educate on effective strategies for making a winning scholarship essay. By going through its content, you will know what to include to ensure you create a compelling essay. If a word-count restriction causes you not to use every single technique exactly how it is taught in this book, that is okay. Realize that the other applicants are faced with the same challenge as well. However, knowing what you know from this book, you are better equipped for writing a successful word-restricted essay than they are. The essay in the Connection Type Ending Notes section is great example of a successful word-restricted essay. Also, there will be other essays toward the end of Step 4 that will be great examples of this as well.

KEY POINT 3: CREATIVITY

Word-count restrictions are a brilliant way to force you to think creatively when writing essays, but don't let that be the only time when you utilize it. When someone is creative, they make something new and unique. A simple concept, but it's one that is vital for you to separate yourself from other scholarship applicants. *You should be striving to write something new and unique that the scholarship judge will read and be intrigued by.* I never took a creative writing class, so my knowledge of being creative is just what I have learned over the course of writing countless scholarship essays.

Although it can be applied anywhere in an essay, I found that I was most creative with my word phrasing, sentence structuring, and idea formulation in my introductions and conclusions. This was primarily because the content of my body paragraphs was, to a large extent, already planned out and accounted for. I knew I would be writing about my personal experiences as supporting points and, therefore, I already knew what I was going to include. When it wasn't personal experiences though, I relied on including connection types as content which, by nature, would require more creativity to formulate them properly. Introductions and conclusions, on the other hand, weren't as intuitive, and I found myself forming far more new and unique pieces of content to fill out those portions of my essays.

Another easy way I incorporated creativity was to use adjectives to vividly describe certain things or events related to what I was writing about. Other ways would be to introduce ideas in non-conventional ways. The best way I can explain this is through an example. Let's take a look at a particular introduction I wrote:

> *"In today's fast-paced environment, keeping up with demands is an essential part for a business to compete in the real world. Ever since Henry Ford's invention of the assembly line in 1913, manufacturing processes have grown exponentially. With this growth comes a high demand for Manufacturing Engineers. These engineers come up with innovative, cost efficient ways to convert raw materials into valuable product, allowing for even the smallest of businesses to thrive. This is why I am excited to pursue a Bachelor's Degree in Manufacturing Engineering at Bradley University. The knowledge I acquire from the rigorous coursework at Bradley will allow me to give back, not only to my community in Winnebago County, but also to the Ogle, Boone, Stephenson, and Rock County regions as well."*

You may recognize the county names in the very last sentence of this introduction. Those names are a part of the same scholarship essay we have covered previously. The scholarship that this example came from was one that I applied for three years in a row and the prompt never changed during that time. I won all three years, so I have many essays and examples to use from this series. Anyway, the main takeaway from this example is in the second sentence. I mention Henry Ford and when he invented his revolutionary assembly line manufacturing technique. I was building up my 30,000-foot-view introduction here, and I used Henry

Ford as a building block. It was something different because I wasn't just talking about manufacturing in vague terms. Instead, I was using a specific, concrete, unique fact that was related to the topic to intrigue the reader. This is a simple example of the small creative twists you can incorporate in an essay that will help you stand out—part of what fills out that final 10% of the essay.

Another example is as follows:

"Being a first-generation college student, I am faced with a lot of pressure to succeed. However, realizing just how great of an opportunity I have, I plan to work tirelessly until I have achieved my objectives."

You may recognize this phrasing as well. It came from part of the first example from the section on personal connections. The main takeaway from this example is in the first sentence. I mention that I am a first-generation college student. That is a very small detail that carries a lot of weight. An ordinary person may think that this is an unnecessary description, but it is quite the opposite. Being a first-generation college student paints the picture that I am underrated and coming up from the bottom, fighting to make a brighter future for myself since my parents did not go to college and lack opportunity because of it. When you are being creative in your writing, you need to look for little details such as this that make you stand out and really catch the reader's attention.

When you're writing for a scholarship centered on your college major, there's an important point to keep in mind. So, for example, my major was Manufacturing Engineering. When I was a freshman and sophomore, I didn't have much manufacturing experience, and I was still new to the material. I didn't yet know the key terms or industry language that signal expertise in the manufacturing field. So, when it came time to actually write about manufacturing, sometimes I found myself stuck with nothing to write about if a prompt asked me why I wanted to study Manufacturing Engineering. Either that, or what I wrote simply came across as inexperienced and far less passionate than I intended. In cases like this, I would look back to my notes and textbooks and looked for certain manufacturing related terminology or phrasing that they used. Doing this helped me fill gaps in my earlier essays and gave the impression that I not only understood the material, but was genuinely passionate in it—even though I was still in the process of learning. *Use whatever resources are at your disposal to help your creative inspiration and you will never run out of things to write about.*

KEY POINT 4: VOCABULARY & PROPER GRAMMAR

VOCABULARY

In high school, I won a small $500 scholarship for an essay that I wrote about veterans. When I talked to one of the judges after the award ceremony they hosted, he told me what he usually looked for in winning essays. He very nonchalantly stated that he really only looks for if the essay is long enough, and if it uses a few big vocabulary words. Before reading on, obviously do not take this to mean that every essay *only* looks for these two things. There is far more to it than that. However, he brought up a valid point about vocabulary. *Having a variety of sophisticated vocabulary words scattered throughout your essay can be a huge benefit.* It's not hard to achieve this either. If you find yourself using the same word repeatedly, look up synonyms or check an online thesaurus for alternatives that express the same idea. When drafting many of my first essays, I remember I would make it a point to use flashy, fancier terms and vocabulary to add some color to my essay. Make this into a habit and it will only help you. Of course, don't congest your essay with obnoxiously complicated words. Everything in moderation. Keep it simple, and use advanced vocabulary on occasion if you need to add some flare to your essay. Often, you'll find that a single, more sophisticated word can replace several simpler ones strung together, resulting in a cleaner, more polished essay.

PROPER GRAMMAR

Make sure you use proper grammar when writing your essays. I'm not trying to make this an English class; I just want to bring it up so you're mindful of it as you write. Having proper grammar in your essay is a non-negotiable if you want to be selected as a winner. It's similar to when we talked about someone reading a résumé. For example, if I am in charge of hiring someone and while reading their résumé I see odd grammar or just silly typos, I am going to immediately not take them seriously because I see that they are not competent enough to pay attention to the details. Therefore, why should I trust them to work for my company? The same goes for scholarship essays. You do not have to be the best writer in the world. *Just make sure your essay makes sense and flows smoothly.* If you need help on this, reach out and find the appropriate resources like a school counselor, an English professor, or even a friend to proofread your work to see if they can find any flaws. Again, you want to avoid all possible reasons why a scholarship judge should not pick you to win. Having bad grammar in your essay should never be one of those reasons.

KEY POINT 5: CUT WASTE & REVISE AFTER FIRST DRAFT

The last key point you need to be aware of is to get in the habit of revising your essays. Your first draft can often be sloppy. *You never want to submit your very first version of your scholarship essay because you will always find something wrong with it afterwards.* Before launching a new product, companies go through multiple iterations, and even after release, customers often uncover bugs that need to be fixed later. I even experienced this when writing this book. The first draft of this book was so hard to read is was laughable! Take these examples as a reminder of why careful proofreading is essential before submitting your work. Also, don't wait to proofread until the very end. As you write, pay attention to whether your sentences make sense and pause to proofread every few lines. Some good tips in finding errors is to read your essay out loud. Hearing the words with your own ears rather than inside your head can often uncover things you may have overlooked. You can also get a family member or a friend to proofread. It's important to be thorough with your final draft, but waiting for perfection will keep you from submitting anything. If you wait until everything is perfect all the time, then you will never get any essays out. The same is true in life: 80% perfect with progress made is better than 100% perfect with no action.

When you proofread, edit, and revise your scholarship essay, *you want to find where there is "fluff" or wasted words that hold no value to what a certain sentence is trying to say*. Ask yourself questions like: "Do I really need this sentence?" and "Is there a better way to phrase this?" Take your time with it. There is no rush to write a scholarship essay so long as you give yourself enough time to submit it before the deadline. Don't be discouraged if you're not coming up with ideas of what to write. Step back, take a break, and tackle it later in the day or the next day. As long as you get your essay to closely resemble what is taught in this book, you will be fine and give yourself the best chance at winning scholarships.

PROPER ESSAY STRUCTURE ENDING NOTES

By this point, you should feel strong and confident in your ability to put together a scholarship essay. Although there are a lot of moving parts, do not get overwhelmed by what was just covered. You do not have to use every single one of these points all at once. At the end of the day, use the proper essay structure points as guiding principles to craft the best possible essay you can. If it makes sense to you and checks most of the boxes that were talked about, you're in a good position. Don't overcomplicate it. There may be a lot of information here, but this is all meant to spark ideas for when you draft your first essays. I keep saying it—writing these essays gets easier the more you do them. Not only will your writing skill improve, but you will find yourself writing *less* with the more scholarships you apply to. In the next section I will show you what I mean.

12

Writing Scholarship Essays

COMBINING ESSAYS

The final major takeaway in What Makes a Good Essay Portion is learning how to combine essays. I am very excited to finally be covering this technique because I have hinted to it over the course of this book. I am also very proud of how I discovered this technique because it will help people like you to win the scholarship money they deserve in order to better their lives in the future. Though very simple at its core, the process for combining essays isn't some revolutionary breakthrough in writing. Rather, how I applied it to exponentially grow my scholarship success is where it is most valuable.

HOW I FOUND THIS STRATEGY

When I talk about combining essays, *I am referring to the process a scholarship applicant takes when they take certain sentences or paragraphs from one or more separate scholarship essays and combine those certain sentences or paragraphs together on one document to create an entirely new scholarship essay*. I originally came up with the idea of combining essays early on in my scholarship journey. At that time I had written, in my opinion, some really great essays and short-answer paragraphs that I saved. As I kept improving my scholarship search skills and finding more scholarships to apply to, I got to a point where I started to run out of new words, sentences, ideas, and topics to write about. Given that the majority of my scholarships centered on manufacturing engineering, there was a limit to how much I could adjust my writing before it became repetitive. The more I tried to reinvent each essay, the longer they took, because I felt like I'd already used every idea I had. I realized I was wasting so much energy on trying to come up with a new essay for the same topic every single time that my quality of writing started to decline. It declined because I had already spent so much energy on my previous essays. I was very proud of those essays because I felt everything came together for them in terms of the structure, examples used, word phrasing, creativity, flow, and the other ideas we have covered in the book so far. I felt like I was out of ideas! I had already developed the habit of saving my work, since I'd learned to keep my short-answer responses and reuse them when the same questions came up. I saved these short answers because I felt they were well written, and I didn't want to risk losing them or having to rebuild them from scratch. Then it clicked. I realized that all of my saved essays up to that point were in somewhat of a standard structure—introduction, body, and conclusion. The introductions and the conclusions were the hardest parts for me to newly draft because this is where you need to be the most creative. I felt like every new essay I started wasn't as good as the one before it. Therefore, I figured I would find the parts that I liked in my old essays and copy and paste them to my new essays. Since the majority of my scholarship applications were from organizations that were not affiliated with one another, it wouldn't matter if I reused a piece of writing from another essay. It is not plagiarizing if I am using my own work!

The interchangeability of my previously written scholarship essays due to the common structure they shared ended up working in my favor. Take car parts for example. You can mix and match countless parts within a car engine, and it will still run. Same with scholarships. I would use different parts of previously written essays to form a new essay that would still meet the requirements of the application. Not only that, but I knew that these newly formed essays were quality written because they came from essays that had previously won, or that I felt I had written very well. Pretty soon I was mixing and matching all sorts of introductions, body paragraphs, and conclusions together that it became a game! As long as I didn't use the same information twice for any scholarship application that I applied to multiple years in a row, I was good. This technique reinvigorated my drive for continuing to find more scholarships to apply for. Combining scholarships opened up an avenue for me to apply to even more scholarships than I originally thought possible because it decreased the amount of time I had to spend writing. I cannot remember how many total scholarships I ended up applying to or essays I wrote during my four years at Bradley University, but as I started writing this book, I was able to find thirty-two saved scholarship essays in my college computer files. It wouldn't have been possible to write thirty-two high-quality scholarship essays had I not discovered how to effectively combine sections together.

HOW TO COMBINE ESSAYS

Let me preface this section by first clarifying that you will still need to be constantly creating new content for new essays. There will never be a point where you stop writing altogether. Instead, you will become more resourceful by making sure your earlier writing doesn't go to waste after just one use. You should strive to always continue to write new content because, as I said before, the more you write the easier it becomes. Not only will it become easier, but you never know when you will write an amazing piece of work that you feel is a very strong, quality scholarship essay. Therefore, do not settle once you have written three or four unique essays. Be mindful of the technique for combining scholarship essays, but always keep writing. Don't let it stop you from writing your best work.

That being said, when you start to combine scholarship essays, *the first thing you need to be aware of is you want to pick parts of your essays that will fit well within the new combined essay*. You know they will fit and flow well if they help answer the prompt you are writing for. You can't forget that answering the prompt is the main goal of the scholarship essay. Don't get caught up in the excitement that you don't have to write anything if you just mix and match paragraphs together to form a new essay. That is the lazy person's route. You need to make sure the essay still makes logical sense. Often, you will find that you can only reuse a certain percentage of a particular essay, and that you have to create the rest of the content because it wouldn't make logical sense otherwise. When you find yourself doing this, refer back to all the sections covered previously. As long as your newly combined scholarship essay fits what was discussed in What Makes a Good Essay Portion, it will make sense and you can feel confident in submitting it. Sometimes you will find that you can reuse the entire essay from one scholarship for a different scholarship. This is the best case scenario because, other than a few minor edits that we will talk about in the next paragraph, there will be little to no effort on your part, and you will still give yourself a great chance to win the new scholarship. On occasion, I was able to completely reuse full essays that ended up winning.

When you copy and paste from different essays, be aware that the majority of the time you cannot copy word-for-word. More specifically, I am referring to when you have a part of an essay you are going to reuse but it has a name or idea related to the original scholarship organization it came from. The worst mistake that you can make when combining is accidentally forgetting to change small details that you wrote for one essay—like the name of the original organization's scholarship—and submit the combined essay to the new scholarship organization. If that happens, the new scholarship organization will know right away that you reused a previous essay of yours and that you were not genuine. When that occurs, say goodbye to any chance at winning that scholarship. Don't make that silly mistake and make sure you review, edit, and revise your essay two or three times before finally submitting it.

That leads me to my next point which is to review, edit, and revise each part of your essay that you combine so it flows smoothly into your other sections. As the upcoming examples will illustrate, I regularly had to make slight modifications to the sections I reused so they aligned with the new essay I was writing. Sometimes you may need to delete or rephrase a sentence or two, or only use a certain part of a paragraph from an old essay rather than the whole paragraph. Use your discretion to ensure the combined essay is coherent and aligned with the guidelines in this book. Usually reused thesis statements and conclusions will be the parts of an essay you will need to revise the most. This is due to thesis statements and conclusions being the most intimately related to the particular scholarship you are writing them for.

The other changes you will mostly make as you combine paragraphs together will be in the form of transitions. Transitioning from paragraph to paragraph, or sentence to sentence if your essay's structure doesn't necessitate paragraphs, is how you will accomplish flow within your essay. A reused paragraph by itself will contain its own internal flow since it comes from a previously validated essay. Therefore, the only flow aspect you need to worry about is the flow between paragraphs. For this, the majority of time you will need to change the paragraph's ending, beginning, or add a whole new sentence or two to successfully connect them. Not every reuse combination will require a transition though. A lot of times when reusing portions of or full paragraphs, especially for body content, I did not need to make any modifications at all because I wanted to keep their main ideas intact. Just know that transitions can help improve flow in your combined essay if needed.

COMMONLY REUSED PARAGRAPHS

I will now start to provide examples of winning scholarship essays and break down each of them. Within each breakdown, we will analyze all areas of each essay including prompts, structuring, connection types, paragraph combinations, reusing content, and other relevant information to truly understand how each scholarship essay came to fruition.

Out of the thirty-two essays that I was able to salvage from my saved college files, I picked eight winning essays to include in this book. Before we get into the essays, I will first introduce eight of my most commonly reused paragraphs that I interchanged with one another to form completely new scholarship essays. The explanations for the techniques and strategies used within these paragraphs will be introduced as they appear in each subsequent essay breakdown. The following commonly reused paragraphs are a mix of introductions, bodies, and conclusions. As you read through these paragraphs, you may recognize patterns as to how these paragraphs were utilized in each of their essays. Once the full essays are introduced, look back to these paragraphs as needed to help your understanding of the full essay. You can view these paragraphs as pieces to a puzzle. The completed puzzle is a new scholarship essay.

PARAGRAPH 1

Out of 32 essays, appears 12 times

"Every day, people are exposed to endless opportunities around every corner but lack the ambition to pursue them in hopes of a better life. Fortunately, I was blessed with the opportunity to receive a college education in order to fully exploit my potential, both as a student and as a person. Manufacturing is used in just about every industry of the world in order to accompany the world's continuous population growth. Seeing how this can have such an impact on society, I decided to study Manufacturing Engineering at Bradley University. The numerous processes for product development and distribution that exist can truly be considered an art. That is why I am excited to learn about how to improve upon these processes and eventually implement my solutions in the real-world. Knowing that I have a chance, for example, to improve a food production operation that results in feeding hungry families that are in need faster is truly well worth the cost of a college education. Also, with my newfound knowledge after graduation, I aim to work within my community of Rockford, Illinois in order to give back what has been given to me all these years; a chance at a new life and new opportunities for the residents, and especially the younger generation. Being a first-generation college student, I am faced with a lot of pressure to succeed. However, realizing just how great of an opportunity I have, I plan to work tirelessly until I have achieved my objectives. Having had two older siblings already graduate college, I am aware of the hefty sums of student loans they have accumulated throughout the years that put their plans on

hold. Therefore, winning this scholarship through SME-EF will help me to keep on track so that my future plans are not delayed."

PARAGRAPH 2

Out of 32 essays, appears 9 times

"This past summer, I was hired to work as a manufacturing engineering intern at Rockford Products LLC, a manufacturing facility that specializes in the making of cold-formed products. Whether it was a specialty fastener, ball stud, or any one of their cold-formed products, it was fascinating to learn how each particular product had its own unique routing and machining instructions in order to be made. These products are then distributed among a number of different markets consisting of automotive aftermarkets, agricultural, commercial vehicles, and key industrial markets, just to name a few. Observing how manufacturing impacts a vast amount of industries is truly amazing and makes me wonder which industry I will end up working for upon graduation.

Working as an intern helped me gain valuable real-world experience very few students are exposed to. While working at Rockford Products, I was assigned a number of different projects including the design and implementation of an ergonomic rake in response to a workplace incident that happened on the shop floor. After numerous hours of research and consultation with fellow engineers and shop floor workers, I designed a rake prototype using SolidWorks that complimented the natural body posture of the workers that used it for the specific task of sorting out parts. I was able to outline the cost of the rake as well as how Rockford Products would go about making it. The rake was designed to reduce the risk of workplace incidents as well as increase shop floor worker health and productivity.

Other projects I worked on included the design and implementation of a procedure to help reduce the likelihood of mixing burnished and non-burnished parts together during the part's routing through the use of a notification lighting system and external attachments to the machine that simplified the worker's duties. Also, I mapped out different forklift lane layouts to accompany OSHA standards without compromising travel times of the parts around the factory."

PARAGRAPH 3

Out of 32 essays, appears 7 times

"In recent years, manufacturing has come to be one of the most pivotal industries in today's economy, accounting for a significant percentage of employment as well as global gross domestic product. In the U.S. alone, the drive for innovation, competitiveness, and constant improvement that comes from our ever-changing manufacturing environment has kept our nation's spot as a worldwide leader in quality and cutting-edge technology. The numerous methods of product development and distribution that exist provide endless opportunities for improving the everyday lives of a world population that continues to grow. Having the ability to contribute to this wave of innovation in which the end result is a better tomorrow is why I have decided to study Manufacturing Engineering at Bradley University. I am ecstatic to have found a college major I can apply my creative and ambitious personality to in the hopes of implementing my own solutions to the world of manufacturing so that I may have a positive impact, not only on society, but manufacturing technology in the Boone, Ogle, Stephenson, Winnebago, and Rock County regions as well."

PARAGRAPH 4

Out of 32 essays, appears 4 times

"Now as a second-year intern during the summer of 2015, I was tasked to work closely with the Quality Engineering Department in order to tackle a massive quality control project. Rockford Products is in the process of transitioning to using a different data collection system, known as InfinityQS that machine operators use in order to input data from dimensional checks they carry out. The first step

was to update numerous control plan documents that list which processes the raw material must pass through in order to become a finished product. Most revisions included pinpointing different dimensions from each part by looking at the engineering prints and labeling the frequency of how often those dimensions would be measured when the part undergoes each process in the routing. Once revisions for a part are complete, that part must then be programmed into InfinityQS."

PARAGRAPH 5

Out of 32 essays, appears 4 times

"Growing up having had two older siblings already attend college, I was able to learn a lot from their accomplishments as well as their mistakes that they made throughout their years of study that really made me ponder what it is I wanted to do with my life. My eldest brother, [REMOVED NAME], who studied Biology at Loyola University in Chicago and who also has been a great role model in my life, made me reflect on whether I wanted to pursue a career in a particular field of science. Taking several advanced science classes in high school made me realize that, although interesting, wouldn't be the right fit as to what field of work I could see myself doing in the future. My sister, [REMOVED NAME], who also studied at Loyola University and majored in Political Science, made me consider a field of study in government or social work but again it did not pertain to my particular interests. As I continued my search, I started to take an in-depth look into how the world itself was moving forward. It seemed like more and more people nowadays have greater demands and expect those demands to be met to achieve a certain standard of living that people fifty years ago would have never dreamed of being obtained. My search ultimately led to the conclusion that without mass-production, the world would not be where it is today."

PARAGRAPH 6

Out of 32 essays, appears 3 times

"My team and I were also required to setup the navigational menus within the software that machine operators would use on the shop floor in order to find the part that they want to add data for. After learning how to operate the software for ourselves, we came up with a simple, straight forward procedure that minimizes the time it takes for them to find where they want to go on the system in order to input the necessary data they collect. By implementing this new procedure, we also lessened the amount of work it takes for our team to program the part numbers into the system."

PARAGRAPH 7

Out of 32 essays, appears 2 times

"During this past Fall 2015 semester I took a materials engineering class in my manufacturing engineering curriculum in which we were tasked with a term project consisting of design modification, materials selection, manufacturing, and cost estimation of an engineering part of our choice. My partner and I decided on looking at how the standard frame of a bike can function under the restrictive and quantifiable conditions of stress, temperature, environment, weight, and other justified assumptions. Those assumptions are: factor of safety, temperature range, max load, mass-producibility, and use of standard pipe sizes.

After we calculated the limits of our bike (For Example: Our bike had a calculated fatigue life of 3,660,000 cycles, where a cycle is defined as a bump or crack in the road that provides a noticeable impact to the rider) and considering the other mechanical properties of materials, we began the process of finding the best material choice for this bike and its application. Our application was that this bike was to function in a city type environment where it would act as a rentable bicycle and see various riders with various loads that experiences multiple uses per day. After much discussion and research as well as considering several additional *factors like amounts of corrosion resistance, if certain materials are lighter/heavier, less expensive, or easier to manufacture than other materials, just to name a few, we concluded our research with finding two ideal material candidates for the bike: AISI 303 stainless steel or 6061 aluminum. Noting the fact that both metals can be used for our ideal purposes, it came down to preferences over a couple factors. Although aluminum is less dense and a bit cheaper, it does not typically last as long as steel frames. In addition, many people have complained that aluminum bikes tend to be much harder to ride, being too stiff and lacking in resilience, thus not storing and releasing enough energy for a smoother ride. So although stainless steel will cost a bit more, since we don't have a preference on any particular weight and would ideally prefer a longer and more comfortable ride, we chose stainless steel as our ideal choice in material for creating our bike frame. We also concluded that the manufacturing process most suited for assembling this bike frame would be Tungsten Inert Gas (TIG) Welding and the cost for the total amount of material required equaled $19.77. Note that the considerations of manufacturing processes and cost were taken into account before final material selection too.*

This project gave me a greater understanding of how to approach the process of choosing the best material for an engineering part I am working with. It also gave me an idea of what I can expect to find in the material-handling industry after graduation. With the knowledge gained from my bike frame project and other classes, as well as the work experience gained through my internship with Rockford Products LLC, I am confident I will be ready to positively contribute to any industry in the manufacturing field, it being material handling, logistics, or supply chain, etc., so that I may help contribute to a better future, in both the industry and the world."

PARAGRAPH 8

Out of 32 essays, appears 2 times

"After my undergraduate studies, I plan to work with a company that fits my interests and who will let me apply my knowledge in order to positively contribute to its future innovations in its respective field and society as a whole. This will also allow me to continue to grow my appreciation for manufacturing as well as start to specialize in a specific field which I have yet to determine. Also, in an effort to keep improving both personally and professionally, attending graduate school is a series consideration in about 5 to 7 years so that I may be one step closer in fulfilling my objective of making my own impact in the manufacturing industry."

INSTRUCTIONS FOR INTERPRETING ESSAY BREAKDOWNS

Each of the paragraphs listed above were written at different times. These were sections that, when written for the first time, I felt were very strong pieces of content. I then began to look for opportunities to reuse them in later essays which will be one of the main lessons of the upcoming breakdowns. As each of the above unique paragraphs appear in the below essays, whether in its full form or a smaller portion, I notated those occurrences by using symbols such as ① followed by brackets shown here: **{ }**. For example, a portion of text that starts off with ① **{** means that it came from Paragraph 1. When you reach the ending bracket **}**, it means that concludes the portion that came from Paragraph 1. When a portion is encapsulated in those brackets, it means that exact wording found in the essay came from that specific paragraph. Within those brackets, you will encounter one final set of brackets show here: *[ ]*.

These brackets are to show that there was a small edit done to the wording from the original paragraph the reused portion was taken from. In addition to how the reuse strategy is deployed, the following breakdowns will also explain what else goes into a winning essay and how to apply all the other aspects of a strong scholarship essay that were discussed in What Makes a Good Essay Portion.

One disclaimer that I would like to mention is after I explain a topic or example in depth when it appears for the first time in one essay, when that same topic or example is brought up in a different essay, I won't go into as great of depth as I did the first time explaining it to save on redundancy of teaching the same lesson. Rather, I will explain in a more concise manner how that example is used in the current essay's context it is used in. My goal behind these breakdowns is to help you recognize where I used the essay concepts I write about in this book so that you, in turn, will be able to apply them to your own writing.

I numbered every sentence of each essay since I refer to them in each breakdown. As you read each breakdown, I encourage you to look back and find the sentence I am referring to in that essay to truly see how the ideas I expand on are formed. Take a picture of the essay on your phone if you have to so that way you don't have to constantly be flipping back through pages. Also, there will be points that I will refer back to previous sections of the book or other breakdowns. Looking back at those sections or other breakdowns will help you to understand the current breakdown you are on. To begin each essay breakdown, I will first list out some baseline information of where the essay comes from and what the prompt is. Then, I will include the original essay that was written for the prompt, after which I will break down that essay into five main parts: Prompt Breakdown, Introduction Breakdown, Body Breakdown, Conclusion

Breakdown, and Final Breakdown Comments. Without further ado, let's get started on the first essay breakdown.

ESSAY BREAKDOWNS

Essay 1	
Organization:	Community Foundation of Northern Illinois (CFNIL)
Title:	Women of Today's Manufacturing Scholarship
Date Written:	01/15/2014
	Freshman Year, 2nd Semester (Spring)
Total Winnings:	$1,000
	Applied to Sophomore Year, 1st Semester Tuition (Fall)
Prompt:	*How will your coursework help you to impact manufacturing technology in the Boone, Ogle, Stephenson, Winnebago, and Rock County regions?*
Word Count:	N/A

INTRODUCTION

" [1]In today's fast-paced environment, keeping up with demands is an essential part for a business to compete in the real world. [2]Ever since Henry Ford's invention of the assembly line in 1913, manufacturing processes have grown exponentially. [3]With this growth comes a high demand for Manufacturing Engineers. [4]These engineers come up with innovative, cost efficient ways to convert raw materials into valuable product, allowing for even the smallest of businesses to thrive. [5]This is why I am excited to pursue a Bachelor's Degree in Manufacturing Engineering at Bradley University. [6]The knowledge I acquire from the rigorous coursework at Bradley will allow me to give back, not only to my community in Winnebago County, but also to the Ogle, Boone, Stephenson, and Rock County regions as well.

BODY 1

[1]*Bradley University has received national recognition for its pristine Manufacturing Engineering curriculum.* [2]*Caterpillar Inc. helps fund this and other engineering disciplines by donating money toward scholarships and state-of-the-art equipment.* [3]*As a student, using this equipment will give me an opportunity to design and conduct various experiments that relate to different manufacturing processes and systems.* [4]*Analyzing and interpreting the data collected will help me understand each component in the particular system as well as give me a hands-on approach to the world of manufacturing.* [5]*This hands-on approach allows me to be aware of the constraints, benefits, costs, and materials associated with several manufacturing problems.* [6]*Ultimately, I will have the ability to take these factors into effect to formulate the best possible solution for the problem.*

BODY 2

[1]*Communication is a vital part of manufacturing engineering.* [2]*Whether it is through oral, written, or technical forms, information must be passed through in order to implement solutions to different problems effectively.* [3]*As I learn about the modern processes for product development, I will gain an understanding of how communication flows within a factory setting and how that factory intercommunicates with its clients in and out of state.* [4]*I can then apply this knowledge to help with networking among the Winnebago, Ogle, Boone, Stephenson, and Rock Counties' different manufacturing firms.* [5]*Therefore, these different regions can work together to reach a common goal, which is to better their communities as well as make a profit.* [6]*Bradley will show me how to facilitate communication on the job and in everyday life.*

CONCLUSION

[1]*Through my coursework at Bradley University, I will be able to apply science and mathematics to the management, design, and materials used in different manufacturing processes.* [2]*Understanding all of these aspects will help me to impact the manufacturing technology that is used in the Winnebago, Ogle, Boone, Stephenson, and Rock County regions.* [3]*I can pinpoint what needs to be changed in a process that will allow it to operate with*

greater efficiency. [4]This will result in newer model designs for the machines used in the factory while reducing the chance for error. [5]These new technologies will take into consideration the ergonomics of the workplace thus boosting employee productivity. [6]My coursework will also help me to abate confusion with reading technical and graphical forms of communication by making them simpler to understand. [7]Firms will then be able to communicate efficiently resulting in fewer problems in the future. [8]Since manufacturing accounts for a large part of the nation's GDP, it is important that we keep our competitive edge. [9]The education I receive from Bradley University will inspire me to continue to improve upon different manufacturing processes and technologies. [10]It will help my community grow in competitiveness and for me to grow as an individual."

ESSAY 1 BREAKDOWN

PROMPT BREAKDOWN | ESSAY 1

This is a unique prompt and essay situation as a whole because this is my first manufacturing-related essay that I ended up writing around the beginning of my second semester freshman year. If you remember the story of how I even chose Manufacturing Engineering in the first place, you'll know that I made the decision to study this major just a few weeks prior to applying for this scholarship, and now I found myself needing to write a detailed essay on the subject! Not only that, but an essay that would be good enough to actually win this scholarship. Contrary to how I am describing it now, those thoughts did not distract from my approach to the task at hand. In reality, I was excited to approach this prompt because I was just coming off of a very definitive and confident decision in choosing that major. That confidence in that decision gave me the courage to approach this essay prompt in the way a true engineer of this field would, and to put my best effort despite my inexperience. So, I encourage you, especially as you are starting out, to not get overwhelmed or derailed if you fall into a situation such as this. That is why I really emphasized how my college major decision was a confident one. That definitive decision helped instill in me a sense of worth and belonging—that despite my inexperience in manufacturing at the time, I *identified* myself as a student of this subject and therefore I am worthy and deserving enough to be writing about this topic. *Use the fact that you, yourself, chose your college major for a reason as evidence to be deserving enough to win an industry-specific scholarship over other candidates who might have more experience than you.* It will allow you to truly concentrate on your writing which will cause creativity to emerge because you will seek the right information and terminology to craft your essay which will thus mask what level of experience you really are at and create an even playing field with other applicants. This was my mindset heading into this prompt and how I was able to craft the output that I did.

Knowing where I stood now, I was able to focus on the prompt for what it was. The theme of this essay is very straightforward in that it will be about manufacturing, and more specifically about the technology related to the field. So, from the start this was my focal point. There was no word-count restriction for this essay. Whenever I encountered essays without word-count restrictions, my mind immediately aired on the side of caution and opted to write more rather than not enough. With the platform that I was applying on, you had to attach either a Microsoft Word document or a PDF file, both of which gave more flexibility with how much content you can include. You don't need to write a long novel. *Instead, focus on strong supporting points and provide enough detail to make your argument clear without slowing the reader down.* Having no word-count restriction is just a pass you get to elaborate more in your writing, and you get to make your point without making sacrifices to your message. That is what I was thinking with this initial prompt, and I defaulted to my standard essay format of an introduction, body paragraphs, and conclusion as my boundaries to help me craft this essay. If you write too little in these instances, you may run the risk of either not answering the prompt as fully or as deeply as the scholarship judge would want. If you write too much, you run the risk of drowning out your message to the point where the reader is left with a weaker impression. *In cases like this with no word-count restriction, sticking with a standard essay structure that was taught in school is your best bet.* That includes having an introduction, two to three body paragraphs, and a conclusion. With a standard paragraph size being around six sentences (this varies with the context), you now have boundaries that can get you to a strong finished product. At the end of this essay, I finished with a one-page document that nearly filled the whole sheet.

INTRODUCTION BREAKDOWN | ESSAY 1

You may recognize this prompt from the earlier sections going over passionate connections, introductions, and conclusions. Albeit different topics about this prompt were covered in those sections, referencing back to those sections—especially the Introduction section since we are breaking down this essay's introduction now—give deeper insight into how I was thinking about this prompt. It is worth noting to refer back to those sections since we are going to again cover this prompt in this breakdown, only this time it will be less on the side of explaining concepts and more on using those concepts in practice.

This essay was the first time I had ever answered this prompt. Starting off with my introduction's attention-getter, I knew I needed to appeal to scholarship judges in the manufacturing industry. The challenge was that I had chosen this field only a few weeks earlier, so I didn't feel I had much to say yet. How should I even start? This is where creativity comes into play. Despite being a novice, I thought, "What is something anyone in this industry, experienced or not, would immediately recognize and relate with?" How about mentioning the guy who practically invented modern manufacturing for what it is today—Henry Ford. Sentences 1 through 3 act as the beginning of my attention-getter, focusing on a higher-level topic that keeps the reader engaged because they are curious what this higher-level topic has to do with the prompt at hand. Briefly at the end of sentence 3 when I mention "Manufacturing Engineers," I am beginning to connect the dots. Sentences 4 through 5 end my attention-getter and create flow into the thesis statement. These sentences form our first connection type of the essay: a passionate connection. Here, I explain why I am excited in my degree choice and that, in turn, will get the reader excited with me. Not only that, but it conveniently flows into my thesis statement in sentence 6.

My main supporting point for my thesis is that "the knowledge I acquire" from the coursework asked about in the prompt is what will help me to impact manufacturing technology. Looking back now, I could have been even more specific with what "exact" knowledge that will be; however, this detail alone is providing the framework for the supporting information in the body paragraphs that will further answer what the judges are seeking. This is coupled with the use of a personal connection: by showing how my coursework will "allow me to give back" to the community, I make it clear that my career goals aren't self-centered. Instead, it shows that I'm keeping my community—and the communities mentioned in the prompt—in mind, demonstrating that I'm not just answering the question but giving my pursuit of this scholarship a deeper purpose.

BODY BREAKDOWN | ESSAY 1

Before starting to write Body paragraphs 1 and 2, I first had to reflect on what supporting points I wanted to include that would support the main idea of "knowledge acquired." I remember writing this essay because this was the point where I had to do research online to get ideas of different aspects of manufacturing since I didn't have a lot of personal experience to write about. My research led me to a broad understanding of the manufacturing system as a whole and how different pieces of equipment process different materials that flow through a supply chain to ultimately meet the needs of their customers. Once I had this broad understanding, I then had to answer the question of how my coursework will have an impact on a manufacturing system. As a freshman, all I really had to offer were the future opportunities Bradley envisioned for me—and I knew that if I wanted any chance at winning, I had to be genuine in how I presented them. So, I concluded that my first supporting point of Body 1 would be surrounding the topic of "equipment exposure" while in school.

Body 1 cascades down from this topic of "equipment exposure" and what it means for my manufacturing impact. Sentences 3 through 6 show both my flow and research in action. I wanted to ensure that all the ideas I brought up in this sequence connected. It is worth to mention about the "hands-on approach" phrase found in sentence 5. This is a use of a passionate connection where I wanted the judges to feel that I am the type of person who is willing to get their hands dirty and fully immerse myself on the manufacturing plant floor rather than hiding behind a computer to solve problems.

Body 2 is where the second supporting point of "communication" is introduced and used to answer the prompt. I centered on communication because, in my research, I read about things such as blueprints, engineering drawings, work instructions, and other means of conveying information that are related to manufacturing equipment. This sounded vital in the industry, and I thought it would apply perfectly to the prompt. I proceeded to structure this topic the same way as done in Body 1, by explaining how I can use the supporting point of communication to have a tangible impact on the communities the prompt mentions. An emotional connection can be found in sentences 4 through 5 where there is talk about this being able to better the aforementioned communities. This is emotional because it talks more of how the communities can benefit directly versus my personal motivation for helping them.

It was all about telling a story, trying to expand my supporting points as much as I could, utilize connection types to help create impactful reading, and sound very thorough and thoughtful when it came down to writing these body paragraphs. I remember really having to proofread and revise my body sentences as they came together because it was my first time writing on a manufacturing subject. *The lesson here is to keep pushing through no matter how rough the writing process is, or how long an essay will take you. Have the grit and willpower to push through.* You'll see my writing evolves with each new essay that comes up. It is fine if you struggle with your writing when you first start. Each challenge will elevate your writing for the next scholarship. You'll be able to learn from the challenges you faced in previous essays to become more efficient and impactful, and truly learn what works when it comes to bringing an essay together.

CONCLUSION BREAKDOWN | ESSAY 1

Speaking of bringing an essay together, let's break down the last portion of this essay—the conclusion. In sentences 1 through 2, you see me restating the thesis statement. Notice how it is phrased differently than compared to the introduction yet still retains the same key concepts of "coursework" and the specific communities of the prompt. Again, the reintroduction of the thesis statement is bringing the reader back to a higher, broader sense of ideas in order to make the closing arguments and solidify the message of the essay.

This solidification begins with sentences 3 through 5 where the first supporting point of "equipment exposure" is revisited; however, it is presented this time in a new light. With sentences 3 through 5, I do not explicitly say the term "equipment." Rather, these sentences were my take at still being able to introduce new ideas and keep a fresh message throughout the essay while keeping the same high-level theming. The same can be said for the second supporting point of "communication" that is brought up in sentences 6 through 7. Although the reintroduction of both supporting points acted as an extension of the body with the way I needed to explain the impact each one would have, they are more about closing off the loops of each point to make a lasting impact to the reader of how *exactly* what I wrote about would yield real-world results. No new ideas. No new tangents. Just sticking to the substance that was elaborated on in both body paragraphs, making sure that all open points are fully understood in a way that sets up the essay to finally come to an end.

You can see the end of the essay start to take shape in sentences 8 through 10. When writing, I always would reach a point where I knew that it was time to end the essay. A "mental signal" of sorts. That signal is felt when you know that you have finished summarizing the last of your supporting points in your conclusion. *Once you know you've made sure that everything you wanted to capture in your conclusion has been captured, it is sort of a mental checkbox that is ticked and that way you know it is time to end the essay.* I guarantee you will experience this in your writing as well. Once I reach that mental signal, two questions guide how I end an essay: "How can I creatively end this essay?" and "How can I ensure the ending is strong and makes a lasting impact for the reader?"

When looking into the first question on creativity, it is almost as if you are back on the 30,000-foot-view thought level that you started your introduction with because you are shaping all the information you have brought to the reader back into a larger perspective. In this essay's case, sentence 8 talks about how large of a foothold manufacturing has on the gross domestic product (GDP) of the United States. It really brings into perspective how critical the topic of manufacturing is in the world. This is then followed by sentence 9 which suggests that the knowledge gained from Bradley's coursework will help me to improve these manufacturing processes. Sentence 10 then flows from that to truly capture the full picture of what I am writing about while leaving the essay off on a high note. Sentence 10 finishes with connecting the impact of the "knowledge" in sentence 9 to the growth of the prompt's communities and also myself. Sentences 9 through 10 form to create both an emotional and personal connection. Emotional because, similar to how it was used in earlier emotional connections, I am mentioning how the local communities will grow—something that the scholarship judges truly care deeply about. Personal because this "knowledge" will allow myself to grow more in my career so I can have a greater impact in the communities I serve. Sentences 8 through 10 act as one final ending point to answer the prompt while leaving a lasting impression for the scholarship judge who is reading this essay, accomplishing the second question described above. Approaching a conclusion in this way allows you to piece together a thoughtful ending to any essay and give you that sense of confidence in your overall finished product as you submit your application. This was a feeling during my scholarship journey that I always wanted to have at the end of every essay and application packet, and my goal is to make sure you are able to reach that as well.

FINAL BREAKDOWN COMMENTS | ESSAY 1

To end our analysis of this first essay, we need to address the elephant in the room. That elephant is that at no point was a paragraph or section of a paragraph reused from a previous essay to craft this essay! Don't worry, the rest of the essays that will be broken down will have this feature. In this essay, there are a few reasons this was the case and why introducing it first matters.

Firstly, as you saw before the essay, this was written on January 15th, 2014, which was near the start of my freshman year second semester and was shortly after making the initial decision to study Manufacturing Engineering as a major. This was the eighth scholarship essay that I had written. The previous seven were from my high school era, so this was the first one from my actual college journey and the first one related to manufacturing. Although great attempts for what they were, the previous high school essays were not at the level of quality that was needed to truly stand out as a scholarship applicant, nor was the content relevant to what I was writing about, so I couldn't reuse anything. Also, I had not even thought about reusing any content because I was so new to this process! At this point, I had nothing to go off of other than what I was taught in my high school English classes about the basics of writing and the determination to win as many scholarships as possible.

Those two points—writing basics and determination—would merge to become the byproduct that is this winning scholarship essay. It is important to talk about how I really got the engine of my mind running when it comes to thinking like a winning scholarship essay writer. Those two points made me slow down, really understand the topic at hand and who I was writing for, how to answer the prompt, and write in such a way that connected deeper than any essay that I would have written in high school. Although there could have been improvements made in the flow and overall story that was told in this essay, a skeleton was formed that would go on to become the rest of the essays that I would write. Especially when it comes to the *determination* part. I had to do some research on manufacturing initially to write an essay like this. I could have tried to take the easy route and write vaguely about the topic, but my gut feeling knew that wouldn't be enough because I inherently knew I wouldn't be fooling anyone that way. *Determination turned into creativity, which turned into workable material that I can build my essay around.* Later, the workable material got easier because I gained more experience at my internships and college classes that I could write about. It will be for you too. Just don't discredit the value of doing a little research or get discouraged when your beginning essays aren't as smooth of a writing process as you think they should be. That is part of the journey. When you feel challenged in the beginning, that is growth happening and I promise if you stick with it, it will pay dividends.

The final point I would like to address to conclude this breakdown is the fact that I didn't end up reusing any of this essay's content in later essays. As I went on to start applying for other scholarships, I was still under the impression that I needed to write brand-new content for each one, and so I did just that. The more new essays I wrote, the more unique and refined material I developed. So, when I finally had the epiphany that I could reuse sections from earlier essays, this one wasn't my first choice—it wasn't as strong, and honestly, I had forgotten about it at times. That doesn't mean this is a bad essay. On the contrary, this is the essay that truly started it all. *What this means is that you will continuously improve the more essays you write to the point that your best work one day becomes lessons learned you look back on.* Be present in the moment. Do your best work at that point in time. Most importantly, trust the process and never give up.

This essay ended up winning $1,000 that I was able to apply toward my sophomore year tuition. I forget how exactly I was notified of the win. All I remember is that it lit a fire in me and made me realize I was on to something that could change my college financial situation if I kept going. I didn't know what the future would hold. All I knew was that I wanted to see how far a win like this could take me if I continued to try. Today, I know the answer to that question, but at the time all I had to rely on was faith and belief that I could repeat this win. Not once. Not twice. Only several times over until I graduated. In the next essays that follow, you'll see the blossoming of these thoughts into the fruit that it bore so that you too can have the faith, belief, and confidence to change your college financial situation as well.

Essay 2	
Organization:	Community Foundation of Northern Illinois (CFNIL)
Title:	Women of Today's Manufacturing Scholarship
Date Written:	01/08/2015
	Sophomore Year, 2nd Semester (Spring)
Total Winnings:	$1,000
	Applied to Junior Year, 1st Semester Tuition (Fall)
Prompt:	*How will your coursework help you to impact manufacturing technology in the Boone, Ogle, Stephenson, Winnebago, and Rock County regions?*
Word Count:	N/A

INTRODUCTION

" ① { [1]*Every day, people are exposed to endless opportunities around every corner but lack the ambition to pursue them in hopes of a better life.* [2]*Fortunately, I was blessed with the opportunity to receive a college education in order to fully exploit my potential, both as a student and as a person.* [3]*Manufacturing is used in just about every industry of the world in order to accompany the world's continuous population growth.* [4]*Seeing how this can have such an impact on society, I decided to study Manufacturing Engineering at Bradley University.* [5]*The numerous processes for product development and distribution that exist can truly be considered an art.* [6]*That is why I am excited to learn about how to improve upon these processes and eventually implement my* } *own solutions not only within my community of Winnebago County, but also the Ogle, Boone, Stephenson, and Rock County regions as well.*

BODY 1

② { [1]*This past summer, I was hired to work as a manufacturing engineering intern at Rockford Products LLC, a manufacturing facility that specializes in the making of cold-formed products.* [2]*Whether it was a specialty fastener, ball stud, or any one of their cold-formed products, it was fascinating to learn how each particular product had its own unique routing and machining instructions in order to be made.* [3]*These products are then distributed among a number of different markets consisting of automotive aftermarkets, agricultural, commercial vehicles, and key industrial markets, just to name a few.* [4]*Observing how manufacturing impacts a vast amount of industries is truly amazing and makes me wonder which industry I will end up working for upon graduation.*

BODY 2

[1]*Working as an intern helped me gain valuable real-world experience very few students are exposed to.* [2]*While working at Rockford Products, I was assigned a number of different projects including the design and implementation of an ergonomic rake in response to a workplace incident that happened on the shop floor.* [3]*After numerous hours of research and consultation with fellow engineers and shop floor workers, I designed a rake prototype using SolidWorks that complimented the natural body posture of the workers that used it for the specific task of sorting out parts.* [4]*I was able to outline the cost of the rake as well as how Rockford Products would go about making it.* [5]*The rake was designed to reduce the risk of workplace incidents as well as increase shop floor worker health and productivity.*

BODY 3

[1]*Other projects I worked on included the design and implementation of a procedure to help reduce the likelihood of mixing burnished and non-burnished parts together during the part's routing through the use of a notification lighting system and external attachments to the machine that simplified the worker's duties.* [2]*Also, I mapped out different forklift lane layouts to accompany OSHA standards without compromising travel times of the parts around the factory.*}

CONCLUSION

[1]*Although still in college, seeing how I was able to positively influence a company that has an impact on my community reassured me that Manufacturing Engineering is for me.* ① {
[2]*Being a first-generation college student, I am faced with a lot of pressure to succeed.* [3]*However, realizing just how great of an opportunity I have, I plan to work tirelessly until I have achieved* [*all my goals*]. [4]*With my newfound knowledge after graduation, I aim to work within my community of* [*Winnebago County and the*

surrounding counties] in order to give back what has been given to me all these years; a chance at a new life and new opportunities for the residents, and especially the younger generation. } "

ESSAY 2 BREAKDOWN

PROMPT BREAKDOWN | ESSAY 2

The next winning essay on our list coincidentally is from the same organization as Essay 1 who used the same prompt for a new application cycle. This means that at the time of writing this essay, I had one more year of experience in writing, college courses, and personal experiences like internships than when I first applied for this application. Also, because I already won from this organization, I had a good idea of what good looks like when it comes to what were the criteria to win. All I would have to do is follow a similar approach as I did in the first application in order to give myself the highest probability of winning once more. It may seem like this is too good to be true and I just had the luck of the draw when it came to this situation in that I already had a winning blueprint. However, that is not the case. Yes, I had a winning blueprint, but it was not because this was the same application and just a different year. The winning blueprint was in the strategy that I followed when I crafted the first essay and what is covered in this book. You could argue that this situation was even more difficult because I had already won this scholarship once. What would stop the judges from having winner-bias and, even if they recognized my application, choosing to award it to someone new instead? I had to prove myself once again through this application. Also, I wouldn't be able to submit the same essay as I did one year prior because they would catch on to that! This posed a new challenge that I hadn't faced yet in my scholarship journey—applying to the same scholarship again. Therefore, my mindset going in was how I can showcase myself in a different, stronger manner while answering the same prompt.

A lot of the same aspects of this prompt exist as well. The theme is manufacturing, so I'll know how to craft the substance of the essay. There is no word-count restriction, so I'll revert to a standard essay structure of introduction, body, and conclusion and the standard length that comes with it to craft the bones of the essay, supported by the fact that this is what helped win the previous year.

INTRODUCTION BREAKDOWN | ESSAY 2

Here I was, staring at a blank Microsoft Word page on my laptop wondering how I am supposed to start a completely brand-new essay. It started to feel like a momentous task because I knew how much effort my previous essays had required. That is when it dawned upon me that I had written a brand-new essay just six days prior for another manufacturing organization. I looked at that essay and asked myself, "Why can't I just use this essay for the one I am writing now?" I started to play around with the earlier essay I wrote and realized a few things. The essay I was trying to reuse came from a completely different prompt, it had word-count restrictions that affected the structure, and the organization—the audience I wrote for—had different values that they were looking for in their answer. At that point, I knew I could not just copy and paste this exact essay and call it a day.

This analysis led to a few important realizations. The first being that the essay I was trying to reuse followed the same 30,000 to 300 back to 30,000-foot-view flow, contained a similar essay writing structure, and was manufacturing related. In any essay you write, the introduction and conclusion ease the reader into and out of the main body. *Their tendency to utilize broader, higher-level thought patterns makes their content reusable across essays instead of being locked to one specific piece.* Since the main issue I faced with this new essay was getting it started, I realized I could reuse the introduction from the earlier essay I had written. This realization opened the floodgates for my essay strategy moving forward and forever changed the way I approached essays. I went from a mindset of pure grind-it-out essay production, to one that valued efficiency in the same production process. The goal was not to lose the grind-it-out mentality. That mentality should always be at your highest levels throughout the essay production process. The goal was not to see how hard a process you can endure when writing. The goal was to maximize scholarship winnings at all costs. *The only way you can achieve that goal is to incorporate the reuse of past scholarship content to increase application output which positively correlates with an increased amount of scholarship winnings.*

The reason that the introduction for Essay 2 is so significant is because this is the first ever instance of me taking a piece of content from one essay and using it in another. The introduction of this essay starts with using Paragraph 1, although it is only the first six sentences of it. This section from Paragraph 1 stuck out to me because it contained all the makings of a solid introduction that I wanted. Sentences 1 through 4 act as the attention-getter. Sentence 5 acts as the transition piece to relate the attention-getter to the thesis statement. Sentence 6 acts as the thesis statement that answers the prompt.

Notice how the original Paragraph 1 continues past the first six sentences found in this essay. Paragraph 1 was actually the full essay I had written six days before the one I'm breaking down now. I stopped at sentence 6 because that's where Paragraph 1 shifted into body content that supported the essay it was originally written for—material that was irrelevant to the one I was writing now. That brings me to a key point in the reuse strategy. *Be mindful of how your reusage fits with the essay you are inserting it into.* You can choose any amount of material and combine it however you like, as long as it complements the new message. In my case, the first six sentences of Paragraph 1 were relevant to the new essay and met all the criteria to be an all-encompassing introduction. Also, notice how sentence 6 ends differently in this essay versus sentence 6 in the original Paragraph 1. I rephrased the ending of this sentence since I needed to apply it to the current essay I was writing. Don't forget to edit all necessary sections you reuse as needed because if you copy and paste the original directly into an essay, it may not make sense unless you fix how it flows overall with your new essay.

Beginning with sentences 1 through 4, we see our attention-getter at work. The theme focused on here is manufacturing, and more specifically manufacturing technology as specified in the prompt. Sentence 1 introduces an emotional connection, hinting at how others may lack ambition to pursue opportunities. Sentence 2 then flips this idea into a personal connection, in that I recognized my opportunity of a college education and am attempting to take full advantage of it, showing the scholarship judges my drive and ambition for their field. Sentences 3 through 4 then further relate this 30,000-foot-view idea of "opportunities missed" started in sentence 1 to the central theme of manufacturing by tying in how my college major will be able to impact society's population growth needs. My college major is a talking point here because, as we've already seen in Essay 1, the prompt is inquiring about "coursework." How these initial sentences come together to seamlessly guide the reader where you want to take them is a perfect example of flow at work.

The flow of the introduction then continues with sentence 5. At this point, our thought level is descending, getting into more specifics and details. Sentence 5 is needed because sentence 6—our thesis statement—would not make sense without it. Our thesis statement in sentence 6 is about me "learning to improve processes and implement my own solutions" to then impact the communities mentioned in the prompt. The question is *why* I am "excited to learn," as stated in the beginning of sentence 6. The answer is in sentence 5 where I explain how fascinating manufacturing processes are, comparing them to an art form. This is a very strong passionate connection, and a great example of how these connection types can be used to really tell a captivating story throughout your essay. You can see how my pattern of thought came together to achieve the standard framework of what an introduction should contain in a way that answers the prompt and connects with the reader. You'll recognize that your own patterns of thought will come as waves during your essay writing. They make writing easy at the end of the day. Recognize when you catch one of these waves. You'll feel it. You'll know you have entered a flow state that is guaranteed to produce a strong essay!

BODY BREAKDOWN | ESSAY 2

You can see here that the body of this essay is Paragraph 2 which was reused in nine other essays. This essay that we are breaking down now is the original essay where Paragraph 2 was first written. When thinking of what to include in the body, I had to divert from the prior year's application where my supporting points centered around what I would be taught in college and how it relates to broad manufacturing topics. Although I made the most of the situation I had at the time, the overall message lacked depth. I couldn't submit a repeat of the same vague supporting points phrased differently this time around. I had to think, "What was different between this year and last year"? That answer is experience.

My thesis statement suggesting "learning to improve processes and implement my own solutions" is supported by talking about the experiences gained at my first ever manufacturing engineering internship that I had the previous summer. Body 1 starts by giving an introduction into the company that I worked for. I give specific examples and try to convey as much technical knowledge as I can to showcase just how much I learned. Body 2 dives deeper into the internship, noting an important project of mine that solved a specific problem. Body 3 then rounds out the overall internship by giving further examples of my impact during my time there. This paragraph exists primarily because I wanted to present as many examples as I could of the impact I made during my internship to make a strong impression to the scholarship judges.

These body paragraphs work together to act as one large supporting point to answer the prompt. They provide examples of how I "learned about processes," "improved processes," and "implemented my own solutions," thus covering every aspect of the thesis statement. *It is always a great idea to write about personal experiences related to the theme of your essay because it shows that you are interested in the topic you are writing about since you specifically sought out those experiences to have.* That speaks volumes to the scholarship judges since your words correlate into actions, really emphasizing how serious you are about the subject of the essay. These body paragraphs come together to form a passionate connection. If you revisit the section earlier in the book where passionate connections are first mentioned, you will see Paragraph 2 used as an example if you need more insight into how this applies as a passionate connection. The fact that you are talking about your experience, reflecting interest and excitement from what you've learned and went through, is what makes the passionate connection work. If you weren't passionate about the subject, you wouldn't put yourself in these scenarios or have as much detail or impact emphasized in your examples. Always put yourself in the scholarship judge's shoes and ask, "If I were reviewing applications, what would I want to see in the best essays and applications?" *By asking yourself questions like this, you will lead yourself to answers that will help guide your writing.* You can never go wrong with personal experience as it paints you as a worthy candidate every time, it is the reason I wrote about it in this body, and it's why this section was reused so many times later.

CONCLUSION BREAKDOWN | ESSAY 2

For the conclusion, I found myself in the same dilemma that I was in with the introduction. How do I end this same essay prompt differently than last year? It would have been easy to write a different conclusion altogether because of how the body ended up being very different than last year's essay. However, I decided to keep with the trend of reusing content, and I looked back to the previous essay I had written six days prior (Paragraph 1) to see if there was anything I could salvage. Sure enough, I found a section that would act as a strong conclusion and flow well with this new essay.

Remember that Paragraph 1 was an essay all by itself. So, when I looked to see what I could reuse, I first looked at the concluding sentences of Paragraph 1. Right away, I noticed that none of the sentences by themselves seemed like a good transition for this new essay, so I couldn't simply copy and paste them in. This leads me to sentence 1 of this essay's conclusion. Sentence 1 was not reused. I had to come up with a creative way to transition my body paragraph's content with the conclusion section I was trying to reuse. Sentence 1 acts as that bridge by revisiting the supporting point of my internship—being "able to positively influence a company"—and relating it back to manufacturing engineering, which is a nod to the prompt being about coursework.

Sentence 2 of the conclusion is where I begin to reuse from Paragraph 1, starting by plugging in sentences 9 and 10 from that original section. One note is I didn't number the individual commonly reused paragraphs, so when you look back for sentences 9 and 10, they will be toward the end of Paragraph 1. Conclusions must have a strong ending, and I thought these sentences fit perfectly because they are very powerful in that they make a personal connection talking about my status as a first-generation college student. I elaborated on this example, as well as other aspects of Paragraph 1, in Chapter 11's Key Point 3: Creativity section and the Personal Connection section if you want to revisit those explanations in more depth. These sentences paint the picture that the odds are stacked against me and that I do not have any help on my path toward striving for a better future. I wanted the judge to feel the fight in my spirit that I am doing everything I can to succeed, not only in the manufacturing industry, but in life! I then end the conclusion with sentence 4 which is sentence 8 from Paragraph 1. Notice that sentence 8 was before sentences 9 and 10 in Paragraph 1, and it shows up after them in this essay. *There is no cut-and-dry way to reuse content. It's however you want to tell the story and guide the reader.* In this case, I noticed how sentence 8 from Paragraph 1 touched on all the points that the prompt was seeking—talking about knowledge gained from coursework and talking about community—that I knew this was a great way to end this essay. Sentence 4 of this conclusion also acts as a restatement of the thesis because of how I brought up "Winnebago County and the surrounding counties," which was edited from its original sentence that used "Rockford, IL" instead. Lastly, the phrasing of sentence 4 continues the personal connection that was started in sentence 2. This is a personal connection because I am explaining how giving back to my community is something that is greater than myself. By talking about giving back, it shows the scholarship judge that I am motivated to continue in my manufacturing education because I will be able to impact those around me and even future generations, which ultimately answers the prompt of how my coursework will impact manufacturing technology in the five counties.

FINAL BREAKDOWN COMMENTS | ESSAY 2

The main takeaway from this essay was showing how reusing content from a previous essay can be implemented successfully. This strategy will save you time in the long run and will also save you the stress of having to write new pieces of content every time. It only makes sense how this strategy came to be. If the goal is to output as many scholarship applications as possible, and the majority of applications you are eligible for are related to the same theme as your college major, it is only natural that after a certain point it would prove harder to write about the same things—especially if you are applying a lot within the same semester or year! New experiences and other topics that would be good to write about come slower than the rate at which you want to be writing and applying. *So, always be on the lookout for how you can be creative and incorporate previously written content into new essays.* Keep in mind that the reuse strategy can take any form, as shown in this essay's conclusion. I took different sentences from Paragraph 1, reordered them, and edited them so they would be able to flow within the new essay successfully. You don't have to strictly follow any sort of rules or guidelines for reusing content. The goal to always remember is the message of your essay. If you find a sentence or phrase, and a string of ideas from one or multiple essays that achieve the right ideas you are trying to incorporate in your new essay, that's all that matters.

The key to this reuse strategy is to not get too complacent with only relying on reusing old content either. I said that new experiences and topics come more slowly—not that they stop coming altogether. When you feel like you have another solid idea to write about—whether it's a new internship, a completed project, a trade show you attended, or another meaningful experience—write about that as a new supporting point. You want to continually write new pieces of content for two reasons: first, every new experience helps you grow, making you a stronger candidate than you were in past applications; and second, your writing and the way you present your ideas improve the more you write. The reuse strategy isn't meant to be a crutch. It is meant to be a compliment to your essay writing. Don't limit yourself to your past writing pieces only. Always search for new and innovative ways to present yourself as the best applicant possible in your writing. You may be one essay away from writing a brilliant essay that is your finest work yet. Don't let reusing past work hold you back from that. Be smart and strategic when reusing past work; however, continue to write new content to add to your arsenal for reuse next time.

One final point on the body of this essay I would like to mention is that it was significantly easier to write about my personal experience of my internship than having to string together supporting points from more of a research-heavy approach like in the case of the previous year's application. Not only was I more confident in the subject matter of what I was writing about since I saw the real impact I made during the summer job and could articulate it better, but also it resonates as a deeper message to the reader. I was able to establish a clear, coherent flow within the body just by telling the story of my summer in chronological order, which made it easy to produce sizable essay content that included passionate connections relevant to the prompt. If you do not have the luxury of having quite the same personal experiences yet, do not worry. Think about what you *can* talk about. Is there a project in school that you got particularly involved in? Are you working on a project in your free time that can apply to the subject you are writing about? Just as described in the Get Involved section of the book, it is easy to manufacture these personal experiences so that you have this type of content to write about. *The point is to try to present something tangible that shows scholarship judges you are not just talking, but rather that you are actively involved in the area that they are giving money to support.*

This essay ended up winning the $1,000 scholarship, proving that you can win the same scholarship multiple times in a row. I have no proof of this, but if I had to attribute one thing that helped me win this same scholarship for a second consecutive year, it's that I was able to show the growth that I underwent in one year. I showed that I applied myself in the manufacturing industry by securing an internship that I contributed positively to, I improved my writing technique to be able to further justify my deservedness of the scholarship, and I had a deeper understanding of how I would be able to use the knowledge from my major to add value to those around me. Whatever the reasoning, I know for certain that I did everything in my power to give myself the best chance to win. This is the reason I want to share this knowledge with you as well so that you too can share in the success that I found winning scholarships.

Essay 3	
Organization:	Association for Manufacturing Excellence (AME)
Title:	Dr. Sherrie Ford - Manufacturing as a Career Path 2015-2016 Scholarship
Date Written:	10/31/2015
	Junior Year, 1st Semester (Fall)
Total Winnings:	$1,500
	Applied to Junior Year, 2nd Semester Tuition (Spring)
Prompt:	*Please describe why you want a career in Manufacturing.*
Word Count:	500 words or less

INTRODUCTION

"⑤{ [1]*Growing up having had two older siblings already attend college, I was able to learn a lot from their accomplishments as well as their mistakes that really made me ponder what it is I wanted to do with my life.* [2]*My eldest brother, [REMOVED NAME], who studied Biology at Loyóla University in Chicago and who also has been a great role model in my life, made me reflect on whether I wanted to pursue a career in a particular field of science.* [3]*Taking several advanced science classes in high school made me realize that, although interesting, wouldn't be the right fit as to what field of work I could see myself doing in the future.* [4]*My sister, [REMOVED NAME], who also studied at Loyola University and majored in Political Science, made me consider a field of study in government or social work but again it did not pertain to my particular interests.* [5]*As I continued my search, I started to take an in-depth look into how the world itself was moving forward.* [6]*It seemed like more people nowadays have greater demands and expect those demands to be met to achieve a certain standard of living that people fifty years ago would have never dreamed of being obtained. [7]My search ultimately led me to the conclusion that without mass-production, the world would not be where it is today.*} ①{ [8]*Manufacturing is used in just about every industry of the world in order to accompany the world's continuous population growth. [9][With this], I decided to study Manufacturing Engineering*} *with a concentration on Lean Manufacturing so that I may help to make my mark for a better and brighter future.*

BODY & CONCLUSION

[1]*Working as an intern over the past two summers for Rockford Products LLC, a local manufacturing firm in my hometown, made me realize that I had made the right choice.* ②{ [2]*I was assigned a number of different projects including the design and implementation of an ergonomic rake in response to a workplace incident that happened on the shop floor. [3]After numerous hours of research and consultation with fellow engineers and shop floor workers, I designed a rake prototype using SolidWorks that complimented the natural body posture of the workers that used it for the specific task of sorting out parts. [4]I was able to outline the cost of the rake as well as how Rockford Products would go about making it.*} [5]*Following through with this project gave me a greater knowledge and understanding of, not only the design aspect, but of Manufacturing Engineering as a whole. [6]Therefore, after graduation I would love to play a major role in the design and production of the next big product or improvement upon an existing product that would see worldwide use. [7]To be a part of something that millions of people use on a consistent basis that improves their quality of life would be an enormous accomplishment that can only be met if I continue to set new goals for myself and strive for excellence in everything I do."*

ESSAY 3 BREAKDOWN

PROMPT BREAKDOWN | ESSAY 3

Here we have another manufacturing themed prompt, but this time from a completely different organization than Essays 1 and 2. With this new organization comes a completely different question. This organization wants to know why I want a career in manufacturing. At the time of writing this essay, I was midway through my first semester of junior year at Bradley and was fully invested in manufacturing as a career path, so I felt very confident I could put together a strong application centered around this essay. Up to this point I had a lot of relevant experience both in and outside of school, so it wasn't finding what I would write about that would be the biggest challenge of this essay. The biggest challenge would be finding a way to capture the right examples to write about in 500 words or less.

This is the first essay that we will cover with a word-count restriction. You would think that having this word-count restriction would affect the scholarship more, but that isn't necessarily the case. 500 words is still a substantial amount of content to write. Again, I would always err on the side of caution, so I planned to use as much of the 500 word allowance as I could. I approached this essay just like any other essay by following a standard essay structure. I started writing how I would normally, only this time I would periodically go back and check ratios of the different parts of the essay like the attention-getter, introduction, body, and so on, to see if it was overall proportionate to the rest of the essay. For example, out of 500 words, you do not want 300 of those to be only your introduction. *The only thing with these types of essays is that you have to be conscious of what you include and expand on, because expanding on a non-*

essential part of the essay could throw off the essay's overall balance. So, with the theme of manufacturing and the word-count restriction in front of me, I started writing.

INTRODUCTION BREAKDOWN | ESSAY 3

Being as far into school as I was, it meant I was equally as far in my scholarship journey and had a history of applications and essays to show for it and reuse for later. That is exactly what ended up happening in this introduction. Sentences 1 through 7 of the introduction come from Paragraph 5 which was written four months prior. I picked this section to reuse because it not only had several strong points, but it also flowed well with what the prompt was asking for. Since the prompt was asking me why I decided to study manufacturing, I figured I would start the essay talking about how I got to that decision as previously described toward the beginning of this book. Sentences 1 through 4 act as the attention-getter and 30,000-foot-view thought pattern. Sentence 1 starts off strong because I mention the strong influences on my life—my brother and sister—which helped me to start asking questions about my future. Sentence 1 leaves the reader asking, "How did they influence you?" and makes them start to read into sentences 2 through 4, which answer that question. Sentences 5 and 6 then start the connection to the main point of the essay, still relating it to a high level topic of the "world's needs" but aligning it with manufacturing. Sentences 5 and 6 are painting how impactful this industry is, and, more importantly, the reason I am phrasing this idea in this way is because it shows how I, as a scholarship applicant, truly realize the impact manufacturing has on the world. I am not saying some low-level idea like that the reason I picked manufacturing as a major was just because I needed a job, or that I thought manufacturing was "cool," or something like that. *Rather, these sentences show that I see the bigger picture.* That picture being that I am not just thinking about myself, but instead of what services the world needs, which translates stronger. This is a great example of how creatively presenting ideas can transcend past a surface-level meaning and leave the scholarship judge with a greater appreciation for why you, the applicant, are applying for this scholarship. This connection to the main point of the essay ends with sentence 7, coming full circle and answering vividly how I ended up where I did as a student of manufacturing engineering. Though sentences 8 and 9 truly finish it off, sentences 1 through 7 are inherently a drawn out passionate connection because it explains how my interest and passion for the field of manufacturing evolved.

The passionate connection wraps up with the final two sentences of the introduction paragraph. Sentence 8 was reused from Paragraph 1. With how sentences 6 and 7 started the flow of connecting to the main point, the next sentence after needed to be the final bridge to the thesis statement. Since I had this sentence written before, I knew of its existence, and knew how I used it in previous essays, so I thought that it would be relevant to this essay. Instead of trying to say the same thing in a different way, I was able to look back at what worked in previous essays and reuse sentence 8 as my bridge to the thesis statement. Sentence 9 then ends our introduction by presenting our thesis statement and main point of the essay which is concluding that I picked Manufacturing Engineering as my major, and the reason why is to help "make my mark for a better and brighter future." The introduction comes full circle with this thesis. Everything in the introduction—from explaining the world's needs to choosing my major—leads up to my main point: I want to shape the future through manufacturing. The question now is *how* I will make my mark, and the answer lies in the body.

BODY BREAKDOWN | ESSAY 3

This body is unique in that it is connected to the conclusion. This is a byproduct of the word-count restriction. Had I separated the body into its own paragraph, it wouldn't have looked proportionate to the rest of the essay and would have just looked like some sentences thrown together. Working outside the typical structure of an essay isn't the end of the world. *So long as you align with the principles of proper essay structuring, your essay will flow the same and still hold the same weight.* Here, we begin our descent into our 300-foot view of getting into the details of *how* I am going to achieve what was stated in the thesis statement. The main supporting point to my thesis statement is, again, my personal experience at my internship. Sentence 1 of the second paragraph of this essay acts as a transition for a couple of items. First, and more obviously, it acts as a transition from the introduction into the body, especially with the phrasing at the end when I say, "made me realize I had made the right choice"—with "right choice" referring to studying my major. The other item is that it acts as a necessary transition piece to successfully integrate yet another reused section from Paragraph 2 into the main idea of this essay. Sentence 1 is a spinoff of the first sentence of Paragraph 2; however, I had to do without the description of the company I worked for due to word-count restriction. I had to get quicker to the point with this beginning sentence, so I simply state the company name. Also, a big difference from Paragraph 2's first sentence is where I mention "over the past two summers." My personal experience over two summer internships at the same company is what will support my thesis because I am putting into action how I am making "my mark for a better and brighter future."

Sentences 2 through 5 are a copy and paste of the main talking point from the second paragraph within Paragraph 2. Although these sentences talk about a project that technically was one I worked on in my first-year internship, the scholarship organization doesn't know that, and so the timetable doesn't matter when it comes to the examples you use so long as the scholarship judge can clearly see the value from your example. I reused this section because it was a tangible example of impact I had, it is a passionate connection, it was my most interesting project there even when compared to my second-year's internship projects, and it was already written. Therefore, it was an easy choice to reuse this section here. The end of this reused section at sentence 4 marks the end of the body of this essay. With the word-count restriction, I had to limit the supporting points to just this because if I continued with examples, I would not have had enough flexibility in my conclusion to end the essay how I normally would want to.

CONCLUSION BREAKDOWN | ESSAY 3

Sentence 5 of this essay's second paragraph marks the start of the conclusion. Again, this isn't its own standalone paragraph due to the word-count restriction causing me to format differently than usual. *Whenever there is a challenge like this, view it as an opportunity instead of an obstacle.* Here, my opportunity is to finish this essay in a way that makes my application stand out. Sentence 5 begins with a transition back into a higher-level thought pattern. I connect the supporting point that was my internship by talking about my takeaways from the ergonomic rake project and relate that back to my manufacturing studies. Sentence 6 and 7 then restate the thesis in a different manner and answer the prompt question when I talk about being part of a product that sees worldwide impact and helps "millions of people." These two sentences really mesh together as both a passionate and personal connection. Passionate because helping so many people through a product that is mass produced is truly inspiring to me, and personal because knowing the opportunity I have in front of me will motivate me to "strive for excellence in everything I do." By approaching the conclusion in this way, we are able to bring our reader back to the 30,000-foot-view thought level that we initially started the essay with. It allows the ideas presented in the essay to truly come full circle for the reader. *Also, ending on a connection type allows you to be perceived not just as a college student looking for extra money, but as a purpose-driven individual with ambitions greater than yourself and the scholarship funds you are applying for will help you accomplish those ambitions.* Despite having little room to include a conclusion, with the right amount of creativity you can end any essay on your terms.

FINAL BREAKDOWN COMMENTS | ESSAY 3

After plugging in this essay to a word counter, the final word count came out to exactly 500 words. Talk about efficiency! The essay didn't just magically turn out like that, though. Although I wasn't checking constantly, I was conscious of the word count going in and would check periodically where I was after adding to the introduction, body, and conclusion. I found myself cutting different parts out from the reused portions and revising phrases and whole sentences in order to meet the word limit as I wrote through this essay. The reason why it ended up being at 500 words was because I initially started with too much and cut just enough to meet the word limit while retaining the quality of the content I wanted to include. Word count is an easy controllable. If they give you a limit, triple-check to make sure you are either under or at that limit. Try to also use as much of the limit as you can. You don't want to add wasted words that serve no purpose just to increase your word count, but by using close to or all of the limit, you are giving yourself another differentiating factor versus other scholarship applicants. Others might leave 15–20% of the limit unused because they're playing it safe or looking for an easy out, and as a result, they don't write as much or go as in depth when a word-count restriction is involved. Don't use word count as an excuse as an easy out like they would. *Just like how you would want to fill up your general essay portion with as many extracurricular activities as I've explained, you want to do the same for your essay with a word-count restriction.*

Another big win from this essay other than meeting the word count 100% is how I was able to reuse virtually all the content of this essay from other scholarships I had written. Even sentences 5 through 7 in the second paragraph were from another scholarship that I had written about four months before this one, although I did not include it as one of the eight most commonly reused paragraphs because it was only used twice—once for the original and once for this essay. I did not use it anymore after that. Not that it was a bad section or anything, it's just that I had so many other sections from different scholarships to choose from that I simply went with others at the time. Notice, though, that as mentioned earlier in this breakdown, I was a few months into my junior year when writing this. That means I had already gotten to the point that I am making completely new essays out of other scholarship sections. Rather than writing completely new essays, I am just picking and choosing what I can include, then just piecing them together and filling in any gaps there may be. It got to the point where mixing and matching scholarship sections turned into a game for me! This meant that I still had virtually two more years of being able to apply for scholarships having this luxury of saving time and energy through the reuse strategy and maximizing my chances for winnings in the process due to the increased amount of scholarships I could apply for by taking advantage of this situation. If it sounds too good to be true, it's not. I am setting up the blueprint in this book; it is your job to execute it now. Don't talk about it—be about it. Take action, because I promise the whole scholarship application process will get easier the further you go along.

This essay is another example of how achieving a flow and telling a story can bring substance to what you are writing about. I ended up answering the prompt of "why you want a career in manufacturing" in several ways. I started off with how the idea of manufacturing even entered my head with explaining how I compared my older siblings' career choices with my interests and how they did not align. I then established the main point of the essay which was how my search for a major led me to manufacturing since it aligned closer with not only my personal interests, but also the needs of the world. I then pretty much had to prove why I wasn't just some college kid that was full of it and writing about things that were superficial. That is when I went into the roots of my personal experiences of my internship to show how I am taking action right now in the industry. Guiding the story I am telling the reader in this way displays to them that not only was my interest in manufacturing perked during my initial research of the major, but that the interest was solidified and further developed through the personal experiences I willingly chose to pursue. I articulated how I grew from the experience and further fell in love with the career field. This shows what I am doing in the present moment. Lastly, I ended the story with how I am looking into applying my knowledge toward the future with wanting to be involved in the next wave of innovation to hit manufacturing. In all aspects of this essay, you can see how I answered the prompt of why I wanted a career in manufacturing. Sure, I could have jumped straight to talking about how I wanted to be a part of future innovations of the industry, but you can see how that leaves a large gap for the scholarship judge. "How did you get to that point" is what they will be thinking. This approach I took covered the past, present, and future views of this prompt, riddling this essay with reasons, and building up my case as one who deserves this scholarship more than someone who, let's say, is the same amount of deserving but doesn't articulate it appropriately in their essay. Maybe they were one of those applicants missing the last 15–20%! At that point, I would even question if they are as deserving like I had previously mentioned because if they have the same amount of passion, they would have also seen the word-count restriction in the same way I did, which was to use all the space I could get. I may be stretching this example; however, it is just getting the point across for you to reflect on your personal, passionate, and emotional *experiences* that you have had and channel them into the connection types of your essay. Combine that with proper flow, transitions, and following the 30,000 to 300 back to 30,000-foot-view thought pattern, and you will come out with an essay like the one we just broke down. I know it is in you, and I hope that examples like this help you to see that essays aren't as scary or intimidating as they seem once you break them down into their basic components.

I ended up winning $1,500 from this scholarship. How would it feel if someone handed you $1,500 in cash out of the blue on a random day? That is how it feels to receive an email or a phone call saying that you won a scholarship. It is an amazing feeling, and is what made me want to continue maximizing my scholarship chances while I was in school. What is not an amazing feeling, though, is when you do not win. That is actually what happened with this scholarship organization. Essay 3 was my second application to this organization's scholarship. The first application was during the summer after my sophomore year and, had I won that, it would have been applied to the fall semester of my junior year, but that was not the case. Losing stinks sometimes, plain and simple. However, don't let that derail your motivation. There is growth from all failures. If you don't win the first time around, it simply means that you have areas to improve on. Whether that is in your writing style, the content within your writing, your general application involvement, or another reason. *A proper scholarship journey requires you to become comfortable with failure.* You're likely going to lose more often than you win. When you face an application in which you do not win, just dust it off, reflect on what you can improve on, and move on. Scholarships are a numbers game. Keep applying. Keep opening doors. In this case with this organization, they stated on their website that if you did not win from a previous application you can reapply. So, that is exactly what I did and look what happened! Never give up. Always keep going. Your future self will thank you later.

Essay 4	
Organization:	Community Foundation of Northern Illinois (CFNIL)
Title:	Women of Today's Manufacturing Scholarship
Date Written:	01/20/2016 Junior Year, 2nd Semester (Spring)
Total Winnings:	$1,000 Applied to Senior Year, 1st Semester Tuition (Fall)
Prompt:	*How will your coursework help you to impact manufacturing technology in the Boone, Ogle, Stephenson, Winnebago, and Rock County regions?*
Word Count:	N/A

INTRODUCTION

" ③ { [1]*In recent years, manufacturing has come to be one of the most pivotal industries in today's economy, accounting for a significant percentage of employment as well as global gross domestic product.* [2]*In the U.S. alone, the drive for innovation, competitiveness, and constant improvement that comes from our ever-changing manufacturing environment has kept our nation's spot as a worldwide leader in quality and cutting-edge technology.* [3]*The numerous methods of product development and distribution that exist provide endless opportunities for improving the everyday lives of a world population that continues to grow.* [4]*Having the ability to contribute to this wave of innovation in which the end result is a better tomorrow is why I have decided to study Manufacturing Engineering at Bradley University.* [5]*I am ecstatic to have found a college major I can apply my creative and ambitious personality to in the hopes of implementing my own solutions to the world of manufacturing so that I may have a positive impact, not only on society, but manufacturing technology in the Boone, Ogle, Stephenson, Winnebago, and Rock County regions as well.* }

BODY 1

② { [1]*[For the past two summers, I was fortunate enough] to work as a Manufacturing Engineering Intern at Rockford Products LLC, a manufacturing facility that specializes in the making of cold-formed products.* [2]*[During the summer of 2014], I was assigned various projects including the design and implementation of an ergonomic rake in response to a workplace incident that happened on the shop floor, [the integration] of a procedure to help reduce the likelihood of mixing burnished and non-burnished parts together during the part's routing, [and the revision of forklift lane layouts on the shipping dock.]* }

BODY 2

④ { [1]*Now as a second-year intern during the summer of 2015, I was tasked to work closely with the Quality Engineering Department in order to tackle a massive quality control project.* [2]*Rockford Products is in the process of transitioning to using a different data collection system, known as InfinityQS that machine operators use in order to input data from dimensional checks they carry out.* [3]*The first step was to update numerous control plan documents that list which processes the raw material must pass through in order to become a finished product.* [4]*Most revisions included pinpointing different dimensions from each part by looking at the engineering prints and labeling the frequency of how often those dimensions would be measured when the part undergoes each process in the routing.* [5]*Once revisions for a part are complete, that part must then be programmed into InfinityQS.* }

BODY 3

⑥ { [1]*My team and I were also required to setup the navigational menus within the software that machine operators would use on the shop floor in order to find the part that they want to add data for.* [2]*After learning how to operate the software for ourselves, we came up with a simple, straight forward procedure that minimizes the time it takes for them to find where they want to go on the system in order to input the necessary data they collect.* [3]*By implementing this new procedure, we also lessened the amount of work it takes for our team to program the part numbers into the system.* }

CONCLUSION

[1]*As I enter my third year in the Manufacturing Engineering curriculum at Bradley University, it is hard to believe how far I have come both as a student and as a person when looking back to when I was just a freshman.* [2]*I am confident that after graduation I will have all the necessary skills in order to succeed in my field of engineering, not only because of my courses completed at school, but because of the experience I gained through my internship as well.* [3]*I cannot wait to apply my knowledge in order to help companies, especially those in Boone, Ogle, Stephenson, Winnebago, and Rock County regions, achieve their goals so that I too may continue to grow and learn how to improve upon manufacturing technology and processes in order to better the community I serve."*

ESSAY 4 BREAKDOWN

PROMPT BREAKDOWN | ESSAY 4

The prompt from Essay 4 is the same prompt that we have already covered in Essays 1 and 2. This was the third year in a row that I applied for this same scholarship since they allowed previous winners to reapply. As a reminder, even though we have covered this same prompt twice already, this essay breakdown section is not necessarily about where the essay comes from. The point of this section is, again, to discuss the details, techniques, and strategies used to formulate the essays used to apply to these applications. Although this essay answers the same prompt, it is still a different essay entirely, and it is worth detailing out how it came together and study its best practices since this ended up being a winning essay.

Since this is the same prompt, we already know that the theme we will be writing about is how my coursework will impact manufacturing technology around the listed counties. It is worth noting that there is no word-count restriction for this once again; however, experience leads me to make sure to write a good amount of content utilizing a full introduction, body, and conclusion. My mindset going into this prompt, and all of the applications that would follow, was I felt confident in my ability to present a strong scholarship application since I was validated by the fact that I had won a few scholarships already and was doing everything in my power to stand out, such as being as involved as I could be in school and also trying to get relevant industry experience in my major via internships. With this being the third application for this same scholarship, I somewhat knew what to expect. I would follow roughly the same approach I did with the previous two, just as I would with any other essay. The last thing, however, that I wanted to make sure I kept in mind was to not underestimate this scholarship, take it for granted since I won the previous two years, or think that it would be an easy win. *Always approach your essays like you are an underdog coming for the top spot. Always aim to write your best work and surpass your previous writing. Don't get complacent or comfortable, because the moment you do is the moment you start to slack, cut corners, and miss details that other applicants will make sure to meet, which will result in them taking the scholarship from you.* So, that is what I did here and with all the other applications I applied for. Each essay is a blank canvas waiting for you to paint a masterpiece that showcases you as the most deserving to win the award.

INTRODUCTION BREAKDOWN | ESSAY 4

Being that this was the third time writing an essay for this organization's scholarship, I was put in a position where I couldn't reuse a lot of content I had already written because I had done so in the previous two applications. Therefore, although the introduction begins with Paragraph 3, it was on this application that I wrote Paragraph 3 for the first time. Again, it is all about turning obstacles into opportunities. Being put in a position to write new content opens up the door to be able to use that newly written content at a later time. In the case of Paragraph 3, this was the first time I had written it and it was then reused six other times after.

To avoid repeating the same explanation, I will direct you to revisit the section of the book going over introductions because it is in that section that I used Paragraph 3's content as the primary example to analyze, breakdown, and explain what a good introduction is. There you will find the exact reasoning for what makes the introduction of this essay work. In this breakdown section, I will just give a quick summary of what is already explained in that section. Sentences 1 through 4 act as the primary attention-getter. It starts with a 30,000-foot-view idea of how manufacturing is so impactful in the world since it touches so many aspects that fuel society as we know it. It works as an attention-getter because that is what the theme is centered around. *When you are writing any attention-getter, take a step back to understand your essay's theme and your audience. After you know those two things, find an idea that would amaze anyone in that space and elaborate from there.* We then see the thought pattern start to descend in sentence 4 by connecting the introduction's high-level idea to how it applies to me and my major of Manufacturing Engineering. Ending sentence 4 in this manner takes the form of a passionate connection because it is showing why this course of study resonates with me specifically.

Keep in mind that attention-getters can be non-linear too in terms of connection types used. A lot of examples in these essay breakdowns show my 30,000-foot view centered around thoughts and ideas that lead to *passionate connections*, and that is because they worked for me the majority of the time. Just remember that your high-level ideas introduced in the beginning of your essays can be different variations that can take a personal or emotional connection route as well. As an example, instead of the high-level ideas of manufacturing I used, I could have started the introduction with an angle that goes down how manufacturing played a pivotal role in the country of my heritage, Poland, at many points in history and connect it to how this helped the immigrants of my family get to where they are today. This would play into a personal connection because seeing the struggles of my family "personally" motivates me to contribute to an industry that helped them throughout the years and subsequently will help other families in similar situations. Another angle could have been centered on an emotional connection. I could introduce a high-level topic such as how there are still parts of the world that are lacking basic life necessities like food, water, medicine, or shelter, and connect it to how I would be able to use my coursework to study practices that can help manufacture products to be shipped to those in need at a faster and greater scale than they were previously sent. No one wants to see their fellow human being struggling, so this would tie into the "emotions" of the reader. *Keep your options open to how you want to start your introductions to your essays.* Find the angles that work for you—the ones that your writing will be able to flow off of in order to give the strongest message for your reader.

To end the summary of this introduction, sentence 5 acts as our thesis statement. Here, the answer to our prompt, as also explained in the Introduction section of the book, is "preparing me to be able to contribute to the wave of innovation." This exact phrasing is found in sentence 4, and then sentence 5 connects that phrasing to the answer the organization is looking for in their prompt. Sentence 5 tells how my coursework will be able to impact manufacturing technology in the counties that the prompt mentions. Now, like with every essay, the body will support that claim.

BODY BREAKDOWN | ESSAY 4

Going into writing the body, I knew my supporting points to my thesis statement were going to be my personal experiences from my internships. Note how at this point "internships" is plural. The main difference between this essay and the other two essays I had written for this organization was that, going into this essay, I had completed a second summer internship at the same company where I had my first internship. Therefore, when looking to start my body, just as I did with the essay I had written one year prior, I wanted to introduce my internship experience. My dilemma was figuring out how to set the stage the same way without repeating myself or copying what I'd written before. The answer to that dilemma is what makes up sentences 1 and 2 of Body 1 of this essay. My main supporting point is going to be my second-year internship. Setting the stage, or in other words the story that I am telling, comes into play when I give backstory of the company I worked for, similar to the previous year's essay. I was hesitant at first, but I ended up reusing portions of Paragraph 2 as the setup—the *transition*—to introduce my second-year internship. I was hesitant because Paragraph 2 was already used in the previous year's essay so the scholarship judges would be seeing the same wording, but without this transition piece, I felt that I couldn't tell the same story. In order to minimize the risk of reusing content they had previously seen, I rephrased and summarized Paragraph 2 into the bare minimum parts I needed for a successful transition. When comparing the original Paragraph 2 section to what was reused in this essay, you see that only two main sentences were reused, and those two sentences were heavily modified to fit the flow of the current essay. How I did this was in sentence 1, I just needed an introduction to the company I was working for, and then in sentence 2 I briefly list all the projects from my first internship. Even though using somewhat of the same wording was a risk, it was still important to my supporting point because revisiting what I had done in the first-year internship gives the reader an idea of how I already had a big impact at the company and makes the reader want to keep reading to figure out how I got better in the second year.

After Body 1 finishes setting the stage, the essay flows into Body 2 where Paragraph 4 is used. Paragraph 4 was new content first written in this essay. Here, the same strategy was used writing about my second-year experience as was used in Essay 2 when elaborating on my first-year internship experience. The focus of Body 2 was to explain, as clearly and intelligently as possible, my role and impact during my second-year internship. That is what makes up the bulk of sentences 1 through 5. Mentioning specific manufacturing tools that I had exposure to such as "quality control," "control plans," and "data collection" give insight into how much I absorbed during my brief time at the job. It is impactful because, again, it is not just about regurgitating what you did for the sake of filling words on the page. Rather, including details like this paints a picture of what I learned during the internship and shows how I can use these skills to then apply them to the overall impact to manufacturing technology that I will bring to the Boone, Ogle, Stephenson, Winnebago, and Rock County regions. That is why personal experiences are so powerful.

The second-year internship supporting point is further expanded on in Body 3 as well. Body 3 is Paragraph 6 of the commonly reused sections and was also written for the first time in this essay. Body 3 continues listing out more examples of how I contributed value toward my projects that translated to real-world benefits the company realized. *When listing out personal experiences as supporting points, always explain the result of your great work. The same wording flow used to write about personal experiences is similar to how you would want to answer a job interview question.* In interviews, they talk about the STAR method. Situation, task, action, result. I like to simplify this slightly by reframing it to be situation, action, and result only. I've found that the "task" part of it generally is talked about in the "action" part of the method anyways. It also helps me when I am actually in an interview because it is easier for me to remember a three-part method instead of four parts, so I tend to lump those together into one. So, in the same way you would answer an interview question, writing about your personal experience in this way will efficiently and clearly describe the value that you provided to your reader, which in this case are the scholarship judges. To apply this to Bodies 2 and 3, sentences 1 and 2 of Body 2 describe the "situation," sentences 3 through 5 and sentence 1 of Body 3 describe the "action," and sentences 2 and 3 of Body 3 describe the "result." At the end of the day, it is up to you to sell yourself in your examples, and your essay as a whole. You need to sell to the scholarship judges the idea that you are the most deserving applicant to win this scholarship. *How you do that is to describe the value that you add as an individual as it relates to the theme of the essay.*

CONCLUSION BREAKDOWN | ESSAY 4

To conclude this essay, I found it best to write a new conclusion instead of reusing content because at this point I had already written a majority of new content that I figured this conclusion would flow best if it were crafted specifically to summarize that new content. Sentence 1 starts the transition from the depth that was described in the body paragraphs to back a higher-level thought where I am relating back to my college curriculum as a whole. This sentence also came about due to the scholarship situation of which I was writing for. Being that this was the third application for this scholarship, they had seen the growth in multiple aspects of my young career thus far. I reflected on how the first application had no personal experiences in manufacturing as compared to this one where I displayed a plethora of manufacturing experience. So, phrasing the transition in this way, talking about "how far I have come both as a student and as a person," was my creative spin to start the conclusion for the reader. Sentence 2 is where I summarize the supporting points of my internships, and sentence 3 is where I restate my thesis in a way that ends the essay on a high note. This exact conclusion was the primary example used in the Conclusion section found earlier in this book. So, just as with the introduction example, to avoid repeating the same information I encourage you to revisit that section as well to find more detail why this paragraph functions well as a conclusion to a scholarship essay. Sentences 2 and 3 are covered in greater detail there than in this breakdown.

FINAL BREAKDOWN COMMENTS | ESSAY 4

In this breakdown, we have again covered the strategies and techniques used to craft a strong scholarship essay. What was unique about this essay was we crafted it knowing that it would be submitted to a scholarship organization that had already reviewed our application twice over. The general essay that was submitted with this application wouldn't have changed other than the new extracurricular experiences I added over the past year. The only thing that would have predominantly changed would have been the essay portion. So, the question becomes: How do you present yourself to someone who has already seen what you bring to the table? We answered this question two-fold. First, ensuring new content was used versus the previous two essays, and most importantly second, that the new content used continued to show growth in our career. "Growth" was a main talking point when writing the second essay (Essay 2). When looking at this essay, "growth" is *still* the only thing that we can double-down on. This would hold true if we applied for a fourth year in a row and would hold true for any other application in which multiple resubmissions exist. It is impossible to know the true reasoning as to why I was selected to win this $1,000 scholarship yet again. It could be because the growth we conveyed in our application beat the rest of the competition that applied. It could be because there weren't a lot of applicants in the first place and they needed to give someone the money. *Whatever the reason, our job, as stated before, is to give ourselves the best chance at winning scholarships, whatever the situation.* So, when it comes to this essay and application, we checked all the boxes of giving us that best chance without letting the situation of being the third time of applying affect the quality of our application. This "growth" should not only be for resubmissions though. It should exist and be shown in whatever application you are submitting. *That is how you always uphold your quality and not get complacent.* "Growth" in the case of this essay, although not limited to, was using both internships in our body as supporting points. This application would be the last application we would send to this organization, and also the last essay breakdown that we will cover as a repeat submission to the same organization.

Although it may have seemed repetitive at times, each essay breakdown answering this same prompt proved that each essay you submit is truly its own entity. In this series of essays toward this prompt, we discussed writing new content and reusing past content to create new essays that answered the same prompt. Whatever the situation, sticking to the fundamentals in this book will allow you to navigate each new essay situation you find yourself in. What was so pertinent about this three-essay series was bringing to light how reapplying to the same organization, if allowed, can open amazing opportunities for the applicant, including the chance to win even more money. One of those opportunities came to me after I graduated from college. A few years after college, this organization called me back to attend an event they were hosting to be a guest speaker on topics involving scholarships. Also, there was a scholarship exposition in Rockford, Illinois, another year where I was in attendance as a guest and this organization had a booth there. At the event, I visited their booth and they recognized me. This presented a great networking opportunity and helped further solidify this organization as a resource I could utilize in the future, for example, if I needed a job lead or support on a project. *At the end of the day, each scholarship you encounter is, at its truest form, a blank slate, regardless of if you have applied to it in the past or not.* Staying grounded in the present and keeping past lessons in mind will help you focus and submit the best application you can at that moment. Upholding this frame of mind will be your main support as you go through your scholarship journey. The byproduct from your hard work and effort throughout the journey could open doors and opportunities that you could never have imagined, as was the case with me and this three-essay series.

<table>
<tr><th colspan="2">Essay 5</th></tr>
<tr><td>Organization:</td><td>Society of Manufacturing Engineers - Education Foundation (SME-EF)</td></tr>
<tr><td>Title:</td><td>Myrtle & Earl Walker Scholarship</td></tr>
<tr><td rowspan="2">Date Written:</td><td>01/22/2016</td></tr>
<tr><td>Junior Year, 2nd Semester (Spring)</td></tr>
<tr><td rowspan="2">Total Winnings:</td><td>$5,000</td></tr>
<tr><td>$2,500 Applied to Junior Year, 2nd Semester Tuition (Spring)
$2,500 Applied to Senior Year, 1st Semester Tuition (Fall)</td></tr>
<tr><td>Prompt:</td><td>• Why do you want to enter this field of study?
• Career Objectives: What are your near and long-term career objectives?
• If you have selected "Engineering" as your major, please describe how your educational plans relate to manufacturing engineering or manufacturing technology?
• Educational Objectives: What are your near and long-term educational objectives?</td></tr>
</table>

	• *How will this scholarship help you achieve your objectives?*
Word Count:	300 words or less

INTRODUCTION, BODY, & CONCLUSION

"③{ [1]*In recent years, manufacturing has come to be one of the most pivotal industries in today's economy, accounting for a significant percentage of employment as well as global gross domestic product.* [2]*In the U.S. alone, the drive for innovation, competitiveness, and constant improvement that comes from our ever-changing manufacturing environment has kept our nation's spot as a worldwide leader in quality and cutting-edge technology.* [3]*The numerous methods for product development and distribution that exist provide endless opportunities for improving the everyday lives of a world population that continues to grow.* [4]*Having the ability to contribute to this wave of innovation in which the end result is a better tomorrow is why I have decided to study Manufacturing Engineering.* [5]*I am ecstatic to have found a college major I can apply my creative and ambitious personality to in the hopes of implementing my own solutions to the world of manufacturing.*} ⑧{ [6]*After my undergraduate studies, I plan to work with a company that fits my interests and who will let me apply my knowledge in order to positively contribute to its future innovations in its respective field and society as a whole.* [7]*This will also allow me to continue to grow my appreciation for manufacturing as well as start to specialize in a specific field which I have yet to determine.* [8]*Also, in an effort to keep improving both personally and professionally, attending graduate school is a series consideration in about 5 to 7 years so that I may be one step closer in fulfilling my objective of making my own impact in the manufacturing industry.*} [9]*Although a college education is a burden financially, it is a great investment for my future and, with the help of this scholarship through SME-EF, will take me to places I never would have imagined.*"

ESSAY 5 BREAKDOWN

PROMPT BREAKDOWN | ESSAY 5

Here, we find our first multi-layered scholarship essay prompt. This prompt consists of five different bullet points all related to my specific college major of manufacturing, which is also the theme of this essay. At first glance, this looks to be an intimidating essay prompt because each of these points by themselves could act as its own standalone prompt in which you could write a one-thousand-word scholarship essay on. The challenge here is they want you to be able to address all of these bullet points at once all within a word-count restriction of 300 words. When looking at this prompt for the first time, I was actually relieved in reading that the essay needed to be 300 words because I knew it wouldn't take as long to write an essay of this length, thus saving on some mental energy. Also, even though you could write a lot of content related to each bullet point individually, the word-count restriction would force me to eliminate as much waste as possible in my writing, requiring me to get straight to the answers the scholarship judges are wanting to hear. Again, it is important to view obstacles as opportunities.

The next thought that crossed my mind was, "What order should I address these in?" *Unless the scholarship specifically tells you to answer them in a sequential order, you don't have to follow the order that these bullet points are listed in when answering them.* All they ask is that you answer the questions. Therefore, it is up to you, when faced with prompts like this, to determine the best order that works for you. *What I would recommend is, out of all the bullet points, see which one sticks out to you where you feel you can speak the strongest too.* Use that as an avenue to start your essay, and then work the rest of the bullet points in once you feel you have written a strong beginning essay portion. For this prompt in particular, bullet points 1 and 3 stuck out to me the most. I felt as if I had already written a lot of essays answering prompts like these two, so I knew how to get an essay off to a strong start centered around these questions. I knew that these two would take up a good majority of my essay since I was restricted to 300 words. My plan was then to use the rest of the bullet points to fill in the ending portion of the essay, incorporating them in using connection types and clever transitions.

It is important to try your best to answer each aspect of prompts like this even if a word-count restriction forces you to keep your answers short. It is better to have answers to each bullet point than to be missing one or two answers because that will give a reason to the scholarship judge to negate credibility from your essay versus a student who was detailed and efficient in their essay and was able to answer all of the bullet points presented. Answering all of the bullet points will give more depth to the story you are telling. If you try to go too deep on only a select few bullet points, leaving out others thinking that it will bolster your message, you are wrong. It weakens your story, making the judge see you as one-dimensional and assume you left answers blank because you had nothing to add, thus leaving your essay feeling incomplete. Again, this would only happen if you had an essay prompt such as this one where they give you the flexibility to fit these bullet points in however you want. Observe how they want you to answer the prompt because that is how their organization determined they would like to score applicants. The best thing you can do with this, and all other essay prompts, is before writing your first word, always ensure you know what the prompt is asking for and plan to incorporate it at all costs.

INTRODUCTION BREAKDOWN | ESSAY 5

For the introduction, I decided to reuse Paragraph 3. When looking at the dates of when Essay 4 and Essay 5 were written, Essay 4 was written two days prior. That means I had just written Paragraph 3 when I decided to reuse it again. The prompt from Essay 4 was asking how my manufacturing engineering coursework would impact manufacturing technology in their local region, which is similar to bullet point 3 of this prompt where they nearly ask the same question. So, I thought reusing from Essay 4 was a no-brainer. Sentences 1 through 5 come from Paragraph 3. Sentence 5 ends earlier when compared to the original Paragraph 3 section. This is mainly due to the word-count restriction and was an edit to cut down so I could get to 300 words. The reuse of Paragraph 3 here was perfect because sentences 1 through 3 are my attention-getter, and sentences 4 and 5 form the thesis statement of the essay.

Considering the fact that this essay is only 300 words, the structure of this essay ended up taking the shape of one large paragraph, deviating from the standard paragraph-specific structure that is found with typical introductions, bodies, and conclusions. *Even in a single continuous paragraph, you can still follow the general flow of a proper essay structure and use the same core building blocks to shape your message*—and that's what you see taking form in this introduction. Sentence 4 begins to answer bullet point 1. It states the reason why I decided to study Manufacturing Engineering was because I wanted to have "the ability to contribute to this wave of innovation in which the end result is a better tomorrow." This "wave of innovation" was described earlier in the attention-getter. Sentence 5 addresses bullet point 3, stating that my educational plans relate to manufacturing because finding "a college major I can apply my creative and ambitious personality to" will allow me to begin "implementing my own solutions to the world of manufacturing." Admittedly, I remember reviewing that bullet point when writing this breakdown and thinking that I could have been a little more specific with exactly *how* my educational plans would relate to manufacturing. In previous essays, I had the luxury of explaining *how* by describing my personal experiences of my internships. However, at the end of reusing Paragraph 3's section, I had already used 152 of my 300 allotted words, so I figured what was currently written in Paragraph 3 addressed bullet point 3 well enough since I needed to still get to bullet points 2, 4, and 5. Also, if I was experiencing having to make these judgement calls, chances are other applicants would also be experiencing making cuts to their essays because of the word-count restriction. Overall, ending the introduction in this way was a strong course of action since this reused section contained a captivating attention-getter and a strong thesis statement that has a passionate connection embedded within in it. The passionate connection was how I detail the amazement I see within the manufacturing industry, and how that amazement is pushing myself to continue to pursue this degree field.

BODY BREAKDOWN | ESSAY 5

The body of this essay takes its most diverse form yet in this book. Due to the word-count restriction, we are forced to basically continue the body "sentences" directly off of the introduction "sentences." Our challenge now is to apply supporting points to our thesis statement, which again if you look back to the Introduction section where Paragraph 3 was explained in detail, our thesis statement in sentences 4 and 5 suggest that our coursework is "preparing me to be able to contribute to the wave of innovation," and our supporting points need to address *how* exactly we plan to become prepared. The situation we have, though, is that the three prompt bullet points we have left to answer ask us to explain our career and educational objectives. When Paragraph 3 was first written, the *how* was the internships I had that "prepared" me. Here, we could technically write about the remaining bullet points in such a way that further support the thesis statement provided in the introduction. However, being that I only had 148 words left, I decided to directly write to answer the prompts, and not necessarily target them to flow as supporting points to the thesis statement. As we will see in the end, this works out to our favor.

Sentences 6 through 8 come from Paragraph 8, which was written for the first time on this essay. Sentence 6 addresses bullet point 2, stating that my career objective was to work at a company and begin contributing to their solutions they provide that affect society as a whole. The reason why I stated "after my undergraduate studies" was because this was my way of explaining my near-term career objectives as asked in the prompt. Sentence 7 then further expands on that point, bringing up how I will "start to specialize in a specific field" of manufacturing. This can be seen as a both near-term and long-term answer to satisfy bullet point 2. Immediately following is sentence 8. Here, I start to answer bullet point 4 by stating how my educational objective is to explore options for graduate school. I give a timeframe of five to seven years because that was my way of having them view that answer as both a near and long-term educational objective of mine. Sentence 8 was the most uncertain point that I had during this essay. Truthfully, my near-term educational objective was simply to pass college and graduate with honors! In hindsight, I probably should have written about that; however, what steered me this direction was the "long-term" aspect of that bullet point. As a side note, my long-term educational objective ultimately became earning various certifications in my field, such as my Certified Six Sigma Green Belt (CSSGB). Although I didn't know how my career would progress at the time I was writing this essay, I gave my best effort in reflecting and writing what I *thought* was going to happen. One thing to add is that long-term education doesn't just stop after a certain point. *The reality of life is that you always want to keep learning, growing, and expanding your knowledge base to stay relevant within your industry.* Learning becomes fun at that point! Being a lifelong student is an amazing mindset that I encourage anyone to adopt. Always challenge yourself to improve, and the moment you feel you are comfortable or stagnant, that is a signal for you to make a change! Having the knowledge I know now, that is what I would have written about, but as with any college student, there are a lot more unanswered questions than answered ones. So, the best thing you can do is approach prompts like this with your best intentions, keeping in mind that plans can change the more you grow in life.

Sentence 8 effectively closes out what you would consider the body of this essay. Remember when I said that writing supporting points for the thesis would prove difficult due to the word requirement and three other bullet points yet to be answered, but that it would end up working out in our favor? If you think about it, the main idea of "preparing me to be able to contribute to the wave of innovation" was answered (though not as directly as we might have preferred) by talking about the educational and career objectives. One could argue that advancing through increasingly challenging educational and career objectives provides the best preparation for contributing to innovation in the manufacturing industry. The answers to bullet points 2 and 4 after the introduction ended up being our supporting points to our thesis statement. This continued the flow within the essay, allowing the reader to keep connecting the essay's ideas in order for them to form a complete view of me both as a student and an applicant. You may be asking what I did that allowed this flow to happen despite me being put in a situation where I went straight for answering prompts directly instead of prioritizing flow of supporting points as a typical essay structure would entail. The answer lies in the constant use of connection types riddled throughout the essay that tie this flow together. I will explain more about these connection types in the Final Breakdown Comments section, so stay with me. I first want to quickly finish the Conclusion Breakdown because the conclusion also plays into effect with how connection types organically achieved flow within this essay.

CONCLUSION BREAKDOWN | ESSAY 5

The conclusion, similar to the body, also takes a different form due to the word-count restriction. We still have the concept of a conclusion present because, ultimately, the essay needs a clear and intentional ending. The end of sentence 8 brought this essay's word count to 264 out of 300. What's more is that we still have bullet point 5 to answer, which asks how the scholarship I am applying for will help to achieve the objectives I stated. I didn't have many options here. In a proper essay structure, we would want to find a way to creatively bring our thought pattern back to the 30,000-foot view in a way that revisits the supporting points, revisits the thesis statement, and provides a strong ending. With 36 words left of flexibility, my best bet was to give an answer to bullet point 5's prompt in a creative way that leaves a strong ending, and leave it at that. Sentence 9 is my best attempt at doing just that. I take the angle that while college can feel like a financial burden, it's ultimately an investment in myself—and without support from resources like this scholarship, I wouldn't be able to reach the objectives I've set for my future. Sentence 9 closes by emphasizing that the cost of college is justified, as the opportunities it provides will advance my life in ways that would not be possible without it. This brought the word count to 299. With the way this essay went, I needed every bit of that 299 because I was constantly reformatting sentences all throughout this essay in order to meet the word-count restriction. This is another example of if given a word-count restriction, use every bit of it as you can. Knowing me, I am surprised that I didn't fit in one last word to make it to 300!

FINAL BREAKDOWN COMMENTS | ESSAY 5

Now that the full essay is broken down, we can finally address what was brought up in the Body Breakdown section with how flow was organically created the way bullet points 2 and 4 were addressed outside of a standard supporting point approach. *Flow was achieved because connection types were used all throughout the essay, just not in the format that you might have realized.* When looking at sentences 1 through 5, the passionate connection used here is the most obvious considering it came from an essay without a word-count restriction and was reused. Just to reiterate, the passionate connection occurs when sentence 4 talks about how my major of Manufacturing Engineering will allow me to be a part of the high-level idea detailed in sentences 1 through 3 of how manufacturing plays a huge role in today's society. I was able to build up the "passionate" feeling with the attention-getter and thesis statement, both helping to prove how impressive manufacturing was to me. Now, look closely at sentence 6, which, again, was the start of the body "sentences." I ended that sentence with the phrase "and society as a whole." Including this little snippet elevates sentence 6 from simply a point about my career's objectives (addressing bullet point 2) into a point in which I am communicating to the scholarship judges that I am mindful of things greater than myself. This snippet hints at the beginnings of what could morph into a true emotional, personal, or passionate connection if given more runway to be explained upon. Emotional because I could have went into how "society" has hungry kids that I can use my studies to help feed with solutions I come up with the deeper I get into my career field. Personal because I could have went into how "society" has flaws in terms of the quality of life it presents to some people's reality. So, including an example here of how *my* quality of life was negatively affected due to resources being neglected on my end somehow because of how manufacturing lacked in a certain segment is one way I could swing this. Passionate because I could have went into how "society" is where it is today due to the manufacturing breakthroughs of the past and how I want to be a part of the breakthroughs of the future.

Obviously, I did not include that level of detail to truly define this phrase as one of those connection types, but the setup is there to get the scholarship judge thinking of how I will be able to affect "society." That is the main lesson here. *When word count is scarce and causes an essay structure to be broken down as much as it was in this essay, even mentioning phrases such as "and society as a whole," when you can't get to a true connection type, acts as a sort of "mini" connection type that ends up bolstering your message.* How flow ended up happening "organically," how this essay still made sense, and how you could argue supporting points existed for the thesis statement despite not directly being planned for was due to the fact that I had gotten so accustomed to tailoring my writing in such a way that emphasized, extracted, and included connection types everywhere I could fit. That, when faced with phrasing challenges in terms of cutting ideas short due to word-count restrictions, the connection type writing style still showed up, albeit in a reduced or watered-down context. *These "mini" connections can then be looked back on and applied to your higher-level thesis statement in such a way that they support it.* So, if we were to isolate sentence 6 only, it's not so much that the phrase "and society as a whole" is the sole supporter of "preparing me to be able to contribute to the wave of innovation." Rather, the higher-level thought of mentioning "society" is related to, and flows with, what was talked about in the introduction. If you look at phrases such as "global gross domestic product" and "improving the everyday lives of a world population" in the introduction, those are broader topics that can connect to a broader "society" term, therefore making the use of a "mini" connection in this manner make sense. So, to end the example within sentence 6, earlier in the Body Breakdown section we mentioned how career objectives could technically be looked at as a supporting point to the "preparation" aspect that was suggested as the thesis. On the other hand, you could also argue how "getting a job," which is the root of what sentence 6 is saying, isn't necessarily answering how that would "prepare" me, *but*, with the "mini" connection used at the end of the sentence, you could then relate this idea of "getting a job" to the greater idea of "society." *Since the reader knows based on my introduction that my focus is to impact society through manufacturing, they will then relate the subject of what sentence 6 is saying to the broader message of the essay, thus making it a supporting point even though sentence 6 was originally crafted to directly answer bullet point 2.* Without this "mini" connection at the end, this sentence wouldn't be as meaningful. Therefore, the use of a "mini" connection in this way created flow this essay so desperately needed. *In this context, flow is the ability to realize supporting points out of sentences that may not fit perfectly in an overall proper essay structure.*

To end this point, let's quickly highlight the rest of the "mini" connections that were used. Sentence 7 contains the phrase "allow me to continue to grow my appreciation for manufacturing." Sentence 8 contains the phrase "so that I may be one step closer in fulfilling my objective of making my own impact in the manufacturing industry." Sentence 9 contains the phrase "although a college education is a burden financially, it is a great investment." Take sentence 9's "mini" connection for example. It wasn't mentioned in the Conclusion Breakdown because I wanted to wait until this point to mention it, but here we see a great beginning of a personal connection, stating how college is a burden due to it being too expensive. Although we couldn't elaborate more on how it affected us personally (hence why it is labeled as "mini"), using this phrasing to accomplish a "mini" personal connection still speaks volumes to the scholarship judge. Tell them how much it stinks to be paying for college! Make them feel your pain! Sentence 9, as well as the other "mini" connections just listed, truly bring out the human aspect within your writing. *The biggest lesson here is you want to elevate your writing to a point where you are always bringing your ideas back to a point that is greater than yourself.* It is not just about you at the surface. Getting into the habit of fitting full connection types in your writing will get you to the point that "mini" connections will happen automatically when put into situations such as the one I found myself in with this 300-word-count essay. It gives layers to the story you tell, and gives deeper reasoning as to why the organization should pick you to win the scholarship. It will be because the story you told in your essay painted you as a person, and not just another name on the list of scholarship applications they must get through.

I ended up winning this scholarship, and originally they told me that it was an award of $1,500 that would only be applied for one year. A few days later, almost like a miracle, the organization reached out to me and said they wanted to change the award to $2,500 which would be automatically renewed every year I had left in college. I forgot the reasoning as to why. All I remember was that they asked me if this was okay to do. I accepted the change without hesitation, as it provided additional funds I could apply toward my tuition. The harder you work toward scholarships, the more you open the door for opportunities like this to happen to you as well. Keep grinding, because in the end it will all be worth it.

Essay 6	
Organization:	Material Handing Education Foundation, Inc. (MHEFI)
Title:	Howard Bernstein Scholarship
Date Written:	02/20/2016 Junior Year, 2nd Semester (Spring)
Total Winnings:	$10,000 $5,000 Applied to Junior Year, 2nd Semester Tuition (Spring) $5,000 Applied to Senior Year, 2nd Semester Tuition (Spring)
Prompt:	• *Future study plans (if applicable).* • *How did you first learn about the material handling, logistics, and supply chain industry? What sparked your interest to study this field?* • *Describe any past experience or planned future work with the industry.* • *Describe your short-term career goals.* • *Describe your long-term career goals.*
Word Count:	N/A

PROMPT BULLET POINT 1

SHORT-ANSWER PARAGRAPH 1

" ⑧ { [1]*[I am a passionate, forward-thinking junior Manufacturing Engineering student seeking new and exciting opportunities to] apply my knowledge [and skills to a driven company] in order to positively contribute to its future innovations in its respective field and society as a whole.* [2]*[Right] after my undergraduate studies, I [aim] to work with a company that fits my interests [in the manufacturing industry so that I may] continue to grow my appreciation for manufacturing as well as start to specialize in a specific field which I still have yet to determine.* [3]*Also, in an effort to keep improving both personally and professionally, attending graduate school will be a series consideration in about 5 to 7 years so that I may be one step closer in filling my goal of making my own impact in the world of manufacturing.* } "

PROMPT BULLET POINT 2

SHORT-ANSWER PARAGRAPH 1

" ⑤ { [1]*Growing up having had two older siblings already attend college, I was able to learn a lot from their accomplishments as well as their mistakes that they made throughout their years of study that really made me ponder what it is I wanted to do with my life.* [2]*My eldest brother, [REMOVED NAME], who studied Biology at Loyola University in Chicago and who has also been a great role model in my life, made me reflect on whether I wanted to pursue a career in a particular field of science.* [3]*Taking several advanced science classes in high school made me realize that, although interesting, wouldn't be the right fit as to what field of work I could see myself doing in the future.* [4]*My sister, [REMOVED NAME], who also studied at Loyola University and majored in Political Science, made me consider a field of study in government, consulting, or social work but again it did not pertain to my particular interests.* [5]*As I continued my search, I started to take an in-depth look into how the world itself was moving forward.* [6]*It seemed like more and more people nowadays have greater demands and expect those demands to be met to achieve a certain standard of living that people fifty years ago would have never dreamed of being obtained. [7]My search ultimately led to the conclusion that without mass-production,* [*in addition to various material handling, logistics, and supply chain techniques*]*, the world would not be where it is today.*}

SHORT-ANSWER PARAGRAPH 2

③{ [1]*Manufacturing,* [*which in essence is the combination of all the factors listed previously*]*, has become one of the most pivotal industries in today's economy, accounting for a significant percentage of employment as well as global gross domestic product. [2]In the U.S. alone, the drive for innovation, competitiveness, and constant improvement that comes from our ever-changing manufacturing environment has kept our nation's spot as a worldwide leader in quality and cutting-edge technology. [3]The numerous methods for product development and distribution that exist provide endless opportunities for improving the everyday lives of a world population that continues to grow. [4]Having the ability to contribute to this wave of innovation in which the end result is a better tomorrow is why I have decided to study Manufacturing Engineering at Bradley University. [5]I am ecstatic to have found a college major I can apply my creative and ambitious personality to in the hopes of implementing my own solutions to the world of manufacturing so that I may have a positive impact, not only on society, but* [*on the material handling, logistics, and supply chain industries as well*]*.* }"

PROMPT BULLET POINT 3

SHORT-ANSWER PARAGRAPH 1

"②{ [1][*For the past two summers*]*, I was* [*fortunate enough*] *to work as a Manufacturing Engineering Intern at Rockford Products LLC, a manufacturing facility that specializes in the making of cold-formed products. [2]*[*During the summer of 2014*]*, I was assigned various projects including the design and implementation of an ergonomic rake in response to a workplace incident that happened on the shop floor. [3]After numerous hours of research and consultation with fellow engineers and shop floor workers, I* *designed a rake prototype using SolidWorks that complimented the natural body posture of the workers that used it for the specific task of sorting out parts. [4]I was able to outline the cost of the rake as well as how Rockford Products would go about making it. [5]The rake was designed to reduce the risk of workplace incidents as well as increase shop floor worker health and productivity. [6]Other projects I worked on included the design and implementation of a procedure to help reduce the likelihood of mixing burnished and non-burnished parts together during the part's routing. [7]Also, I mapped out different forklift lane layouts to accompany OSHA standards without compromising travel times around the factory.*}

SHORT-ANSWER PARAGRAPH 2

④{ *[1]Now as a second-year intern during the summer of 2015, I was tasked to work closely with the Quality Engineering Department in order to tackle a massive quality control project. [2]Rockford Products is in the process of transitioning to using a different data collection system, known as InfinityQS, that machine operators use in order to input data from dimensional checks they carry out. [3]The first step was to update numerous control plan documents that list which processes the raw material must pass through in order to become a finished product. [4]Most revisions included pinpointing different dimensions from each part by looking at the engineering prints and labeling the frequency of how often those dimensions would be measured when the part undergoes each process in the routing. [5]Once revisions for a part are complete, that part must then be programmed into InfinityQS.*}

SHORT-ANSWER PARAGRAPH 3

⑥{ *[1]My team and I were also required to setup the navigational menus within the software that machine operators would use on the shop floor in order to find the part that they want to add data for. [2]After learning how to operate the software for ourselves, we came up with a simple, straight forward procedure that minimizes the time it takes for them to find where they want to go on the system in order to input the necessary data they collect. [3]By implementing this new procedure, we also lessened the amount of work it takes for our team to program the part numbers into the system.*}

SHORT-ANSWER PARAGRAPH 4

⑦{ [1]*During this past Fall 2015 semester I took a materials engineering class in my manufacturing engineering curriculum in which we were tasked with a term project consisting of design modification, materials selection, manufacturing, and cost estimation of an engineering part of our choice.* [2]*My partner and I decided on looking at how the standard frame of a bike can function under the restrictive and quantifiable conditions of stress, temperature, environment, weight, and other justified assumptions.* [3]*Those assumptions are: factor of safety, temperature range, max load, mass-producibility, and use of standard pipe sizes.*

SHORT-ANSWER PARAGRAPH 5

[1]*After we calculated the limits of our bike (For Example: Our bike had a calculated fatigue life of 3,660,000 cycles, where a cycle is defined as a bump or crack in the road that provides a noticeable impact to the rider) and considering the other mechanical properties of materials, we began the process of finding the best material choice for this bike and its application.* [2]*Our application was that this bike was to function in a city type environment where it would act as a rentable bicycle and see various riders with various loads that experiences multiple uses per day.* [3]*After much discussion and research as well as considering several additional factors like amounts of corrosion resistance, if certain materials are lighter/heavier, less expensive, or easier to manufacture than other materials, just to name a few, we concluded our research with finding two ideal material candidates for the bike: AISI 303 stainless steel or 6061 aluminum.* [4]*Noting the fact that both metals can be used for our ideal purposes, it came down to preferences over a couple factors.* [5]*Although aluminum is less dense and a bit cheaper, it does not typically last as long as steel frames.* [6]*In addition, many people have complained that aluminum bikes tend to be much harder to ride, being too stiff and lacking in resilience, thus not storing and releasing enough energy for a smoother ride.* [7]*So although stainless steel will cost a bit more, since we don't have*

a preference on any particular weight and would ideally prefer a longer and more comfortable ride, we chose stainless steel as our ideal choice in material for creating our bike frame. [8]We also concluded that the manufacturing process most suited for assembling this bike frame would be Tungsten Inert Gas (TIG) Welding and the cost for the total amount of material required equaled $19.77. [9]Note that the considerations of manufacturing processes and cost were taken into account before final material selection too.

SHORT-ANSWER PARAGRAPH 6

[1]This project gave me a greater understanding of how to approach the process of choosing the best material for an engineering part I am working with. [2]It also gave me an idea of what I can expect to find in the material-handling industry after graduation. [3]With the knowledge gained from my bike frame project and other classes, as well as the work experience gained through my internship with Rockford Products LLC, I am confident I will be ready to positively contribute to any industry in the manufacturing field, it being material handling, logistics, or supply chain, etc., so that I may help contribute to a better future, in both the industry and the world.} "

PROMPT BULLET POINT 4

SHORT-ANSWER PARAGRAPH 1

" [1]My short-term career goals start with finding an exciting internship at a company where I can relate to what they produce and what they believe as a company. [2]Although I am looking mainly for internships either in Peoria or Chicago areas, I am open to relocating to a company that is in a different location because I want the best possible chance to get to experience and learn from a different city and a different field of manufacturing other than my internship I have held for the past two years in Rockford, Illinois. [3]Entering my senior year, I will strive to pull off straight A's and succeed in my Senior Project course requirement. [4]Also, I will continue to try and find as much possible financial aid outside of my university since I am in charge of paying off my own tuition. [5]After graduation in May of 2017, I will start the process of finding my first full-time position as a Manufacturing Engineer with a concentration in Lean Manufacturing."

PROMPT BULLET POINT 5

SHORT-ANSWER PARAGRAPH 1

"[1]My long-term career goals are after gaining experience at a company for a few years, I will seriously consider attending graduate school so that I can further my expertise of lean manufacturing. [2]Also, I plan to look into starting some form of investing, learning to master the Polish language, and maybe starting to pursue some invention ideas that I have been writing down throughout the years. [3]After several years in the industry, I hope to have been promoted to higher positions within the company I work for, eventually landing the position of manager or executive one day."

ESSAY 6 BREAKDOWN

PROMPT BREAKDOWN | ESSAY 6

Essay 6 is another multi-layered scholarship essay prompt that was written one month after Essay 5. During my scholarship applications, I encountered prompts of this nature less frequently than the standard one-question prompts discussed in Essays 1 through 4. They may seem intimidating because, as mentioned in Essay 5's breakdown, just one of the prompt bullet point questions could be expanded on to form an essay by itself. The challenge then becomes how one should handle writing an essay that points them in several different directions. Although it depends on the organization's prompt requirements, generally the essays I have encountered involving multiple questions expect you to answer all of the bullet points in one essay unless told otherwise. This was the case for Essay 5. Essay 5's bullet points acted as the building blocks for what should be included in one singular essay. They inherently gave you the blueprint for how your essay should flow. Similarly in Essay 6, we see multiple bullet points being asked of us; however, there is one stark difference. When working through the online application, this organization gave five different text boxes to type each bullet point answer in separately. This meant that essentially they wanted five short-answer paragraphs instead of one large essay.

Knowing this, my mindset when approaching this essay was two-fold. Number one, I wanted to be mindful of the content that each of these short answers provided. Since none of these sections had word-count restrictions, I could have written one thousand words for each, but doing so would have weakened my overall message. So, I decided to stick to a short-answer format, going in-depth as needed. Number two, I wanted to keep the style of using connection types wherever possible to strengthen the message of the short answers I write and accomplish the "mini" connection type effect that was described in the breakdown of Essay 5.

The reason that I am still considering this an essay even though the paragraphs are split up is because you are still writing the same amount of content that you would write in a scholarship essay, only this time each section is unrelated. Unlike an essay, the content you write in a multiple short-answer format won't tie together to become one cohesive message. With this, you will see that it is more difficult to follow a proper essay structure involving an introduction, body, and conclusion even if you tried thinning them out into sentences within each paragraph like Essay 5. Therefore, my approach for each of these bullet points was to concentrate less on the essay structure, flow, and transitions, and instead focus on providing a strong, straight-to-the-point answer that utilized connection types where appropriate. *Writing short answers is like writing body sections of an essay where you can elaborate on your supporting points right away.*

Each prompt bullet point that is provided acts like its own thesis statement, and your short-answer response acts as the body with an opportunity to close with a conclusion if desired.

We can also observe that this prompt introduces a slightly different theme. This organization is primarily focused on what is known as "material handling." Material handling is a systematic process that involves moving, storing, protecting, and controlling materials and products throughout a manufacturing or distribution process. It's how goods get from point A to point B for a process to function. As it applies to my field of manufacturing, material handling includes processes such as delivering raw materials to a manufacturing line in a way that continually feeds production, or transferring finished goods from the end of the line into warehouse storage. Although material handling is distinct from manufacturing, I still qualified for this organization's scholarship because the manufacturing field inherently incorporates numerous material-handling practices. That said, I made a point to frame each idea in terms of its material handling relevance rather than viewing it purely through a manufacturing lens. With this, let's dive into how this multi-layered prompt was answered. Instead of the standard essay breakdown we have normally been following, I will break down each of the prompt's bullet points individually since no proper essay structure exists between them.

BULLET POINT 1 BREAKDOWN | ESSAY 6

Bullet point 1 starts off by asking about my future plans followed by the phrase "(if applicable)." This was the first question that appeared on this scholarship's online submission page; however, the scholarship itself did not present it as one of its primary questions. I knew this because, although it is not explicitly shown in this book, the scholarship's website had this bullet point as pre-curser to what they truly wanted to know in the latter bullet points. The latter bullet points all were numbered while this one was not, implying that it was of lesser importance to the organization. Also, the fact that it says "(if applicable)" indicates that a scholarship applicant could skip this section entirely if they truly did not have any future plans. Knowing what the teachings are in this book though, we want to take every opportunity the scholarship gives us in order to stand out from the rest of the applicants, so you already know that we are going to answer this prompt no matter what.

This section came easily because I had finished Essay 5 one month earlier, and its prompt included similar bullet points about future plans. Therefore, I looked back and reused what turned out to be Paragraph 8 of the commonly reused sections. Sentence 1 was heavily modified from the original Paragraph 8 although still kept the same flow. The beginning of the original Paragraph 8 contained the phrase "after my undergraduate studies," which technically refers to "future plans"; however, Paragraph 8 was written in the middle of Essay 5 and was already part of that essay's flow. I thought that if I reused Paragraph 8 as-is, it wouldn't flow right. So, I added a better introductory sentence that introduces the topic of "future plans" in a way that also shows my passion for what is to come and presents this idea in a "mini" connection style. The "mini" connection being "and society as a whole." After this sentence restructuring, I make small edits within sentence 2 before ultimately leaving the rest of Paragraph 8 intact to let it speak for itself. This was a simple answer to a simple question, and it was time to move on to the next bullet point.

BULLET POINT 2 BREAKDOWN | ESSAY 6

Bullet Point 2 was technically the first primary bullet point since the online submission page numbered it officially as "1," had larger text, and did not say the phrase "(if applicable)" after it. This meant that I needed to give a more detailed short answer for this question. The prompt asks how I learned about the material handling, logistics, and supply chain industries, and what sparked my interest in it. This is similar to the prompt in Essay 3 where it asks why I wanted a career in manufacturing. Both roughly ask why I choose the field I am in. Looking back at Essay 3, I saw that Paragraph 5 answered this question perfectly, so I reused that section to start this short-answer paragraph. For a detailed breakdown of the intricacies of the techniques used in Paragraph 5, revisit Essay 3 where they were covered earlier. Here in Essay 7, I mainly want to focus on the reuse aspect of this section. The only edit I needed to make to Paragraph 5 was in sentence 7 where I added a snippet to include the exact phrasing of "material handling, logistics, and supply chain." This was so the scholarship judges knew I am keeping their theme at the forefront of the subject since this reused section was originally written based on manufacturing only. This serves as another clear example of the importance of revising reused sections to ensure they align with the application at hand. If I had forgotten this small edit, I probably would have lost the scholarship, since the section wouldn't make sense without mentioning "material handling, logistics, and supply chain."

Reusing Paragraph 5 helped me answer the first question in bullet point 2, which focused on how I *first* learned about the industry. The second question of bullet point 2, which asked "what sparked my interest to study this field," still needed to be addressed. This is where I looked to my old content and found that Paragraph 3 had the exact phrasing that stated why I decided to study the major that I currently was in college for.

It included specific examples of what sparked my interest in the field of manufacturing, so, I elected to reuse Paragraph 3 to answer the second part of this short answer. Again, we will only be focusing on the reuse aspect of this section because Paragraph 3 was broken down in more technical detail about the strategies contained in its writing in Essay 4 and 5. Please revisit those breakdowns as needed. Regarding the reuse of this section, I only needed to make slight edits to sentences 1 and 5 to make sure the section applied to the material handling theme and that was all it took to complete answering bullet point 2.

BULLET POINT 3 BREAKDOWN | ESSAY 6

Bullet point 3 is the second primary question of the application and asks to describe any past experience or planned future work with the material-handling industry. My first course of action was to see if I could continue to reuse past content for this short answer. *One advantage of writing short answers is that reusing paragraphs is easier, since they don't need to integrate as seamlessly as they would in the middle of a full standard essay.* They are a bit more forgiving in this way because, again, it is more about making your point directly versus telling a story to make yourself stand out as a candidate. This is the approach I took for bullet point 3. I didn't have a lot of "planned future work" as the prompt implied. However, I had a lot of content written about my past experiences that I could apply here. As a reminder, the focus here is on the reuse aspect. As Paragraphs 2, 4, and 6 are reintroduced for this short answer, you can revisit Essays 2 and 4 if you want a refresher on why these paragraphs align with the scholarship guidelines discussed in this book.

You will notice that the first paragraph of this short answer is a reuse of Paragraph 2. This section had a strong description of what I had done at my internships that I thought it would fit well here to start. Sentences 1 and 2 show the minor edits I made to clarify that I was differentiating between two internships rather than one. My next step was then to combine all of the sections found in Paragraph 2 into one. If I had just copied all of Paragraph 2 for what it was, it would have been too spread out and also contained too much information. This is followed by the second paragraph of bullet point 3, which reuses Paragraph 4 in its entirety without any edits needing to be made. Paragraph 4 was a perfect addition because it was a continuation of the supporting points of my past experiences. Continuing to the third paragraph of bullet point 3, Paragraph 6 is reused here to finish talking about my internship experiences, also without any edits needed. Paragraphs 4 and 6 didn't require any changes because they were already concise and to the point.

My primary objective in responding to bullet point 3 was to present substantial past experience, demonstrating to the judges that I had been proactive in developing within their industry. The problem was that, at this point in the answer, I had copied almost all of my manufacturing experience but hadn't included any material handling examples or edited the manufacturing content to apply to material handling. I could have easily gone back and completed the latter—editing the content to apply to material handling—but I decided to write a brand-new content piece instead. I recognized that relying on weak material handling connections by merely repurposing my manufacturing content would make my examples less effective. Therefore, the fourth, fifth, and sixth paragraphs of this short answer use Paragraph 7, which was written on this short answer for the first time. There is something rather amusing when looking back at this added piece of new content I'd like to point out. Paragraph 7 was written with a great intention to give as strong of an example as I could about material handling. I wrote about a very technical project that I had just completed, and thought that it would really impress the judges. Don't get me wrong, I think it did since this essay ended up winning; however, the amusing part was that I actually made a mistake at the time of writing this short answer. I thought my project, which was from a materials engineering course, was the same as what the material-handling industry worked with. I saw the words "material" and thought they were the same thing when in reality they are two completely different subjects! The project I wrote about was part of a materials *engineering* course, where we study how the properties of different materials are changed and manipulated. This is drastically different from material *handling* which deals with how raw and finished goods are transported in a production system. For whatever reason, when I was applying for this scholarship, I had missed that simple fact, and that is why you see Paragraph 7 go in a direction that seems to differ from the overall theme.

Mistakes aside, Paragraph 7 is yet another example of how you could write about a personal experience you had in a way that forms a passionate connection for the reader. It is also an example of how you can write about a personal experience that isn't necessarily an internship, yet is still as impressive if you find yourself missing actual internship experience. To summarize how Paragraph 7 was written, I walked through how the project came together and tried using as many technical references as I could. Again, I thought these were technical references for material *handling*, but instead they were for materials *engineering*. The concept here is the same though. If you want to impress scholarship judges with your personal experience for *any* theme, go into detail with the terms, ideas, and solutions people in *that field* would recognize. Doing so shows that you take the industry seriously, are genuinely interested in it, and have high potential within it. Despite making this mistake with writing about a different "material" topic, I'd like to think the project I wrote about impressed them enough to have them look past my blunder!

By the end of Paragraph 7, I felt I had included enough proven experience that addressed bullet point 3 to make me stand out in my application. Although this short answer ended up being longer than I expected, I felt it needed a brief conclusion to tie together the ideas presented. The sixth and final paragraph of this short answer is three sentences that bring the reader back to a 30,000-foot-view thought pattern. Sentence 3 also demonstrates a "mini" passionate connection by showing my fascination with manufacturing, material handling, logistics, and supply chain, and my desire to use that knowledge to create a better future.

BULLET POINTS 4 & 5 BREAKDOWN | ESSAY 6

I am going to keep this breakdown brief and combine bullet points 4 and 5 together since there is not much content to explain here. If you look closer at the nature of the questions of bullet points 4 and 5 themselves, it makes sense why we do not need such a deep analysis. First of all, these bullet points ask about short and long-term career goals. These questions are more student-centric versus the primary bullet points of 2 and 3 where those questions were more industry-centric. Since the organization is focused on material handling, they naturally place more emphasis on the accomplishments you've had in their industry so far. Short and long-term goals matter, but what really sets a candidate apart is the impact they've already made and continue to make in their industry. That is the whole reason why the organization even exists. They don't exist because students have goals; they exist because businesses in the material-handling industry justify the need for an organization like this. So, it would make sense why more weight would need to be put on the specific questions that ask about the industry. They want to know that the future generations will be taking their industry to the next level, *and how you do that is to figure out and thoroughly answer the questions they find more meaning in*.

A second indication that I shouldn't go too in depth on bullet points 4 and 5 was their placement at the end of the question sequence. They want to know about questions related to the industry first, then about future plans after. This isn't to say you can't write more than I did if you encounter prompts like this. I am just bringing to light why I started to lessen my message when I got to these questions. Also, earlier I mentioned that the sum of the short-answer sections essentially make up an essay. Since the bulk of the "essay" was already taken up with bullet points 2 and 3, the remaining can be used as a conclusion of sorts. That said, I didn't use any formal strategy or technique when answering about my short or long-term goals. For each bullet point, I simply gave an honest answer about the best idea I had for my future after reflection and tried describing it as best I could. The worst thing I could have done is not say anything, or be very minimal with my ambitions. Even though they are short in length, the answers I wrote provide various examples of future plans. I did not just limit myself to one thing. This was the best approach I could take considering I had minimal content. Listing out a few different career plans gives the impression to the scholarship organization that I am keeping my options open, I am striving to learn the most I can, and I truly want to become the best I can be as a student within the industry. That is where I ended these bullet points which brought me to the end of this scholarship application.

FINAL BREAKDOWN COMMENTS | ESSAY 6

The biggest takeaway from this scholarship is observing how easy putting together these short-answer responses was using all of the reused sections from past scholarships. It wasn't until over halfway through that I finally had to write a new portion to the essay. On top of that, the short-answer aspect of this scholarship's essay portion made the reuse even easier due to no essay structure being needed. Notice how far I was into my college journey at the time of writing this essay. I was just beginning my second semester of my junior year. By that time, I had submitted so many applications and had written so many essays that I had a plethora of previous content to choose from to reuse. Not only that, but because this was the first time applying to this organization's scholarship, I was able to reuse all of my best content since this is the first time they would be seeing my writing. All this is to say that when you keep applying and writing scholarship essays, you will reach a point in your scholarship journey, just as I did with this one, where you will be able to apply similar reuse strategies to lessen the burden of writing essays.

Ironically enough, I was sitting in my materials engineering class—the subject I mistakenly wrote about on the essay instead of material handling—when I received an email saying I had been selected to win this scholarship. Despite being seated in the front row of the classroom, I subtly opened the email on my phone to reveal that not only had I won $5,000 for my junior year, but that this same scholarship would repeat the same winnings my senior year for a total of $10,000. The reason I vividly remember what class I was in, where I was sitting, and how I reacted was because this was the largest scholarship payout I had ever received. I was in absolute shock that I had won such a significant amount! I remember writing on a piece of my note paper the words "I just won $5,000!" At that moment it seemed unreal. I felt a wave of relief, joy, and excitement when reading this news. It truly felt as though the years of exhaustive effort I had devoted to scholarships were finally bearing fruit. It was an amazing feeling, and one that I will never forget. Thank you for allowing me to relive that brief moment of joy once again as I write about it here in this book. I expand on this feeling because I want to share with you what is waiting for *you* down your scholarship journey. When you experience moments like this—as if a weight is lifted off of your shoulders knowing a large amount of tuition is paid off—that's when you realize all the hard work was worth it. Every word written. Every application submitted. All these things can come together to open a door that can truly change your college financial situation. This was the door that opened for me, and I hope yours will be one even greater.

Essay 7	
Organization:	Grand Lodge of A.F. & A.M. of Illinois Ancient Accepted Scottish Rite (AASR)
Title:	Sherwood and Evelyn Kresin Memorial Scholarship
Date Written:	02/21/2016
	Junior Year, 2nd Semester (Spring)
Total Winnings:	$1,000
	Applied to Junior Year, 2nd Semester Tuition (Spring)
Prompt:	*Provide your thoughts regarding your choice of career field, your aspirations, and your plans for the future. Any insights that you provide will greatly assist the committee in making its evaluation. Please make your statement as legible as possible. Attaching a separate page or writing on the back is acceptable.*
Word Count:	N/A

INTRODUCTION

" ③{ [1]*In recent years, manufacturing has come to be one of the most pivotal industries in today's economy, accounting for a significant percentage of employment as well as global gross domestic product.* [2]*In the U.S. alone, the drive for innovation, competitiveness, and continual improvement that comes from our ever-changing manufacturing environment has kept our nation's spot as a worldwide leader in quality and cutting-edge technology.* [3]*The numerous methods of product development and distribution that exist provide endless opportunities for improving the everyday lives of a world population that does not cease to stop growing.* [4]*Having the ability to contribute to this wave of innovation in which the end result is a better tomorrow is why I have decided to study Manufacturing Engineering at Bradley University.* [5]*I am ecstatic to have found a college major I can apply my creative and ambitious personality to in the hopes of implementing my own solutions to the world of manufacturing so that I may have a positive impact, not only on society, but* [*to the community I serve*] *as well.*}

BODY 1

②{ [1][*For the past two summers*]*, I was* [*fortunate enough*] *to work as a Manufacturing Engineering Intern at Rockford Products LLC, a manufacturing facility that specializes in the making of cold-formed products.* [2][*During the summer of 2014*]*, I was assigned a number of different projects including the design and implementation of an ergonomic rake in response to a workplace incident that happened on the shop floor.* [3]*Other projects I worked on included the design and implementation of a procedure to help reduce the likelihood of mixing burnished and non-burnished parts together during the part's routing* [*as well as the revision of forklift lane layouts on the shipping dock which had to comply with OSHA's safety standards*].
}

BODY 2

④{ [1]*Now as a second-year intern during the summer of 2015, I was tasked to work closely with the Quality Engineering Department in order to tackle a massive quality control project.*

[2]Rockford Products is currently in the process of transitioning to using a different data collection system, known as InfinityQS, that machine operators use in order to input data from the setup, in-process, and end-of-run dimensional checks they carry out. [3]The first step in undertaking this project was to update numerous control plan documents that list which specific processes the raw material must pass through in order to become a finished product. [4]Most revisions included pinpointing different dimensions from each part by looking at the engineering prints and labeling the frequency of how often those dimensions would be measured when the part undergoes each process in the routing. [5]Once revisions for a particular part are complete, that part must then be programmed into InfinityQS.} *[6]Every part in Rockford Product's product line calls for different dimensions, characteristics, and routings that have to be separately entered so that all critical data is recorded properly and, based off that data, can be used for improving machining processes in the future.*

BODY 3

⑥{ *[1]My team and I were also required to setup the navigational menus within the software that the operators would use on the shop floor in order to find the part that they want to add data for. [2]After learning how to operate the software for ourselves and numerous discussions of how we would want the operators to use the software, we came up with a simple, straight forward procedure that minimizes the time it takes for them to find where they want to go on the system in order to input the necessary data they collect. [3]By implementing this new procedure, we also lessened the amount of work it takes for our team to program the part numbers into the system.*}

CONCLUSION

[1]Although still in college, seeing how I was able to positively influence a company that has an impact on my community reassured me that Manufacturing Engineering is for me. ①{ *[2]Being a first-generation college student, I am faced with a lot of pressure to succeed. [3]However, realizing just how great of an*

opportunity I have, I plan to work tirelessly until I have achieved [all my goals]. [4]With my newfound knowledge after graduation, I aim to work within my community of Rockford, Illinois in order to give back what has been given to me all these years; a chance at a new life and new opportunities for the residents, and especially the younger generation.} "

ESSAY 7 BREAKDOWN

PROMPT BREAKDOWN | ESSAY 7

The prompt starts by asking about my choice of career field, as well as my aspirations and plans for the future. Also, no word-count restrictions are imposed on this essay. Notice how this is the first prompt that is not directly related to manufacturing. This scholarship came from an organization I stumbled upon during one of my online searches, buried deep in the later pages of Google's results. I didn't really understand what their organization was at the time. All I knew was that they were offering financial aid I was eligible for, so I went ahead and applied! The fact that this prompt was more generic than the previous ones didn't throw me off, because the scholarship's theme would still end up being manufacturing-related—that was my career field after all. What I did notice, though, when looking deeper at this prompt, was that I answered prompt questions similar to this in the past, both about why I am in the career field I am in as well as what my future plans are. This immediately triggered alarm bells in my head! I knew this essay would be another great opportunity to apply the reuse strategy again, so, I proceeded to investigate which pieces of previously written content I could dust off and potentially reuse. That's when I centered on an essay from an earlier breakdown we had covered—Essay 4. It wasn't so much the similarity between Essay 4's prompt and the prompt I'm covering in this breakdown; rather, it was the substance within Essay 4 that made it stand out. In that essay, I found everything this prompt was looking for—my thoughts on my career field, my aspirations, and my plans for the future. The more I read through Essay 4, debating on what bits and pieces to salvage to begin writing this new essay, the more I realized that I could keep the majority of Essay 4 as it was, and, after a few tweaks, submit it. That is what I ended up doing. You see that, similar to Essay 4, this essay uses the same sequence of Paragraph 3, 2, 4, and 6, in that order, with the conclusion being the only large section that was changed. This is the strongest example so far of almost entirely reusing a previous essay for a new organization's application. That being said, due to this being a near-copy of Essay 4, I won't overanalyze this essay and rehash the same points that were already covered. I will provide brief summaries of the ideas captured as an overview; however, if you want the full explanation once more, I encourage you to revisit Essay 4's breakdown if you would like a reminder on how exactly that essay came together and why it functions well in a scholarship setting. For this essay's breakdown, I'll go deeper into the reuse aspect and explain how I managed to submit a brand-new scholarship application that still yielded winnings—all while avoiding the hardest part: writing the essay.

INTRODUCTION BREAKDOWN | ESSAY 7

To start the introduction of this essay I reused Paragraph 3, which was originally drafted as a new piece of content in Essay 4. Paragraph 3 pairs a great attention-getter with a high-level thought where sentences 1 through 3 talk about the broad scope of manufacturing in the world. Using this as an attention-getter for this essay is riskier because the scholarship audience isn't necessarily manufacturing fanatics as compared to previous manufacturing-specific organizations that I applied to. The draw and allure of manufacturing would be less-so with these judges considering they are coming from a more non-bias background, being that their organization doesn't center on any specific college major. *This is precisely why you would want to use a 30,000-foot-view angle as an attention-getter before going into 300-foot-view detail.* The reason this still works as an attention-getter is that it prompts the reader to ask, "Where is he going with this?" It's as if, even though the reader is not from a manufacturing background, we are taking their hand and immersing them briefly into the world—our career field of choice—in which we are fascinated, and our passion will subsequently rub off onto them, thus grabbing their attention. We then start to descend into the main reason—our thesis statement—as to why we are writing this essay, which begins in the transitionary sentence of sentence 4 and then explicitly stated in sentence 5. The prompt asks about thoughts of my career field, my aspirations, and my future plans. Our thesis statement answers and gives direction to all three of these inquiries.

For thoughts on my career field, I describe how I think manufacturing is one of the most important pillars to society there is. For aspirations, I talk about how I want to contribute to the wave of innovation within manufacturing. For future plans, I suggest implementing my own solutions within the manufacturing space. Despite this introduction not initially being written for this essay, you can see how it can be applied to this completely new prompt. *The sections of content that you go on to write about are not just a one-time-use commodity.* Using the structuring techniques taught in this book, like the high-low-high thought pattern flow and connection types, will allow your message to tie into any prompt subject you may encounter and, although the amount of editing may vary, your overall flow will carry over. In regard to editing Paragraph 3 to apply to this essay, all we had to do was change the very last sentence since the original section included the names of specific counties that were being discussed at that time. Now, with a strong introduction in place, we want to move on to telling the scholarship judges *how* we plan to answer the prompt and thesis statement.

BODY BREAKDOWN | ESSAY 7

As seen in Essay 4, Paragraphs 2, 4, and 6 are all used to provide the supporting points to answer the "how" of the thesis statement. As was discussed in earlier breakdowns, we see that these reused sections are all centered around my personal internship experience in which we can extract passionate connections from the takeaways of my projects completed. Body 1 takes the same approach as seen in Essay 4, where I take Paragraph 2 and summarize it into a smaller, more condensed version of my first-year's internship. This was not a direct copy from Essay 4 since sentence 3 of Body 1 provided more detail than in Essay 4. However, there is nothing too significant to take away from this edit since both are just summarizing the same thing. *Many of the edits I made to refine reused sections were ultimately guided by what sounded and flowed the best.*

Next, Body 2 uses Paragraph 4, which is a word-for-word reuse of that section—the only difference being sentence 6. Sentence 6 was newly written for this essay and is just an improvement to the flow of Paragraph 4, as it explains in better detail the purpose and benefit behind the project that I worked on. This improvement was also prompted due to my knowledge that the scholarship judge wasn't directly tied to manufacturing, so, if I am able to connect the manufacturing ideas in a way that the reader can better connect the overall impact of my work, that would only be to my benefit. *It is always important to know the audience that you are writing for.*

Lastly, Body 3 uses Paragraph 6 as a true word-for-word reuse section. Also, this is the last supporting point to the body section of this essay. Paragraphs 4 and 6 often appear together because they were first developed side by side in the same essay, both focused on the same topic. I decided to categorize them into their own reuse paragraphs since, during my scholarship journey, I saw each past essay's individual paragraphs as building blocks that could be separated and integrated independently at any time. No edits were made to this reuse of Paragraph 6. This paragraph simply concludes the supporting points of my career thoughts, aspirations, and future plans. By highlighting my internship experience across all these body paragraphs, it suggests to the organization's scholarship judge that this is just a taste of what is to come for my career, aspirations, and future plans all into one. Ultimately, my message is that I aim to be the best manufacturing engineer I can be and make a meaningful impact on the industry, and the experiences I share here reinforce that.

CONCLUSION BREAKDOWN | ESSAY 7

The end of Body 3 concludes the exact repeat of Essay 4 content. Using the introduction and body paragraphs of Essay 4 brought me this far, so why would I stop there and not use the same conclusion as well? The main reason lies in the context of why Essay 4's conclusion was written.

If you remember, Essay 4 was the third time I had applied to the same scholarship organization's application. That scholarship organization had seen nearly all of my content up to that point, which forced me to write a new ending for Essay 4 so they wouldn't encounter anything reused. In this instance, it's not that I couldn't have used Essay 4's conclusion. It's that I felt the brand-new conclusion that was written for Essay 4 was weaker than previous conclusions I had used in the past. The conclusion that I ended up using to end this new essay was actually the same conclusion from Essay 2. In this conclusion, we see that Paragraph 1 was reused, but that it was edited from its original section to form a new conclusion flow. For more information on the specifics behind how this conclusion functions well in a scholarship format, please revisit Essay 2's breakdown. Since I had the flexibility to reuse any of my past content for this essay, I chose this conclusion because I felt it contained an impactful message that fit with the overall flow. I liked the conclusion used in Essay 2 in particular because it contained powerful personal connections, such as being a first-generation college student and how giving back was a main motivator of mine.

Also, considering how we know this reused conclusion came from an essay that achieved both a high-low-high thought pattern and successful use of connection types, let's see how this carried over flow in such a way that answers this essay's prompt despite being a reused section. In the eyes of a scholarship judge, our thesis statement is revisited and answered related to the three prompt directions that were given. Sentence 1 talks about how I was reassured that Manufacturing Engineering was "for me," which satisfied my career field thoughts that were asked for. Sentence 3 ends with suggesting I am striving to achieve all my goals, which is a high-level way of answering the prompt that asked about aspirations. Sentence 4 ends the essay by answering the final prompt inquiry, saying that my future plans are to "work within my community of Rockford, Illinois in order to give back." Again, although this conclusion wasn't originally written for this exact prompt, the style of writing within it combined with proper assessment of if the reused sections would flow properly made it easy to connect it to this essay's prompt. This conclusion brings us to the end of this essay—an essay where every section was reused to form a *completely new essay* for a *completely new organization* for *completely new prize money*.

FINAL BREAKDOWN COMMENTS | ESSAY 7

You can see the power of the reuse strategy at full force here. Every piece of content was reused to craft this essay, which saved time and stress. As a student, it already seems like you don't have enough time and are stressed out due to school anyway, so anything to help in this avenue is welcome. The total scholarship winnings totaled $1,000, which was applied to my junior year second semester. When I say that it took very minimal effort to craft this essay and still won these funds, don't think that I am phrasing it in a way that I just earned it for nothing. Although this essay was indeed much quicker and easier to submit because of the reused content, the bulk of the work had already been completed up front when I first wrote these sections. I paid my dues earlier. It's just like paying a doctor or contractor a high price point for a service that takes thirty minutes. You are not paying for the time. You're paying for the thirty years of experience that enable them to provide that service. It's the same concept here. *Don't feel bad for reusing any of your scholarship content. Feel empowered to look for opportunities to do so.* You wrote the content already, so make it work for you and let it pay dividends.

Essay 8	
Organization:	Foundation of the Fabricators & Manufacturers Association, Intl. (FMA)
Title:	Nuts, Bolts and Thingamajigs Scholarship
Date Written:	03/18/2016
	Junior Year, 2nd Semester (Spring)
Total Winnings:	$2,500
	Applied to Junior Year, 2nd Semester Tuition (Spring)
Prompt:	• *What experiences have influenced your decision to pursue a career in manufacturing and the specific field of study you selected?* • *What type of work do you see yourself doing after you graduate and what motivates you to pursue this specific career?*
Word Count:	N/A

PROMPT BULLET POINT 1

INTRODUCTION

" ③ { [1]*In recent years, manufacturing has come to be one of the most pivotal industries in today's economy, accounting for a significant percentage of employment as well as global gross domestic product.* [2]*In the U.S. alone, the drive for innovation, competitiveness, and constant improvement that comes from our ever-changing manufacturing environment has kept our nation's spot as a worldwide leader in quality and cutting-edge technology.* [3]*The numerous methods for product development and distribution that exist provide endless opportunities for improving the everyday lives of a world population that continues to grow.* [4]*Having the ability to contribute to this wave of innovation in which the end result is a better tomorrow is why I have decided to study Manufacturing Engineering.* [5]*I am ecstatic to have found a college major I can apply my creative and ambitious personality to in the hopes of implementing my own solutions to the world of manufacturing.* }

BODY 1

[1]*Now as my third year within the Industrial & Manufacturing Engineering and Technology (IMET) department at Bradley University comes to a close and I prepare for senior year, I could not*

be happier with choosing Manufacturing Engineering, with a concentration in Lean Manufacturing, as my course of study. [2]*As an undecided freshman, stepping onto Bradley's campus for the first time was frightening since I did not know what path to take at the time.* [3]*My older brother and sister, who both went through college before me, were great influences as far as aiding me in my decision of what my major should be but it wasn't until I took an Academic Exploration Program for Undecided Engineering that really shed light on my future.* [4]*This pass/fail class introduced me to the various options of engineering Bradley provides by bringing in speakers from the mechanical, electrical, and civil departments, just to name a few.*

BODY 2 & CONCLUSION

[1]*The day Industrial and Manufacturing Engineering was presented, [REMOVED NAME], who is the current IMET department chair, came to speak.* [2]*[REMOVED NAME] was so enthusiastic and passionate about the subject that he made me think, "I should be that excited about what I want to do for the rest of my life!"* [3]*Later, I met up with [REMOVED NAME] where he personally invited me out to lunch and described to me the different opportunities and advantages associated with studying either Industrial or Manufacturing Engineering.* [4]*Since then, [REMOVED NAME] has been a great role model to me as I continue toward receiving my Bachelor's Degree.* [5]*Seeing [REMOVED NAME]'s contributions and innovations in manufacturing inspires me to work as hard as I can in order to achieve a successful career as a Manufacturing Engineer so that I may eventually implement my own solutions in the real-world as well."*

PROMPT BULLET POINT 2

BODY 1

" [1]*After my undergraduate studies, one area of manufacturing that I hope to work with is lean implementation in a manufacturing system.* [2]*I am currently in a class taught by [REMOVED NAME] that looks at many ways a manufacturing system can be converted from a standard job shop into a lean, linked-cell manufacturing system that outputs products using one-piece-flow.* [3]*I think it is absolutely fascinating how a manufacturing engineer can go into a factory*

floor, pinpoint where waste is being produced that does not add value to the company, and provide solutions using Kaizen methodologies and lean strategies in order to convert a system from mass production to just-in-time manufacturing. [4]Some of these strategies include development of U-shaped manufacturing cells, setup reduction, integration of production, quality and inventory control systems, and improvement of manufacturing and assembly processes, which I hope to be a part of. [5]I am interested in this type of work because it will allow me to collaborate, not only with other engineers, but also with the workers and operators on the shop floor in order to involve them in implementing lean since the internal customer is the company's most important asset.

BODY 2

[1]In addition to lean implementation, engineering of materials would be another facet of my job I could see myself doing in the future.

⑦ { *[2]During this past Fall 2015 semester I took a materials engineering class in my manufacturing engineering curriculum in which we were tasked with a term project consisting of design modification, materials selection, manufacturing, and cost estimation of an engineering part of our choice. [3]My partner and I decided on looking at how the standard frame of a bike can function under the restrictive and quantifiable conditions of stress, temperature, environment, weight, and other justified assumptions. [4]Those assumptions* [included] *factor of safety, temperature range, max load, mass-producibility, and use of standard pipe sizes.*

BODY 3

[1]After we calculated the limits of our bike [as well as considered] *the other mechanical properties of materials, we began the process of finding the best material choice for this bike and its application. [2]Our application was that this bike was to function in a city type environment where it would act as a rentable bicycle and see various riders with various loads that experiences multiple uses per day. [3]After much discussion and research along with consideration of several additional factors like amounts of corrosion resistance, if certain materials are lighter/heavier, less expensive, or easier to manufacture than other materials, just to name a few, we concluded our research with finding two ideal material candidates for the*

frame: AISI 303 stainless steel or 6061 aluminum. [4]Noting the fact that both metals can be used for our ideal purposes, it came down to preferences over a couple factors. [5]Although aluminum is less dense and a bit cheaper, it does not typically last as long as steel frames. [6]In addition, many people have complained that aluminum bikes tend to be much harder to ride, being too stiff and lacking in resilience, thus not storing and releasing enough energy for a smoother ride. [7][Therefore], we chose stainless steel as our ideal choice in material for creating our bike frame. [8]We also concluded that the manufacturing process most suited for assembling this bike frame would be Tungsten Inert Gas (TIG) Welding and the cost for the total amount of material required came out to be $19.77.

BODY 4 & CONCLUSION

[1]This project gave me a greater understanding of how to approach the process of choosing the best material for an engineering part I am working with. [2]It also gave me an idea of what I can expect to find in the material-handling industry after graduation. [3]With the knowledge gained from my bike frame project and [lean class], as well as [my] work experience gained through my internships with Rockford Products LLC, I am confident I will be ready to positively contribute to any industry in the manufacturing field so that I may help create a better future, in both the industry and the world.} "

ESSAY 8 BREAKDOWN

PROMPT BREAKDOWN | ESSAY 8

Our final essay breakdown has us end with another multi-layered prompt that involves two bullet points. Since this essay was written after Essay 6, which was our first multi-layered prompt, we can compare our approaches between the two. When initially thinking of how best to approach writing an essay that answers these two bullet points, I recognized that I would not need to spread out my written content as much as I did in the five bullet points of Essay 6. Instead, I opted to elaborate more within these two prompts to ensure that both bullet points have proper substance.

Identifying a more important bullet point doesn't apply here because this prompt only asks two questions versus the five in Essay 6. In Essay 6, we wanted to identify our most important bullet points because we wanted to give them the most substance versus the lower-priority bullet points to avoid overwriting. Out of the five bullet points in Essay 6, only two were identified as high priority. Being that this essay only has two bullet points, we can safely assume that both are equally critical. Along those same lines, the application wanted me to write separate answers for each bullet point instead of one large essay because the scholarship's online submission portal separated them. Therefore, similar to Essay 6 where we needed to get to the point and answer the prompt questions more directly due to its bullet points' separation, taking a short-answer approach here would also be ideal.

Knowing that we have more leeway when it comes to the length of content we can include in these two bullet points, we can approach them as if they were "miniature essays" with shortened word counts, just as in Essay 3 or 5. With a word-count restriction, you naturally develop your essay's main idea faster, and you can apply that same approach to "longer-form" short-answer questions as well. With this "longer-form" now available, I knew that I could include more proper essay structuring within my answers versus Essay 6's short answers where that was not an option. *This type of planning allows me to start visualizing how the end result of these "miniature essays" will look like, and, as a result, will help in the execution of the writing.* It gives the framework of a plan that you can follow instead of being lost and not knowing where, or how, to start.

The two final notes I would like to mention about this prompt's bullet points are about word-count restrictions and theme. Regarding word-count restrictions, none were specified for either of these bullet points. Although, from our above planning, we want to approach these "miniature essays" as if they have theoretical word-count restrictions imposed on them. Having each short answer in the form of a "miniature essay" will provide more length than a typical short-answer response and will help to avoid writing too little. Having a theoretical word-count restriction will help to avoid overwriting. Regarding theme, this is yet another manufacturing-related scholarship, reflected in both the organization and the prompt questions. Therefore, we know our audience, and will frame our message to appeal to scholarship judges who prioritize manufacturing ideals versus other industries. With this knowledge, we are equipped to successfully output answers to each of these questions.

For this essay's content breakdown, I will take a similar approach to that of Essay 6, in which I will separate each bullet point into its own respective breakdown. However, one thing that is different between this and Essay 6's breakdown is how each essay paragraph is titled. In Essay 6, each essay paragraph was titled as "Short-Answer Paragraph," followed by a corresponding number. This was because each of Essay 6's short answers lacked proper essay structuring. In the essay we are covering now, even though these are short-answer responses, proper essay structuring is present. Therefore, the essay paragraphs will be titled accordingly, indicated by whether each one functions as an introduction, body, or conclusion, consistent with all other essay breakdowns except Essay 6.

BULLET POINT 1 BREAKDOWN | ESSAY 8

Being that I am approaching this first bullet point as a miniature essay, I needed a strong introduction. So, I looked to my arsenal of past scholarship content, and once again I decided to include Paragraph 3 to start this essay off with. Again, please revisit Essay 4's breakdown as well as the section covering introductions if you need more detailed information on what makes this introduction powerful. Bullet point 1's prompt begins by asking about the experiences that have "influenced your decision to pursue a career in manufacturing." When it comes to how this introduction fits within this scope, sentences 4 and 5 introduce the thesis statement in a way that frames the main idea as how the experiences I have had helped me to view the manufacturing industry as critical to today's world and how I want to be a part of that. Keep in mind that although the introduction's main idea was tailored differently to the prompt it was first written for in Essay 4, the style of writing achieved in this reused section allows this section to be looked at in various ways. In the case of what this bullet point's question is inquiring about, it can be framed as a set up that leads to talking more about the particular experiences that shaped me in the body of the essay.

Body 1 moves on to the supporting points of *how* those experiences shaped my decision to pursue manufacturing. This was a section that was written solely for this essay. The first thing to note here is that Body 1 talks about my life before all of the internships and personal manufacturing experiences that I had. Sure, I could have reused prior content that directly discussed my internships here, but it wouldn't have quite fit with what the prompt was looking for. If I had gone with a reused section about my internships, that doesn't answer *how* I got started in the first place. Internship experience would be an example of experience that would further strengthen my willingness to continue to pursue manufacturing, but it doesn't give an explanation of how it "influenced" me to study the subject in the first place. Internship experience would have implied that I had already made that decision, which would miss answering the bullet point entirely. That is why I deemed it necessary to write a new section that explained my earlier decision-making process of selecting my major. Sentence 1 of Body 1 acts as a transition sentence to a 300-foot-view thought level from the introduction by going into my present situation in school, which is being a third-year student of my manufacturing curriculum. I follow this sequence by going into sentences 2 through 4, which introduce my siblings' influence as well as the academic exploration class I took. These sentences summarize, in brief, the story I shared earlier in this book about how I chose Manufacturing Engineering. In sentence 2, notice how I give life to the story I was telling by mentioning it was a "frightening" time for me. Frightening in the sense that I was already in college, responsible for thousands of dollars in tuition, yet had no academic direction that seemed likely to lead to a job capable of helping me repay it. This acts as an emotional connection for the reader because everyone has felt their stomach get sick with anxiety when faced with uncertainty in their future related to a large, life-altering situation that they got themselves into. Sentences 3 and 4 then introduce the first supporting point to the thesis which was my academic exploration class I enrolled in and why it helped influence my decision-making process.

Body 2 introduces our second supporting point to the thesis—my experience with my mentor at Bradley University. Their name appears removed; however, this was the dean of the IMET department. Sentence 1 is a transitionary sentence, flowing from the idea of Body 1's academic exploration class into what came from that class, which was meeting the IMET dean. Sentences 2 and 3 go into further detail of this encounter, explaining my interactions with him that shed light on the possibilities that come with a career in manufacturing. Presenting the examples shown in these two sentences with creativity and descriptive words add to the impact that I make with this supporting point. The better you are able to highlight your experiences, the more they will stand out against other applicants' experiences. This wasn't hard to write about either, since personal experiences are easier to develop than research-centric essay answers. *Speaking from the heart and trying to convey what you felt in those moments will allow you to produce some great writing!* This sequence of sentences also conveys the passion I felt for manufacturing for the first time, creating a passionate connection the scholarship judge will pick up on. Body 1 then ends with sentence 4 where we start to transition back to a higher thought pattern that brings the topic back to my degree choice as a whole.

With this being a miniature essay, we don't necessarily have room for a full-blown conclusion; however, we do utilize sentence 5 to act as our concluding idea. I could have written or reused a full conclusion paragraph, but since this answer follows a short-answer style, I didn't want it to become too wordy. Being that both of these bullet points make up one scholarship prompt, I am looking at the sum of these two answers as two separate parts of one "full" essay, so going too in detail too early would run the risk of over-explanation. Sentence 5 does its best to capture all the critical parts that a conclusion should include. There is a tie to my experience with the IMET dean, thus restating a portion of the supporting points I brought up. The sentence loops back around to answer the thesis statement by explaining why I want to become a manufacturing engineer. Also, it contains a strong ending using "mini" connection wording, where I explain the impact I want my career to have on the real world, thus cementing the passionate connection idea discussed in the essay.

BULLET POINT 2 BREAKDOWN | ESSAY 8

We now move on to bullet point 2, which asks about what type of work I would want to be involved in after graduation and the motivation behind that work. To begin this second short-answer essay, I opted to forgo a traditional introduction and move directly into body content that elaborates on the supporting points. This decision was primarily due to already having a strong introduction in bullet point 1. Even though it appears earlier in the essay, the two bullet points together function as one full essay, so the introduction in the first bullet point already checks that box, engages the reader, and allows bullet point 2 to continue the 300-foot view flow established earlier. Therefore, we can call the first paragraph of bullet point 2 as Body 1. Within sentence 1 of Body 1 we see our first supporting point to answering bullet point 2's question, stating that implementing lean manufacturing concepts is the type of work I see myself doing after graduation. Sentence 2 then gives the "why" behind this statement, expressing that I was introduced to this facet of manufacturing from a lean concepts class taught by the IMET dean that showcased the value this skillset has in a manufacturing environment. Sentences 3 and 4 then take a more research-based approach because I had very little personal experience with implementing lean at the time. Here, I discuss specific key points that I learned in class, delivering terms such as "kaizen," "U-shaped cells," and "just-in-time," all of which are integral to that subject. This creates a passionate connection, as I am going one level deeper than most when it comes to my interest in lean manufacturing, further strengthening the point as to why I want to do this type of work. Sentence 5 acts as the concluding sentence to Body 1 by summarizing one final reason I'm interested in this type of work, ending with the specific phrase "the internal customer is the company's most important asset." This was me giving a strong ending to conclude the point about lean because this specific phrase comes directly from the lean manufacturing book that I read in its entirety. It stuck out to me at the time because, well, it's somewhat important to know what a company's biggest asset is! So, by including this, I knew it would impress the scholarship judges when they read this, and hopefully surprise them if a student this early on is already making these types of connections!

Take note of how I talk about the topic of the prompt, which in this case is my major, and how I always aim to go as in-depth as I can. *Whether you're writing about research-based content, personal experiences, or other supporting points, going into detail, providing specific examples, and tying them back to your main points is essential—and it will elevate your application in the eyes of the scholarship judges.* Just for reference, this same Body 1 paragraph is also explained earlier in the book under the Passionate Connection section if you would like further insight into this portion's wording.

At this point in the essay, I knew that ending with only one example for bullet point 2 would feel incomplete and not strong enough. I wanted to provide one more example of the type of work I would be doing to give more substance to my answer and give another reason for the scholarship judges to pick me as the winner. If you look back at bullet point 3 of Essay 6's prompt, you will see that it asked about "planned future work with the industry." In Essay 6's answer to that bullet point, I saw the phrasing of Paragraph 7 was written to answer virtually the same question that what was being asked in this prompt. Even though Paragraph 7 was written to talk about the material-handling industry instead of manufacturing, I thought this section was a good candidate for reuse with how these two industries are so closely intertwined. Therefore, I decided to reuse Paragraph 7 as my second supporting point to this essay, giving the answer that the type of work I see myself doing after graduation would be centered on materials engineering.

Body 2 begins with sentence 1 acting as a transition between my supporting points. Paragraph 7 then picks up at the start of sentence 2 and throughout the rest of Body 2, Body 3, and Body 4, giving enough content to close out the short-answer essay with the way it was already phrased. Please see the breakdown of Essay 6 for more insight into the mechanics behind Paragraph 7. As it is used here, Paragraph 7 goes into a 300-foot-view personal experience of a college project related to my major that I thought captured my technical aptitude well and would be thought highly of in the eyes of the scholarship judges. One important point to mention is that the use of Paragraph 7 came with some minor edits that I made throughout the three body paragraphs it spans. When initially inserting this section and proofreading the essay to ensure proper essay flow, I noticed that the original Paragraph 7 was a bit wordy and included some non-essential information. Though I deemed the information essential for Essay 6 at the time, rereading this section and how it fit into this essay made me seek some improvement opportunities. These improvements weren't drastic and just included minor cuts and combinations to sentences. Refining Paragraph 7 in this way achieved a more seamless flow to the supporting point.

The way the third paragraph of Paragraph 7—Body 4 of the bullet point 2 essay—was written, it acted as a conclusion for the prompt it was being used for in Essay 6. Therefore, it could act as the conclusion for this essay as well. I sort of got lucky too, because if you notice in sentence 2, the phrase "after graduation" is used, which is phrasing used in bullet point 1's prompt. Both bullet points deal with life after graduation, so having this phrasing already included was a plus. It creates the impression that, even though this section was reused, it was written specifically for this essay. Also, sentence 3 really summarizes bullet point 2's supporting point, and the "full" essay as a whole, by using "mini" connection phrasing such as "create a better future, in both the industry and the world." Sentence 3 serves as the answer to bullet point 2's question about my motivation for pursuing this career and leaves the "full" essay—meaning the combined short-answer content of bullet point 1 and 2—and the reader on a high note.

FINAL BREAKDOWN COMMENTS | ESSAY 8

In this essay, several strategies come into play: adjusting essay format, producing new content, reusing old content, mixing standard and modified essay structures, inserting connection types, refining flow, and addressing prompt requirements. This is an excellent example to end the final essay breakdown with, especially since it was the second-to-last scholarship essay I wrote and submitted during my scholarship journey, completed near the end of my second semester of junior year. We have covered a lot in this book. However, as you move through the breakdowns and arrive at Essay 8, you'll notice that despite being one of the most technique-driven essays, it doesn't come across as such. With everything you've learned up to this point, using these strategies to craft a strong essay will feel nearly instinctive, which is exactly what this last breakdown demonstrates.

I still found myself writing new content despite this being the second to last scholarship application I would ever submit. It truly shows that you cannot be complacent when it comes to scholarship applications. *Maintaining consistency in the application of these techniques in order to maintain quality throughout will be key to your success.* In this essay, I recognized that the quality would have suffered had I taken the easy route and tried to force reused content into every part of it. My past content didn't quite meet the needs for what this new scholarship required. Don't get me wrong, there will be times when you will recognize that you can reuse previously written content for the entirety of an essay, as was the case with Essay 7. I didn't feel I was forcing any of the reused content to fit when I was writing Essay 7. Rather, the essay flow naturally progressed due to how the subject matter of the reused content answered what the prompt was asking. Even though this essay required a different level of involvement and didn't offer as many "easy" opportunities to reuse content, it was still straightforward to put together. This straightforward nature came from the fact that I consistently applied the scholarship techniques in this book, and that consistency helped me reach a solid final result. That is the final lesson of this final essay breakdown. *Stay true to the process.* Respect the scholarship game for what it is. Never try to cheat it. How you do anything is how you do everything. The more you keep producing high-quality content by applying these scholarship strategies, the more trained and well-versed you will become in your essay writing. That way, when you face challenges along your scholarship journey, you'll be able to handle them with relative ease to the point where, just like in this essay, you will have used nearly every strategy in the book without even realizing it because it becomes your default approach to writing!

As a reward for staying true to the process for this scholarship, I was selected as the winner of $2,500 to be applied to my second semester of junior year. At the end of the day, winning that extra cash will be your only motivation. Don't worry about making mistakes or overthinking when it comes to applying these techniques for the first time. Just like learning to ride a bike: early on you stumble, but with time you gain enough confidence to chase the steepest hills for the adrenaline rush. The same applies here. *Keep trying your best, learning and improving with each scholarship essay regardless of whether you win or not.* Before long, you'll be able to respond to even the most complex of scholarship prompts, all leading to the adrenaline rush of receiving that email or phone call confirming that you, among countless applicants, were chosen as the winner. Truly, there is no other feeling like it.

ESSAY BREAKDOWN ENDING NOTES

Congratulations on reaching the end of all the essay breakdowns! By going through each of these unique examples I provided, you were exposed to all of the tools that I used to create the scholarship success I experienced. These essay breakdowns were the final major topic I intended to address in this book, and they formally conclude Step 4. However, there are a few ending points that I would like to leave you with.

DON'T FEEL BAD FOR REUSING CONTENT

As you've seen time and time again, one of the major themes of the essay breakdowns was the strategy of reusing previous content to form new essays and make your writing process easier when applicable. *One note to this I would like to mention is not to feel bad when reusing previous written sections to form new essays.* You may think that copying and pasting your already written content is cheating in a way. You may think that it gets away from the authenticity of writing and that it is not genuine. This could not be farther from the case. As previously stated, your main focus is to win as much money as possible. How you do that is by applying to as many scholarships as possible in the quickest way possible. Reusing content can help you increase your scholarship application rate in a way that writing everything from scratch cannot. The point here is not to become reliant on the reuse strategy. How would you be able to reuse content if you are not writing anything new in the first place? *The point is to use this strategy as a tool, not a crutch.* When you reuse content, those are still words that you, yourself, wrote. You have already captured the authenticity of your message when you wrote it the first time. When you reuse that same piece of writing, you are bringing your new essay to the same quality level that you had in your previous essay. It also gives you an opportunity to elevate your new essay by pairing that reused section with transitions, additional new content, and edits to ultimately form a new masterpiece.

HANDLING LOSS

What you saw in this book were eight winning scholarship essays. What you did not see was all the losses, failures, and denials that I experienced along the way. During my scholarship journey, I lost a lot more than I won. Do I wish this was the case? Of course not. However, that is the very nature of scholarship applications. You are not going to win every one of the applications you submit. You have to be *resilient* in order to reach the level of scholarship winnings that I experienced. You have to be comfortable with failure and losing. It is okay to lose. It is **not** okay to give up and stop trying when you lose. What differentiated me from other students was that I did not get discouraged the moment something didn't go my way. I thought I was going to win every single application I submitted. I always felt that I put my best work in to provide a quality application that would give me a great chance at being the winner. The scholarships that I thought I was guaranteed to at least win once ended up being the ones that rejected me the most! One in particular that stands out to me was a scholarship provided by the Community Foundation of Northern Illinois. Out of the hundreds of scholarships that they offer to students, one of them was a scholarship from the company Rockford Products, LLC. This was the very same company that I worked at during my first two college summer internships. I thought I was guaranteed to win this considering the fact that during my time there I was the only intern at the company! All I thought I had to do was write about my experience at the company and that alone would make me stand out versus the rest. I applied for this scholarship three years in a row and never won. This shows just how volatile scholarship applications can be. I could have grown bitter after not winning the first scholarship and behaved as though I were entitled to it, but I chose not to. The best thing to do in cases like this is to just keep applying year after year. *All you can do is give yourself an opportunity.* Open as many doors as possible. I opened this door three times. It did not lead me to any winnings; however, other doors that I opened eventually made up for and offset the losses from this "guaranteed" scholarship. It was a humbling experience.

Also, the organization's applications from Essays 3, 5, and 6 were all winners from the second time I applied. They all rejected me the first year that I applied to them. Essay 3's organization, after winning the second time, rejected me the third year I applied to them as well. Imagine if I gave up applying after the first rejection from these scholarships. I probably wouldn't be writing this book because I would have nothing to show for it! *The lesson is I didn't give up.* I learned from my mistakes. I got better. I realized I needed to continue writing new essays and improve as an all-around applicant until they chose me as a winner. Failure was truly not an option. Even if I never won anything while in college, that would not have stopped me from applying to every single opportunity that presented itself. Growth comes from failure. It is not how many times you get hit and fall down. All that matters is that you pick yourself up, dust yourself off, and keep standing up and fighting for the scholarship funds you deserve. Effort beats talent every time. People are celebrated in public for what they do in private when no one is looking. No one will care if you lose, but the moment you win they will be asking how you did it. It's not about proving others wrong. It is about proving yourself right. You are your only competition. Adopt a continuous improvement mindset when it comes to applying for scholarships. *If you lose, think about the areas you are lacking in and seek to improve them to give yourself the best chance you can next time around.* At the end of the day, no matter how many scholarships you win or lose, the true winners are those that never gave up.

BY ANY MEANS NECESSARY

At the end of the day, regardless of the type of financial assistance, the goal is to find a way to pay for college that doesn't require you to shoulder the cost alone. I have a younger sister in college at the time of writing this book that I am helping with her scholarship journey. Her story is drastically different than mine and, with that, her scholarship success is taking a different shape. She is a sophomore in college right now and is currently applying for scholarships using the same process I was. However, the majority of her current financial aid she was able to capture thus far came from a different avenue. Growing up, our parents involved her in violin and piano, with violin being her specialty. She is currently a double major in college—one of the majors being Violin Performance. She was able to locate a school and negotiate a substantial amount of additional funding that she did not find at any of the other schools she applied to. We sent letters to the directors of financial aid at the school similar to what I did at Bradley, and I even helped get on a phone call with the administrative team of her music department to strategically negotiate and plead for extra funding, justifying our position by explaining our family's current circumstances. Out of all the schools we used this strategy on, the school she is at right now was the most receptive to delve out extra financial aid to her original scholarship offering. One of the reasons being was that the school was in a position where they needed violinists in their program. There was an incentive for them to offer my sister a greater amount in order to have her make the decision to go to their school and join their music program. I looked at her freshman year's tuition and scholarship breakdown, and I was amazed just how much they were able to find in extra funding for her to attend. If we hadn't started the conversation by reaching out to them the way we did, they would not have adjusted their assistance package.

The story of my sister is heavily summarized and doesn't cover all the variables, like the fact that it was an out-of-state school, which alone exponentially increases the cost of attendance and is the reason why we had to go back-and-forth with them. However, the extra funding she was able to secure is a form of winning scholarships. She was able to put herself in this situation of being wanted by the school due to her skill as a violinist, which caused them to be able to increase their scholarship funding to make her cost of attendance reasonable. Notice how her skill opened up this opportunity for her. Since she was five years old, she was around the violin and the years of discipline and practice she put in paid off in this moment for her.

Now, I know what you are thinking. Not everyone will have a skill like hers that would be able to be marketed like it was in this example. I didn't have one either. That is not the point, though. *The point is that there are different ways to achieve scholarships that can help fund an education.* Your job while in school is to find those other ways. Obviously, your first priority is to focus on school and graduate, but the second priority is to figure out how to creatively pay for it. By the time she ends her college, she may not win as many different external scholarships as me, but she found a way to be able to gain a substantial amount more in total scholarship financial assistance through her school than I did. Therefore, I consider her story already a success in winning scholarships because, when it is all said and done, she found a way to lower her tuition bill. Sometimes it is being at the right place at the right time too! If the school hadn't had a need for violinists like they did, then maybe they wouldn't have budged with their financial aid offering. The important part here is that my sister, through the rigorous efforts and choices she made leading up to her attending college, opened doors that would have otherwise stayed closed had she taken the easy route and not developed herself, her skills, or her value throughout the years. This book explains how I found my own way to reduce my college costs, and it's the most realistic option for everyday students, since not everyone has a skill they've been building since age five like my sister. Ultimately, both my sister and I found a way to pay for school **by any means necessary**. That is one viewpoint that I want to leave you with as well. In today's world, there are numerous avenues you can take that can help you accumulate funding for school. Although finding scholarships is my favorite, *always be on the lookout for other forms of financial aid that you can achieve*. So long as you find a way to reduce your tuition bill, you are an "everyday scholarship winner."

Step 5

REPEAT

13

Executing Step 5

We have reached the final step in the process of winning scholarships. *Once you have conducted Steps 1 through 4, the final thing there is to do is simply repeat what you have done that got you this far.* Step 1: Know Your "Why" should already be in place to keep carrying you throughout your journey. It is always good to remind yourself of the motivations behind "why" you need to win scholarship funding, but it isn't something you necessarily need to take action on unless your motivations change. More specifically, you will need to repeat Steps 2 through 4. Step 2: Improve Yourself should be a reflection point throughout your time as a student. Be vigilant toward where your opportunities for growth and improvement are. Double down on your areas of strength, and build on them as a foundation for your scholarship applications to stand on. Adopt a continuous improvement mindset so that you are always able to put yourself in the best position to be the most deserving candidate to win the scholarships you apply to. Always be in constant search mode for new scholarships using Step 3: Find Scholarships. Once you have found a new scholarship, carry out Step 4: Apply using the strategies in this book. Step 5: Repeat is the simplest step of this process, and yet is the most time consuming because you will always be cycling through Steps 2 through 4. For as long as you are a student, you will have the opportunity to apply for scholarships.

Therefore, continue repeating Step 5 for as long as you're in this position to maximize your chances of receiving the most financial aid possible. Now, it is up to you to take action.

CALL TO ACTION

One of my absolute favorite quotes comes from Joe Rogan. I am only going to include snippets here, and it goes something like this:

> *"Pretend there's a documentary crew filming your success story and they're following you around right now. What would you do? What would you do if you knew there was a crew following you around with cameras documenting your future incredible success, and they want to catch you in the act of it all."*
>
> *"Live your life like you're the hero in your own movie. If your life was a movie and it started now, what would the hero of your life's movie do right now? Do that. Do those things."*
>
> *–Paraphrased from Joe Rogan, "Be the Hero of Your Own Movie"*

In the back of our minds, we know the things we should be doing. We should eat healthy. We should exercise often. We should keep learning. The list goes on. If you are in school, the thing you know you should be doing is applying for and winning scholarships. I have met students before who never thought to apply for scholarships because they were never told about them. If that is you, and no one ever told you the importance of winning scholarships while you are in school, *then that changes today because I will be that person to tell you that you should be prioritizing winning scholarships*. You are the hero of your own movie.

Reflect on your "why." For me, my "why" for winning scholarships was my mom telling me our family had no money to pay for school, and that I was on my own once their savings for my college dried up after the first year. Think about how much good will come from winning scholarships. Imagine how hard your parents or guardians worked to get you to the point in your life where you are at today. Imagine that you can tell them that they don't have to worry anymore because you found a way to help your family with the financial burden of an education. If it is just you on your own, imagine the story you can tell about how you beat the odds by finding resourceful ways to fund your education even when all the odds were stacked against you. Imagine how, instead of funding a bank's private loan interest payments, making them rich in the process, those payments you normally would have made went into an investment account that netted you hundreds of thousands of dollars in gains over thirty years if you started young. Imagine how the scholarship money you won would be able to fund your education and, instead of needing to pay loans back, you used that money to start a business for yourself with the skills you learned in school. Imagine the peace of mind. Imagine you getting that first email, phone call, or letter in the mail saying that **you** were the one selected to receive free money just because you are a student and you applied for it. *You are the author of your story, and the pen is in your hand. What kind of story will you write?*

This book equips you with all the tools you need to know to win scholarships. As you progress through your scholarship journey, use this book as a guide to help you down your path. Refer back to it whenever you need guidance or clarity about how to navigate a certain scholarship scenario you find yourself in. My goal is to impart all my knowledge to you so that you can share in the same scholarship success that I found. You can do it. There is nothing stopping you from achieving greatness other than yourself! It is you against you! Go out and find as many scholarships as possible. Never stop improving, writing, and applying. Vigorously open as many doors to scholarship opportunities as you can. There are millions of dollars in scholarships that exist in the world today that are out there waiting to be claimed. All you have to do is apply. All you have to do is ask. Ask, and you shall receive.

> *"Ask and it will be given to you; seek and you will find; knock and the door will be opened to you. For everyone who asks, receives; and the one who seeks, finds; and to the one who knocks, the door will be opened."*
>
> *–Matthew 7:7-8, New American Bible (NAB)*

Appendix

SCHOLARSHIP ESSAY CHECKLIST

SCHOLARSHIP ESSAY CHECKLIST

INSTRUCTIONS:

Use this checklist to ensure all required key characteristics are included. Make adjustments as needed depending on prompt, writing style, connection types, content, etc. This checklist is meant to act as a guide to facilitate the essay writing process.

PROPER ESSAY STRUCTURE

INTRODUCTION:

- ☐ 30,000-Foot-View Attention-Getter
- ☐ Connection to Thesis Statement
- ☐ Thesis Statement / Main Idea

BODY:

- ☐ 300-Foot-View Supporting Point(s)

CONCLUSION:

- ☐ Restate Thesis Statement / Main Idea
- ☐ Restate Supporting Point(s)
- ☐ 30,000-Foot-View Closing

ESSAY ENHANCEMENTS

CONNECTION TYPES:

- ☐ Emotional Connection(s)
- ☐ Personal Connection(s)
- ☐ Passionate Connection(s)

KEY POINTS:

- ☐ Transitions Between Paragraphs
- ☐ Flow Between Sentences
- ☐ Within Word-Count Limit
- ☐ Creative Detail
- ☐ High-Level Vocabulary
- ☐ Proper Grammar
- ☐ Proofread & Revise

www.ingramcontent.com/pod-product-compliance
Lightning Source LLC
LaVergne TN
LVHW100253210926
848480LV00003B/911